Dear Reader,

Please note that on page 73 of this book, Iron Imperator, *there has been an illustrative omission. Please find the complete information here.*

For purposes of clarity, Tiberius's confirmed major campaigns during the Augustan period are listed below:

PERIOD	AREA OF OPERATIONS
26–25 BC	Northwestern Spain (Cantabrian Wars)
20 BC	Mission to Armenia
16 BC	Campaigns in Gallia Comata (Long-Haired Gaul) and maybe Germania
15 BC	Pacification of the Alpine regions and Raetia (with Drusus)
12 BC–2 BC	Campaigns in Illyricum (the present-day Balkans)
9–6 BC	Campaigns in Germania
4–5 AD	Campaigns in Germania
6–9 AD	Tiberius represses the revolt in Pannonia (region stretching from Hungary to Croatia) and Illyricum
10–11 AD	Campaigns in Germania

BOKFÖRLAGET STOLPE

IRON IMPERATOR

Roman Grand Strategy under Tiberius

IRON IMPERATOR

Roman Grand Strategy under Tiberius

ISKANDER REHMAN

BOKFÖRLAGET STOLPE

For Barry and Jessica McArdle.

CONTENTS

II.

THE RELUCTANT RULER
Tiberius as princeps

Tiberius Julius Caesar Augustus, second emperor of Rome, has a greater reputation for personal excess than for methodical defence of Rome's empire. Despotic behaviour at home is part of everyone's picture of Roman autocracy; determined decision-making abroad not so much. Which of the two we prefer to stress today says more about us than it does about Tiberius. If we think we can learn from history at all, then, at a time of high strategic anxiety, we should perhaps be less anxious about a leader's offences to moral values than about their capability to protect all our values from outside threat. If we choose to study Tiberius, what can be learned from him about present policy towards NATO, Ukraine, or China? Nothing? Everything? And if the answer is something, how do we find what that something is?

Not since the collapse of communism in eastern Europe has the "then" of ancient Rome been so attractive for those studying the "now" of the Western world. The discipline of "applied history" is having a renaissance. When the issues are liberty and tyranny, leaders and allies, the warfare of multiple fronts and the links between politics at home and abroad, Rome's is the history that thinkers have often chosen to apply—and this book is a fine example of that.

But how to find that "something" worth practical study is still a hard question. Look back two thousand years, and there are many clear and easy parallels between then and now. A few of these are very tempting. Trump vs Biden has echoes of Caesar vs Pompey in the dying decades of the Roman Republic, the rule-smashing populist against the former young gun who now bears the hopes of a desperate establishment on his back. Trump is so often caricatured as an emperor (not often a good one) that his wreaths of olive leaves, like his orange hair, are almost routine.

Rehman, whose applications of history to today extend from the Hundred Years' War of the late Middle Ages to sixteenth-century Spain, seeks a more subtle approach, examining stories, mostly war stories, from distant history while noting all the time the "eerie relevance" to our own times as a "small, scrappy monarchy along the Tiber" becomes a powerful republic and "one of the world's most enduring hegemonies." Relevance is the key word here. Many different forms of relevance are ready to be explored. The applied historian is like a tightrope walker, tiptoeing over the past, looking down and seeing on one side human behaviour that we recognise as relevant—the search for food and freedom, friendship, purpose, and safety—and then looking down on the other side at what is alien but still perhaps relevant, if sometimes hard to understand: the very different approaches to freedom from Romans who so vigorously preach liberty, mass enslavement, different understandings of money, and of so much that is now known as "policy."

Sensitivity to evidence, whether his modern subject is India, China, or the United States, is the key to Rehman making persuasive comparisons, not those that merely entertain. Nuance is his weapon of choice. In both contemporary and classical times, for example, it can be argued that little united a people as well as a single enemy. For two hundred years of its history, until the destruction of Carthage in 146 BC, Rome had an enemy which both threatened and united it. Once the walls of Carthage were down, Rome had its hegemony, its economic boom, but also the seeds of new internal divisions. That was the analysis of its own historians, most of all Sallust, who added as a further example the final conquering of Greece. Both events occurred in the same year, the one removing a military and economic rival, the other a cultural superior.

Rehman's lost enemy is Soviet Communism. Like so many of his colleagues, he has spent his academic life in the shadow not of the Berlin Wall but of the absence of the Berlin Wall. The chief anxiety now is present policy towards China. The West's future unity and moral purpose is on trial—and there is no sign of Chinese absence from debate any time soon.

Rome was an empire long before it had emperors. The idea of that empire came from its writers as well as its fighters. The early historians had a free hand to apply a narrative that suited a common purpose—all the more free because so much of the city's own evidence of its past, its early records on metal and papyrus, were destroyed around 386 BC, when invading Gauls did to Rome what Rome would later do to Carthage. Livy began his 124-book history when Rome's republican civil wars were finally over, and brilliantly welded the best Greek stories of heroism onto the conveniently bare bones of Rome's past. The poet Virgil, semi-official prophet of the victorious first emperor, Augustus, took the same stories and at the beginning of his epic, the *Aeneid*, put in the mouth of Jupiter the prediction of *imperium sine fine*, empire without end.

Propaganda, as so often in centuries to come, produced problems for the next generation. Tiberius was an accomplished general in his youth, but as emperor (a job he was never certain to get until he got it) he needed to be a consolidator, not a conqueror. Finance, the fear even then of imperial overstretch, demanded caution. His more glamorous predecessors—Pompey, Caesar, and Augustus—had had the glory of expansion. Augustus could have chosen an heir who would continue extending Rome's reach but selected Tiberius as one who most likely would not. Tiberius' legacy from his adopted father included strong advice to stick to what had already been won.

The reputation of Tiberius has been damaged—in some accounts obliterated—by the vices of this inactivity, his cruelties and alleged sexual depravity in Capri. More important, for an applied historian if not a popular one, is examining the problems of ruling an empire without the momentum of conquest. These include the necessary level of administration, the management of allies, the balancing of expenditure and cost, the sharing of profit and burdens, the inevitable embarrassment of retreats—and the still present ideal of a moral purpose, which is hard when the glamour has gone. These are issues which today's tightrope-walking historian, conscious of apparent humiliation in Afghanistan, costly attrition in Ukraine, and single-minded rivalry from China, can readily look down and see—and note as familiar in our own time.

Tiberius had also to manage an elite whose functions were so very different from that of the previous generation. Men who would once have sought glory in political conflict at home and conquering abroad had to be given new roles or none. Tiberius became famed for his perceived duplicity and hypocrisy. But he can also be seen as a father of bureaucracy and an uncertain master of management arts. This was new court politics, the inexorable shift of power from the law courts in the Forum to those prepared to be courtiers in the sprawling corridors of the Palatine Hill above.

Tiberius was a traditionalist by nature. He tried to encourage senators to take back some of their previous responsibilities, but most were too nervous to do so. Those who did often found that they had made a mistake, or feared that Tiberius was bluffing, that he never intended to give up power. Real power slipped towards palace advisors, some of whom, to the horror of fellow traditionalists, were foreigners, women, and the formerly enslaved. Over subsequent reigns it would slip further still.

Apart from sticking to Augustus' advice not to expand the empire, there was little defined policy as a modern commentator might understand it. Roman rulers had the army but little else of what later came to be termed the levers of power. Managing Augustus' legacy—as this book shows— was a major problem in itself, requiring, as Rehman notes, "portfolio planning" and "adjudication between myriad competing risk assessments and force structure variants."

The extent to which Tiberius, or any emperor, was able to adjudicate consistently to a plan has long been contentious among classicists. In 1977, the Oxford scholar Fergus Millar promoted an influential theory that emperors had no policy and were almost wholly reactive to individual problems, responding specifically to ambassadors from distant provinces and weighing arguments case by case like a judge. On this analysis, and the principle that "an emperor was what an emperor did," most inhabitants of the empire would barely know who the emperor was, let alone what his plans for them might be.

Other scholars have been more generous in seeing grand strategy. An emperor was undoubtedly more than what he did. An emperor was also what he did not do: his restraint, his preparedness to let others fight to Rome's advantage, either against shared enemies or against each other. At the very minimum he was what he seemed to be doing, what his subjects thought that he might do. The promotion of an imperial image by coins and by statues and portrait busts, by adding his predecessors' names to his own, was as strategic as any modern application of soft power. In some places the medium was literature—poetry and history—increasingly provided by artists working on a tighter rein than Augustus allowed Livy and Virgil. There were also imperial cults, places to worship an emperor: the further a citizen lived from Rome itself, the more likely that he (and in some places she, too) would have access to a place where their ruler could be petitioned as a god.

Whatever Tiberius' interest at any particular time, he was especially concerned when members of his own family had a plan, or seemed to have a plan, that was different from his own. He objected strongly when his glamorous nephew Germanicus, who some thought might have been a more active successor to Augustus, interrupted a holiday in Egypt, a country of great wealth and strategic importance, to cut the price of grain and mingle with people as though he were seeking their votes. When Germanicus died while ruling large swathes of the eastern empire from Antioch in Syria, there was strong suspicion in some quarters that Tiberius, who took his name, had had him poisoned. A public trial of the alleged killer raised questions about what the emperor had done, what he wanted to seem to have done, and who would decide the answer.

Further east from Antioch lay the Parthian Empire, a diffuse and dangerous threat, especially when carelessly roused by Rome into unity. Beyond that was what was already the Silk Road to China, home of the Seres, the silk people, whose customs and manners were then hardly less mythical than those of Romulus and Remus. Survivors of a humiliating defeat of Rome by Parthia in 53 BC were said to have settled there.

Commercial contacts with China began soon after Tiberius' death in AD 37, and maybe before. But no Roman knew how much more bureaucratic China was than Rome, how many more people were writing rather than fighting, managing wars rather than making war. Did management matter even more than manpower and the character of the men who ruled? Roman historians did not apply lessons from the far east as they did from the examples of Carthaginians, Greeks, Gauls, and those nearer to home. They could not. That would be left to their successor historians, like Iskander Rehman, now walking their tightrope.

Rehman is a masterful student of long wars, here between Romans and Germans, elsewhere between Britain, Spain, and France. The West is in the midst of many struggles today that look set to be long—and his authority brings light to their understanding.

Sir Peter Stothard, October 2023

Author's photograph of Villa Jovis,
Capri, May 2022.

INTRODUCTION

There are two Capris. There is the Capri familiar to any visitor to the Amalfi coast—the Capri which, day after day, siphons ferry-loads of sun-dazed tourists from the glistening waters of the Tyrrhenian Sea, disgorging them onto its rock-ribbed shores. The isle of extravagance, the playground of the wealthy, the siren land of the sybaritic.[1] And then there is the other Capri, that ancient Arcadia of beetling crags, muffled pine groves, and ghostly gorges. The Capri of Cybele, goddess of the primordial earth, worshipped deep in its flickering grottoes; of wily Odysseus and brave Aeneas; of Rome's first emperors.[2] To find it, one must climb. Past the squares with their packed restaurants, bronzed Instagram influencers, and glittering boutiques. Up narrow, snaking roads hemmed by stone-walled farmhouses and drenched in violet, tumbling cascades of wild bougainvillea. Through cool, shadowy pathways cushioned by pine needles and rent by twisting roots, where shaggy goats still roam. It is there, behind a pair of rust-encrusted gates, perched aerie-like atop the island's northeastern peak, that one can find the sprawling remains of Villa Jovis, one of Tiberius' many palaces on Capri. It was up on these soaring cliffs, with their sweeping view over "the circling expanse of open sea," that Rome's second emperor, weary of the great mother city's foul air, grasping senators, and choked streets, chose to spend the last decade of his reign.[3] Historical accounts and archeological evidence testify to the site's former magnificence: a colossal, labyrinthine structure teeming with hundreds of praetorians and servants, flowing over multiple levels, complete with huge water cisterns, cavernous kitchens, and luxuriant sloping gardens.

To visit Villa Jovis today, however, is to be overcome, first and foremost, by a sense of melancholy. The grounds are ill-kempt, the signage sparse and poorly maintained. Few tourists have the energy or willingness to haul themselves up the jagged hillside to the ruins. Those few that do stand huffing and puffing, iridescent with sweat, reaching with clammy hands for crumpled water bottles and dreaming of chilled *aperitivi*. Climbing over time-warped stone steps, they wander through gutted chambers and weed-choked alleyways. Crumbling walls, speckled with clumps of bright yellow sea fennel, fan out over thousands of square meters, interspersed here and there with blackened clusters of stunted columns. Depending on the time of day, one can easily find oneself completely alone amid the sun-scorched vastness, with only the gently humming cicadas and skittering geckoes for company. Resting on a bench in the rosemary-scented shade, eyes half-closed and the distant, rhythmic sound of the waves crashing several hundreds of feet below, one can almost see the aging emperor, pacing along the cliff edge, "neck stiff and bent forward," deep in conversation with his trusted advisors, stopping periodically to peer, with rheumy eyes, out across the glassy bay toward the mainland.[4] Almost everything about the decaying palace—from its faded grandeur to the gloaming sense of loneliness and neglect that seeps through its pockmarked limestone—seems to reflect the troubled legacy of its former occupant one of Rome's most overlooked and perhaps misunderstood, rulers.

Indeed, Tiberius, who served as Roman emperor from AD 14 to AD 37, is perhaps one of the most enigmatic figures of antiquity. Unlike the resplendent Augustus or the triumphant Trajan, he has not traditionally been viewed as an embodiment of imperial grandeur and martial glory. Nor has he been associated with the quiet wisdom of Rome's philosopher kings, the emperors Hadrian or Marcus Aurelius, or with the baroque madness and orgiastic savagery of the likes of Nero and Caligula. Instead, the portrait that surfaces from the palimpsest of historical accounts is one of unabashed and frustrating complexity—one whose contours can prove exceedingly difficult to discern, let alone understand.

The most famous narration of Tiberius' reign is that in the *Annals* of the great historian Tacitus, writing more than seven decades after the second emperor's death. While acknowledging many of his biographical subject's military and intellectual qualities, the normally dispassionate historian seems at pains to conceal his personal antipathy toward the brooding autocrat. The net result, note two modern classicists, is that

Tacitus's portrait of Tiberius consists of a whole series of modifications or adjustments, as if he were photographing his subject from a

Marble bust of Tiberius,
National Archaeological Museum, Naples.

series of different angles and in different lights: none of the frames, whether in close-up or not, is contradicted by another, but each produces a different effect.[5]

It is perhaps due to this ambiguity—and to this veil of flickering shadow that has often seemed to obscure any evaluation of the emperor's rule—that Tiberius has constituted such an object of fascination for strategic thinkers and commentators across the ages.

Contrasts have thus repeatedly been drawn between the relative tranquility and moderation of life across the empire under his reign and the (alleged) grotesque depravity of the reclusive monarch's private life on Capri, which—from Suetonius to Robert Graves' wildly popular duology of novels on the life of Emperor Claudius—has always exerted something of a lurid fascination on chroniclers of the period.[6] Whether these graphic accounts of the "old goat" of Capri's debased rutting are accurate, grossly exaggerated, or simply fantastical is another question—and one that few contemporary historians, including this author, would know how to answer.[7] What mattered is that an emperor chose a rustic karstic islet over the marbled promenades of the Palatine, and the close company of a shrunken entourage of foreign astrologers and philosophers over that of his fellow Roman senators. As the historian Tom Holland observes in his gripping history of the Principate, this stubborn quest for privacy was perhaps one of Rome's second emperor's greatest political flaws, for, "to the Roman people, privacy was something inherently unnatural. It permitted aberrant and sinister instincts free rein."[8] As the years went by, and Tiberius maintained his distance from Rome, the figure of the aging misanthrope became, for the general public, ever more stygian, its blurry outline increasingly shrouded in caliginous myth and heinous rumor. As a result, soon "no rumor of his perversities was so hideous that it could not be believed in Rome."[9] In any case, whether true or fabricated, these whispered aspersions, however disturbing or titillating, had little bearing on the lives of millions of men and women eking out their daily lives in the provinces, or on the conduct of Roman grand strategy more broadly.

Meanwhile, chroniclers of ancient Rome have struggled to reconcile Tiberius' apparent reluctance to rule and early deference for republican norms with the dark blossoming of a viciously paranoid brand of tyranny in the later years of his life.[10] Perhaps most importantly, for many writers and political philosophers Tiberius has come to represent something of a curious archetype: that particular breed of authoritarian and misanthropic leader who—despite his moral shortcomings and tendency toward tyranny—also demonstrates a surprising degree of temperance and competence in the conduct of foreign policy.[11] Thus for Alexander Pushkin, Tiberius was "one of the greatest administrative minds of antiquity," whose saturnine wisdom inspired the Russian playwright's memorable depiction of the sixteenth-century tsar Boris Godunov.[12] Montesquieu, for his part, favorably compared Tiberius to the fifteenth-century French king Louis XI, or "Louis the Prudent"—the so-called "spider king" renowned across Europe for his endless webs of intrigue.[13] In the nineteenth century, the great Nobel Prize-winning historian Theodor Mommsen famously drew parallels between Tiberius and Frederick the Great.[14]

For all of these thinkers, it was clear that one of the Rome's most overlooked and unpopular emperors was also one of its most capable—at least with regard to the formulation of grand strategy and foreign policy. Indeed, under Tiberius the administrative apparatus of the Principate was strengthened, and the parlous state of the Empire's economy—which had been weakened by decades of profligacy, predatory usury practices, and heightened military expenditure—was remedied. Tiberius arrested the process of imperial expansion into Germany, which had previously resulted in disaster with the battle of the Teutoburg Forest in AD 9, when three entire legions were brutally annihilated by German tribesmen, and began the process of delineating the Roman imperium's extensive boundaries with a constellation of fortlets and watchtowers.[15] Content with solidifying control over the empire's existing territory, he sought wherever possible to preserve Rome's dominance through the exercise of subtle diplomacy and military pressure rather than armed annexation. Mindful of the ever-looming possibility of provincial unrest, he sought to maintain stability through a policy of fiscal moderation, famously reminding some of his more rapacious governors that "it was the role of a good shepherd to shear his flock, not flay it."[16] No major battles ended in calamity during Tiberius' reign, no legions bled their last on Parthia's sands or vanished into Germania's sylvan gloom, no sacred standards were soiled by barbarian hands. At the same time, however, he proved powerless to prevent the eruption of certain large-scale uprisings, whether in Gaul or in North Africa, remained deeply unpopular, and was subsequently accused by many Roman historians of weakness or negligence in the defense of their imperium's international credibility and interests.

By engaging in a detailed, nuanced, and multidisciplinary analysis of the iron imperator's attitude toward foreign policy, military affairs, and imperial management, this book will seek to peel off some of the layers of mystery surrounding Tiberius' reign. It draws on an earlier, unpublished research project for the Office of Net Assessment (ONA) at the U.S. Department of Defense. Since its creation in 1973 under the Nixon administration, the ONA has played a discreet but invaluable role at the heart of Washington's national security ecosystem, championing the virtues of deliberate reflection and classical erudition, even—and perhaps especially—in the fast-paced world of defense planning and national security. Along the way, it has nurtured generations of historically minded defense strategists, and sponsored myriad detailed monographs and studies of past military campaigns, strategies, and concepts of operation.[17] This study of Tiberian grand strategy, in the tradition of ONA research products, is a work of applied history, i.e. "an explicit attempt to illuminate current challenges and choices by analyzing historical precedents and analogs."[18] Although it engages in a deep analysis of the vibrant academic literature on the period in question, it also seeks to remain in continuous conversation with our troubled present. Applied historians do not believe in perfect analogies, nor do they expect history to mechanically repeat itself, although it may sometimes rhyme. And they certainly do not subscribe to the notion, so prevalent among contemporary American political scientists, that our combined historical experience forms a sterile vat from which neatly self-contained case studies can be surgically extracted and then grafted onto some grand architectonic theory of human behavior. Rather, what is of primary value for policymakers is the intellectual process of historical inquiry itself—how it teaches one to manage complexity and detect shifting patterns of cause and effect, in essence forming a kind of calisthenics of the mind. As historians such as Robert Crowcroft have eloquently noted, a sustained immersion in the past has much to recommend it, primarily as an intellectual habitus, cognitive stimulant, or general "mode of thinking":

It facilitates the rigorous testing of assumptions; seeks to discern the underlying, long-term dynamics of a given situation; identifies patterns; explores the history of relevant groups or institutions; probes the way in which actors think and formulate their goals, draws inferences, assesses what is known; what is presumed, and what is unknown; and hones our ability to react to the unexpected. The formulation and execution of policy is the exploration of possibilities, and a good working knowledge of the database of past human experience might help us to nudge possibilities into probabilities.[19]

This book will seek, in particular, to gauge whether the Tiberian era—during which the international system's leading power seemingly succeeded in consolidating its recent gains and avoiding a potentially ruinous geopolitical overextension—holds any instructive insights for the early- to mid-twenty-first-century United States. In so doing, it will grapple with a series of important and strategically resonant questions relating to the exercise of Roman imperial leadership, and to the challenges inherent to the preservation of military primacy more broadly.

For example, how did the early Principate manage to control such a vast empire with such comparatively small forces? How did these means of territorial control resemble or differ from other, later hegemonies?[20] How did the memory of certain recent and traumatic defeats—whether the loss of Crassus' army in Parthia or the destruction of Varus' legions in the rain-lashed forests of Germania—condition Rome's subsequent attitudes toward overseas intervention and/or shape its grand strategy? How did the early Principate's military machine adapt its force structure and tailor its operational concepts to different theaters and adversaries? Did Roman thinkers and strategists clearly distinguish counterinsurgency and policing actions from high-intensity campaigns, and if so, how did they plan and train for such variations in combat contingencies?

How did early imperial Romans define the concept of peace, and was the empire really as quiescent during the Tiberian period as some would have us believe? What role did allies and auxiliary troops play in Roman military strategy, and what were the risks associated with an overreliance on "green" rather than "blue" forces in certain restive border regions? What defensive frontier system did Tiberius put in place, and how did his policies differ both from those of his predecessors and those of his successors? Last but not least, to what extent should these developments be imputed to the choices made by one individual—the Emperor Tiberius—rather than to the nature of the political system within which he operated, or to the broader physical and geopolitical realities that acted as a brake on Rome's strategic reach?

This study is not a traditional biography—rather its biographical focus is intended to serve not only as a framing narrative device but also, and perhaps more importantly, as a prism through which to engage in a thorough and nuanced examination of the early Roman Principate's strategies for imperial control and primacy preservation. It is structured in two main parts. The first section explores the tumultuous, conflict-ridden world into which Tiberius was born and raised, and provides a *tour d'horizon* of the early imperium's geopolitical environment. It delves into Tiberius' long political career prior to being anointed as Augustus' successor in his mid-fifties; and explores how various life experiences, intellectual debates, and philosophical influences may have furnished the ideational underpinning for some of his later actions. It details his decades of intense campaigning throughout the empire, during which he rose to be considered as one of the Principate's most talented generals. Attention will be drawn, in particular, to the composition of Rome's armed forces, to the nature of its force deployments during the Augustan period—and to how Tiberius' extensive operational experience across a series of complex combat theaters may have shaped his subsequent attitude toward foreign and security policy.

The second section examines Tiberius' rule as Rome's second emperor. It will detail the various uncertainties tied to Rome's first dynastic succession, and explore Tiberius' complex, sometimes fraught relationship with a senatorial establishment ill-accustomed to his more hesitant and cryptic form of governance. It will explore his differences of opinion with certain members of the imperial family with regard to territorial expansion, along with his attitude toward provincial administration and management of key peripheral zones—such as Armenia, Commagene, and Cappadocia—which he successfully (and durably) turned into Roman buffer states. Throughout his reign, and even once he had moved the imperial court to Capri, Tiberius retained an iron grip on the conduct of Roman foreign policy. Focus will also be laid on Rome's military operations during the Tiberian era, as its forces fully transitioned from the armies of the late Republic to those of the early Empire, along with its evolving attitude toward sovereignty and border security.[21] The second section will then engage in a systematic evaluation of Roman grand strategy during the Tiberian era. It will point to the growing reliance on allied and auxiliary forces as a seemingly more cost-effective mode of military primacy and debate the merits and risks of Rome's long-term adoption of such delegative strategies for territorial control and frontier management, along with its move toward an increasingly bifurcated military force structure.

The book will conclude by drawing on some of the contemporary literature on grand strategy, unipolarity, and imperial overextension, and will suggest that the Tiberian period does indeed offer a number of valuable insights for contemporary security managers. Indeed, as Washington's strategic community traverses its own period of self-doubt, pondering the nature of the U.S.'s security commitments and debating the extent and elasticity of its strategic perimeters, the need for rigorous applied history has rarely been more urgent.[22]

I.

GUARDIAN OF THE EMPIRE
Tiberius during the reign of Augustus

Augustus then brought a world exhausted from civil dissension under his authority, with the title of First Citizen. [...] After Brutus and Cassius were killed, there was no longer a state military force; and when Sextus Pompeius had been vanquished in Sicily, Lepidus discarded and Mark Antony killed, even the Julian Party was left with no leader other than Caesar Octavian [the future Emperor Augustus]. Dropping the title "triumvir," Octavian presented himself as a consul, and as a man satisfied to hold tribunician authority in order to safeguard the people. Then, by seducing the military with donatives, the masses with grain allowances, and everybody with the pleasure of peace, he gradually increased the powers, drawing to himself the functions of Senate, magistrates and laws. He met no resistance. The most dynamic men had fallen in battle or through the proscriptions; and the remaining nobles rose to wealth and offices in proportion to their appetite for servitude. Having benefited from the revolution, they preferred the security of the current regime to the dangers of the old.

Tacitus, Annals, I.1–1.2

Marble bust of Livia Drusilla, wife to Augustus and
mother of Tiberius, Vatican Museums, Rome.

IMPERIAL ROME
AND THE BIRTH OF A NEW ORDER

The Roman Republic died the year Tiberius was born. Only a few weeks before the future emperor came into the world, his maternal grandfather had staggered back to his dusty campaign tent, wearily drawn his sword, and taken his own life. Marcus Livius Drusus Claudianus, a senator and former partisan of Pompey, had fought alongside the forces of Brutus and Cassius—two of the leading conspirators in the murder of Julius Caesar—at the Battle of Philippi, and had lost.[1] A proud member of the *gens Claudia*, the Claudian family, the venerable aristocrat could trace his lineage back to the early years of the Republic.[2] It was in this remote corner of northern Greece that the aged patrician, unwilling to bear the humiliation of defeat or countenance the disgrace of capture, had decided his own fate. In the days leading up to his suicide, the serried ranks of two Roman armies, caught in a narrow patch of land wedged in between scrubby gorges and a fetid marsh, had met in a series of brutal clashes.

To many of those taking part in this cataclysmic struggle—Rome's largest land battle to date—it may have seemed that behind the din of arms and braying of trumpets there rang another, fainter sound; the somber death knell of a five-hundred-year-old system of government. Involving more than two hundred thousand combatants, the final melee devolved into a vicious bout of fratricidal bloodletting as the armored columns of legionaries—smothered under great clouds of dust—hacked, stabbed, and bludgeoned away at each other at close quarters.[3] "They did not now remember that they were fellow-citizens of their enemies," lamented the second-century Greek historian Appian of Alexandria, "but hurled threats at each other as though they had been enemies by birth and descent, so much did the anger of the moment extinguish reason and nature in them."

Cato's Death at Utica,
painting by Jean-Paul Laurens (1838–1921),
Musée des Augustins, Toulouse.

Both sides divined equally that this day and this battle would decide the fate of Rome completely; and so indeed it did. [...] The onslaught was superb and terrible. They had little need of arrows, stones, or javelins, as is customary in war, for they did not resort to the usual maneuvers and tactics of battles, but, coming to close combat with naked swords, they slew and were slain, seeking to break each other's ranks. [...] The slaughter and groans were terrible.[4]

Yet although the carnage at Philippi may have marked the collapse of structured republican opposition to the Caesarist faction, it did not signal an end to Rome's bloody civil wars. War "worse than civil [...] when kindred fought against kindred [...], eagles were matched against other, and pilum threatened pilum" would continue to rage across the Mediterranean world for another twelve years.[5] The butchery would only come to an end when Octavian finally prevailed over all of his remaining rivals, defeating both Sextus Pompeius—the swashbuckling son of Pompey who led for a few years a hub of resistance on the island of Sicily—and then his brother-in-law and fellow triumvir, Mark Antony, in a series of large-scale military operations on land and at sea.

Tiberius was born into this maelstrom, and as a result his earliest years were traumatic and eventful, as his blue-blooded parents sought to navigate roiling factional waters, crisscrossing the Roman *oikoumene* or known world, shifting and trading their allegiances in a desperate bid for survival.[6] Tiberius' father, Tiberius Nero, had taken to the Senate floor to argue in Cassius, and Brutus' defense following Julius Caesar's murder, and a vengeful Octavian had subsequently added his name to the dreaded *proscriptiones*, a detailed register, or "hit list," of all newly declared enemies of the state.[7] Fleeing Rome with his heavily pregnant teenage wife, Livia Drusilla, Tiberius Nero first joined the short-lived Italian revolt of Lucius Antonius (Mark Antony's brother), before offering to lend support to Sextus Pompeius' maritime reavers in Sicily. Roman chroniclers later provided dramatic retellings of these years of forced exile and frantic itineracy, with Suetonius recounting how the infant Tiberius' wails almost betrayed his parents' hiding place in Neapolis, or how one night he and his mother nearly perished in a forest fire while skulking through the lands of Spartan allies of the Claudian clan.[8]

The family's errancy finally came to an end in 39 BC with the signing of the Pact of Misenum, which enacted a policy of amnesty for political refugees. After three harrowing years on the run, Tiberius' family was at last allowed to return to Rome. There, the beautiful Livia caught Octavian's eye at a banquet. The hapless Tiberius Nero was strong-armed into annulling his marriage to his young wife, then six months pregnant with his second child, Drusus (later known as Drusus the Elder), and into handing her over to Octavian as a payment for his past opposition.[9] In what must have constituted an excruciating moment of self-abasement, the former senator allegedly took on the ceremonial role of the "father" at the wedding of Augustus and Livia, publicly giving away his ex-wife to her wolfish young suitor.[10] As we shall see, this was to be the first of several instances when the future imperator's personal whims and dynastic ambitions threw Tiberius' personal life into turmoil—durably affecting his relationships with the women and family members he most loved.[11]

Brought up with his younger brother Drusus as a member of the imperial household, Tiberius made his first public appearance in 33 BC, when he delivered the funeral oration for his father. A few years later, following Octavian's resounding victory over Mark Antony at the battle of Actium, the thirteen-year-old was invited to ride alongside his stepfather through the streets of Rome during his triumph. He was placed on the left side of the victor, with the place of honor—to the right of the quadriga—reserved for Marcus Claudius Marcellus, Octavian's nephew.[12] This was to be Tiberius' somewhat awkward position for decades to come: one of prominence but not preeminence, a protégé, companion, and patron of the planned Augustan dynasty rather than one of its fully anointed members.

From 31 to 27 BC, Octavian moved slowly but purposefully to consolidate his rule and entrench the "delicate compromise of supervision and control" that constituted the early Principate's system of government.[13] In this he was greatly aided by—as Tacitus famously noted in his opening to the *Annals*—the Roman populace's state of sheer moral exhaustion. Ever since that watershed moment a half-century earlier, when Sulla had marched his troops into Rome, the city had fallen prey to bouts of severe political unrest (such as the Catilinarian conspiracy), with its cobbled streets playing theater to endless running battles between rival gangs.[14] The civil wars, with their feuding strongmen, savage political purges, and mammoth armies, had decimated Rome's political elites, and repeated interruptions to the city's grain shipments had frequently led to widespread famine. At the time of the Battle of Philippi, no less than sixty-six legions were under arms, and it is estimated that this accounted for an unprecedented 260,000 to 270,000 Italians—or more than 25 percent of the peninsula's youth—serving under the Eagle.[15] To this one must also add the forces of innumerable provincial allies, auxiliaries, and various client kingdoms, which had been sucked—sometimes voluntarily, but more often against their better judgment—into the Mediterranean super-power's internecine struggles. A consummate politician, Octavian framed himself as the defender of plebeian interests, while respectfully emphasizing the power and prestige of the Senate. Capitalizing on Roman society's collective war-weariness, the young warlord—rich with the plunder acquired during his recent Egyptian campaigns against Mark Antony—could count on the loyalty of the legions, as well as on the superlative military skill of his top commander and old friend, Marcus Vipsanius Agrippa. In 27 BC, during the so-called "Augustan settlement," the Senate voted to grant Octavian the honorific title of "Augustus," and formally delegated much of Rome's military and political power to the new princeps, or "first citizen." Under the terms of the Augustan settle-ment, Augustus received a grant of proconsular imperium over the most heavily militarized provinces (all of Gaul, Syria, Egypt, and much of Spain), thus retaining direct control over most of the Roman legions.[16] He was also granted continuously renewable grants of tribunician power, which enabled him to both pass legislation and to veto initiatives that were not to his liking. It is generally from this date that historians mark the true beginning of Rome's imperial era.

The complexity of the first emperor's character—along with the many ambiguities nested within his political program and regime—have con-founded generations of commentators, and it is not possible to do this his-toriographical debate full justice here.[17] Much of the challenge lies in the fact that while the rule of Augustus was unquestionably revolutionary (most notably in its permanent institutionalization of Roman autocracy), it also relied to a great degree on complex forms of co-management with the senatorial elite, and on the revival of many previously abandoned republi-can rites and traditions. The great twentieth-century classicist Sir Ronald Syme memorably portrayed the painful contradictions—the "conspiracy of decent reticence"—that floated over this pivotal moment, writing that

> it would be an elementary error to fancy that the ceremony of January 13th [the transmutation of Octavian into Augustus and the resultant political settlement] was merely a grim comedy devised to

deceive the ingenuous or intimidate the servile. On the contrary, the purified Senate, being in a majority the partisans of Augustus, were well aware of what was afoot. To secure the domination of the Caesarian party, the consolidation of the Revolution, and the maintenance of peace, it was necessary that the primacy of Caesar's heir should be strengthened and perpetuated. Not, however, under the fatal name of dictator or monarchy. On all sides prevailed a conspiracy of decent reticence about the gap between fact and theory. It was evident: no profit but only danger from talking about it. The Principate baffles definition.[18]

Once combined with his assiduous courting of Rome's most venerable patrician families, the outwardly conservative aspects of Augustus' political agenda—most notably his curbing of the more radical reforms imposed by his uncle Julius Caesar upon the functioning of the Senate—did much to help to secure its broader acceptance.[19] Over the centuries, many commentators have—while admiring the ruler's political skill, bureaucratic dexterity, and intellectual acumen—pointed to Augustus' ultimate hypocrisy.[20] Edward Gibbon, in a characteristically acerbic *bon mot*, thus quipped that "Augustus' tender respect for a constitution which he destroyed can only be explained by an attentive consideration of the character of that subtle tyrant," before adding that

> to resume, in a few words, the system of government, as it was instituted by Augustus, and maintained by those princes who understood their own interest and that of the people, it may be defined as an absolute monarchy disguised by the forms of a commonwealth. The masters of the Roman world surrounded their thrones with darkness and humbly professed themselves the accountable ministers of the senate whose supreme decrees they dictated and obeyed.[21]

It is perhaps wiser, however, to view Augustus not so much as a somber tyrant (although there was certainly a cold, cynical dimension to his persona), but as a power-hungry counterrevolutionary, no doubt somewhat sincere in his social and moral conservatism, in his desire to privilege order over liberty, and in his attachment—however selective—to certain political traditions of the Republic.[22] In this he was both the artisan and product of his era, more commonly known as the "Augustan Restoration."[23]

Indeed, many of the greatest writers and poets of the age—often operating under the patronage of Maecenas, the emperor's close friend and cultural advisor—openly and enthusiastically celebrated the advent of the Principate as a period of national renewal following the horror and hardships of Rome's civil wars.[24] At the same time, Augustus gradually enacted a series of socially conservative policies, penalizing celibacy, punishing adultery, and promoting natalist policies.[25] As one classicist notes, this legislative program was central to Augustus' reign, and meant that

> the private life of virtually every Roman now became a matter of the state's concerns and regulations. The state massively intruded on matters of private conduct such as marriage—the question was no more whether to marry, but how soon and whom or whom not—and divorce and adultery; the latter was taken out of the jurisdiction of the family and transferred to a public court. Other palpable effects on people's everyday lives included the prohibition for unmarried men and women to attend the spectacles. It was, in short, the most pronounced attempt at moral and even moralistic leadership, which in this case transcended the mere exercise of auctoritas.[26]

Over the years, certain core themes, or arguments, were to develop as a means of explaining away this passive acceptance of the abandonment of cherished civil liberties and centuries-long traditions, and of what the great German scholar Walter Eder memorably called the "eerie silence" that greeted Augustus' imposition of one-man rule.[27] One widely held explanation was that the Republic's system of government was simply no longer viable—it had failed to keep pace with Rome's rate of territorial expansion. The former city-state's military success and continuous campaigning overseas had bred complacency and corruption, weakened traditional social mores, and empowered belligerent strongmen. This idea—that uncontrolled foreign expansion led to domestic decay—was hardly novel. Indeed, it had repeatedly been expressed by a variety of classical thinkers, ranging from Polybius to Posidonius, since at least the end of the Punic Wars.[28] Famously, for Sallust, the destruction of Carthage, Rome's prime peer competitor, and the resultant flow of riches and dissipation of a "fear-rooted" internal consensus had led to hubris, division, and decadence as a "host of [wealthy] private men"—the future Sullas, Pompeys, and Caesars— took it upon themselves to "level mountains and build upon seas."[29]

This literary topos became even more common during the first few decades of the Principate, as expressed in the works of Horace and Virgil, and perhaps most eloquently by Lucan in the *Pharsalia*, when he writes the following:

> Among the people there were hidden causes of war—the causes which have ever brought down ruin upon imperial race. For when Rome had conquered the world and Fortune showered excess of wealth upon her, virtue was dethroned by prosperity, and the spoil taken from the enemy lured to extravagance: they set no limit to their wealth or their dwellings; greed rejected the food that once sufficed, men seized their wealth or their dwellings; men seized for their use garments scarce decent for women to wear; poverty, the mother of manhood, became a bugbear; and from all the earth was brought the special bane of each nation. Next they stretched wide the boundaries of their lands, till those acres, which were once furrowed by the iron plough of Camillus and felt the spade of Curius long ago, grew into vast estates tilled by foreign cultivators. Such a nation could find no pleasure in peace and quiet, nor leave the sword alone and grow fat on their own freedom. Hence they were quick to anger, and crime prompted by poverty was lightly regarded; to overawe the State was high distinction which justified recourse to the sword; and might became the standard of right. Hence came laws and decrees of the people passed by violence; and consuls and tribunes alike threw justice into confusion; hence office was snatched by bribery and the people put up its own support for auction, while corruption, repeating year by year the venal competition of the Campus, destroyed the State; hence came devouring usury and interest that looks greedily to the day of payment; credit was shattered and many found their profit in war.[30]

Rome's hegemony had become so absolute, and its "interests so vast that it was very difficult to administer them," absent a strong executive in the form of the princeps, argued the various defenders of the new order.[31] Indeed, the legitimation of one-man rule—both as an immediate curative to Rome's fissiparous tendencies and as a bulwark against future disorder—was at the heart of the Augustan project, forming a core element of the regime's propaganda. Rome's first emperor thus continuously stressed

his role in bringing about peace and stability, whether via the construction of the Ara Pacis, or "Altar of Peace," an exquisitely carved marble monument celebrating Augustus' role in ending the civil wars, or through declarations such as those contained in the famed *Res Gestae Divi Augusti*, or *Acts of Augustus*, a detailed account of his achievements, which he bequeathed to the Vestal Virgins before his death and which was chiseled postmortem into the walls of the Temple of Rome and various other locations around the ancient world. In the *Res Gestae*, Augustus thus establishes a direct link between his war termination abilities and his political elevation:

> In my sixth and seventh consulships, when I had extinguished the flames of civil war, after receiving by universal consent the absolute control of affairs, I transferred the res publica from my own control to the will of the Senate and People of Rome. For this service on my part I was given the title of Augustus by decree of the Senate.[32]

One of the many paradoxes of this devilishly complex era, however, lies in the delicate coexistence—and at times intermingling—of such outwardly pacifist and staidly authoritarian sentiments with a more expansionist, idealistic brand of Roman exceptionalism; one which, to quote Virgil in the *Aeneid*, advocated for an "*imperium sine fine*," or an empire without end.[33] For some of these writers, the end of Rome's civil wars was not so much the end of history as a new era full of promise, one which now provided a window of opportunity for an ambitious redefinition of the empire's borders, and for the renewed pursuit of glory in a series of foreign ventures.[34] At the same time, a hazy nostalgia for the fabled sense of unity and purpose that had animated Rome during its darkest hour—when it was facing potential destruction at the hands of Hannibal—continued to shape the thinking of Rome's elites, and not in a way necessarily conducive to policies of restraint. Indeed, Roman thinkers continuously fretted that, in the absence of a great power war, their martial prowess would atrophy, their shared virtues would erode, and their society would slide back into a state of general dissoluteness. The greatest historian of the Augustan Age, Livy, argued that if Rome had chosen to initiate a war with Liguria in 187 BC—during the fifty-year gap between the Second and Third Punic Wars—it was in part to "keep alive the military discipline of the Romans during the intervals between their great wars."[35] Like some winemakers who insist that only vines that have painfully clawed their roots deep through rocky soil can actually produce good wine, Rome's great patriotic narratives were all stories of struggle, sacrifice, and victory against insuperable odds.[36] And while war's reality was often tragic, its prolonged absence was frequently perceived as corrosive.

Lucan may have railed against the hubris that resulted from the imperium's expansion, but he also wistfully drew attention to how the great battles of the civil wars had prevented Rome from fully channeling its energies outward, and from asserting its domination over lands as distant as India.[37] Similarly, the poet Horace—who had deplored the wasteful slaughter of the past few decades in his earliest poems—now began eagerly to anticipate the addition of Britain and Parthia to the empire.[38] As we shall see, it was the continuous tension between these two competing impulses—the urge to dominate and the concern to consolidate—that was to characterize so much of Rome's grand strategy during the reign of Augustus, and—to an even greater extent—that of his successor, Tiberius.

Engraving by Nicolas Beatrizet, *Roman Soldiers Fighting Against Dacians* (after a bas-relief on the Arch of Constantine, Rome), 1553, The Metropolitan Museum of Art, New York.

STRATEGY AND CONFLICT
IN THE AUGUSTAN AGE

Despite Augustus' repeated emphasis on peace, Rome's armies were almost continuously at war during the forty-odd years of his rule. As many classicists have noted, the Augustan concept of *Pax Romana*, or "Roman Peace," signified above all the absence of great power war and civil unrest.[1] It was associated first and foremost with the establishment of *Concordia* at the core of the empire. The skirmishes, raids, and counterinsurgency operations fought along the imperium's ill-defined and porous boundaries were viewed as part of the everyday management of fractious subject peoples, or dismissed—sometimes, as we shall see, in an overly hasty fashion—as mere policing operations against "bandits."[2] As British classicist Neville Morley has noted, this systematic downplaying of armed resistance movements across the empire served both an ideological and bureaucratic purpose:

> Resistance to Roman rule was generally presented as brigandage; that label stripped it of any legitimacy as a movement of protest, but it also offered the local commander a valid excuse for requesting reinforcements and resources, whereas admitting to the existence of a serious revolt would invariably be taken as a personal failure of the governor.[3]

Rome's legions and auxiliaries were expected to operate across a broad spectrum of conflict—not only training for high-intensity "conventional" force-on-force confrontations, but also engaging in policing actions and counterinsurgency .[4] Roman legions stationed in critical provinces were not only static garrison forces, they were also armies of occupation that radiated military power across hundreds of miles, profoundly and durably transforming the economic and social fabrics of their deployment zones.[5] Roman soldiers were thus dispatched for all manner of nonmilitary duties, ranging from road, canal, and aqueduct construction to

Mare Germanicum
Mare Seubicum
GERMANIA MAGNA
BRITANNIA SUPERIOR
Londinium
BELGICA
OCEANUS ATLANTICUS
Mare Cantabricum
GALLIA
AQUITANIA
ILLYRICUM
Masselia
Corsica
Rome
Mare Adriaticum
Baleares
Sardinia
Mare Tyrrhenum
Gades
Sicilia
Mare Ionium et Siculum
Mare Ibericum
MARE
MAURITANIA
NUMIDIA
Carthago
Syrtis Minor
Syrtis Major
N
0   500 km
0   500 miles

The Roman Empire c. 44 BCE - 117 CE
Empire at death of Caesar
Empire at death of Augustus
Empire at death of Trajan
Regional capitals
Cities
Roads
CIA
THRACIA
Byzantium
ONIA
Mare
Aegeum
Athens
Milétus
Pergamum
Crete
Cyprus
ERNUM
Cyrene
ANAICA
Alexandria
AEGYPTUS
Lacus Maeotis
Pontus Euxinus
GALATIA
Antiochia
SYRIA
Palmyra
Damascus
JUDAEA
Hierosolyma
ARABIA
Sinus Arabicus
ARMENIA
ASSYRIA
MESOPOTAMIA
Babylon
Mare Caspium
REGNUM PARTHORUM
Tropic of Cancer

census holding, tax collection, and geographical surveying. In some cases, Roman officers even acted as judges, settling local and tribal disputes. Over time, as we shall see in more detail in a later section, something of a division of labor occurred, with Rome's growing number of auxiliaries increasingly being entrusted with special warfare, counter-insurgency and everyday frontier management, while its legions served as a more conventional deterrent and heavy infantry reserve. This was a gradual process, however, and it was never absolute, with auxiliaries and legionaries continuing to fight in complex "joint" operations throughout the early Principate.

Tensions often simmered within formally conquered territories and provinces for generations, if not centuries—tensions which would sporadically erupt into large-scale confrontations involving thousands of combatants. As Susan Mattern has stressed,

> despite some modern perceptions to the contrary, the history of Rome's expansion is not a story of effortless, brilliant successes. Most places had to be conquered not just once, but more than once, sometimes several times; and the Romans seem to have known and expected this.[6]

Even the strict maintenance of the empire within its present boundaries therefore required the continuous use of military force—peace was never absolute. Augustus, however, was not only bent on preserving Rome's writ—he was also intent on expanding it. Indeed, the early years of Augustus seemed to radiate an "almost euphoric expansionism," with the young emperor spending much of his time on campaigns outside Rome and adding more territory to the empire than any of his successors, barring perhaps the Emperor Trajan (see page 44–45), who ruled a century later, from AD 98 to 117.[7] For a man such as Augustus, who had cemented his control over Rome's institutions following a bloody civil war—and who had not hesitated to display, on occasion, a certain savagery in the prosecution of his fellow citizens—foreign wars served a useful diversionary as well as unifying purpose.[8] Under his rule, the steady trudging sound of thousands of caligae—the ubiquitous hobnailed leather sandals worn by the legions—was thus heard across the ancient world, from the scorched deserts of Arabia to the snowcapped mountains of Raetia (a Roman province encompassing parts of present-day Switzerland, the Tyrol, and portions of Bavaria).

Before launching his campaigns of conquest, however, the emperor engaged in a profound reorganization of the Roman military apparatus. As mentioned earlier, Rome's military manpower had grown exponentially in the course of its civil wars, numbering up to sixty-six legions, along with countless auxiliary and allied forces. Early on, Augustus moved to substantially downsize and professionalize the army, paring it down to twenty-eight legions. Each legion usually comprising somewhere between five and six thousand men, this represented a force of about 155,000 legionaries and a number of auxiliaries that historians such as Tacitus portrayed as roughly equivalent. To this one must add approximately ten thousand praetorians, spread not only across Rome but also across various points throughout Italy, and a newly revamped imperial navy which had been streamlined from about seven hundred warships at the height of the civil wars to less than half that size, comprising about thirty thousand sailors.[9] This meant that the Roman empire's standing army amounted to, at the very most, about 350,000 men, with some estimates suggesting that at least 40 to 50 percent of the state's overall income was funneled into its upkeep.[10]

In his *Roman History*, Cassius Dio famously described a spirited discussion between Augustus' two closest advisors, Agrippa and Maecenas, as to the merits and drawbacks of the evolution toward a fully professionalized force, rather than one based on citizen levies. Agrippa, a staunch traditionalist and republican, argues in favor of the conscript armies of the Republic, pointing to their positive ramifications for societal unity and resiliency, and warning of the considerable expense involved in maintaining a professional force. Maecenas, the fervent monarchist, on the other hand, eloquently makes the case for a permanent standing army of volunteers, arguing that their greater degree of specialization would make for a far more effective and disciplined fighting force:

> A standing army should be supported, drawn from the citizens, the subject nations, and the allies, in one case more, in another less, province by province, as the necessities of the case demand; and they ought to always be under arms and make a practice of warfare continually. They must have secured winter-quarters at the most opportune points, and serve for a definite time, so that a certain period of active life may remain for them before old age. For, separated so far as we are from frontiers of the empire, with enemies

living near us on every side, we should otherwise no longer be able to count on auxiliaries in the case of emergencies. Again, if we allow all those of military age to have arms and to practice warlike pursuits, quarrels and civil wars will always be arising among them. However, if we prevent them from doing this and then need their assistance at all in battle, we shall always have to face danger with inexperienced and untrained soldiers at our back. For this reason I submit the proposition that most of them live without arms and away from forts; but that the hardiest and those most in need of a livelihood be registered and kept in practice. They themselves will fight better by devoting their leisure to this single business; and the rest will the more easily farm, manage ships, and attend to the other pursuits of peace, if they are not forced to be called out for service, but have others to stand as their guardians. The most active and vigorous element, that is, which is most often obliged to live by robbery, will be supported without harming others, and all the rest of the population will lead a life free from danger.[11]

Augustus, ever the tactful manager of men, is described as thanking both of his advisors "for their many ideas and the exhaustiveness of their exposition, and their frankness," even as he "inclined, however, toward the proposition of Maecenas."[12] Most modern historians understand this dialogue to be largely fictitious, one of the many instances of artistic license strewn across the work of ancient thinkers for whom history was just as much a medium of moral instruction as an accumulation of facts.[13] The narrative device does, however, serve a useful function—indeed, there were no doubt similar, and equally vivid, discussions among Augustus and his advisors as to how to right-size the future imperial force. The *dilectators*—officials charged with enforcing conscription—had become dreaded figures in town forums, and it would have been politically challenging for Augustus to maintain the levy-based system now that the civil wars had come to a close.[14] Throughout the early imperial era it even became difficult to recruit Italians into the professional armed forces, until gradually most cohorts (barring those of the praetorians, who offered better pay and conditions) came to be composed of citizens drawn from the provinces.[15]

Furthermore, the gargantuan size of the army post-Actium rendered it both prohibitively expensive and organizationally unwieldy.[16] A recast, leaner and meaner force would not only allow former soldiers to reenter civilian life and thus boost sectors of the economy (such as agriculture) that had greatly suffered during decades of civil strife, it would also perhaps prove more personally loyal to its princeps than a host of citizen-soldiers organized along the lines of the former regime.[17] By 29 BC, up to 120,000 former legionaries had been discharged and settled in veteran colonies. These colonies were to play a crucial role in reshaping provincial landscapes, and in supporting Rome's imperial expansion. Often situated in newly acquired territories, they acted as self-sufficient hubs of economic activity and, much in the vein of the rugged settler communities on the wild American frontier, helped expand colonial dominance over contested or ungoverned spaces—all while frequently being targeted by indigenous insurgents.[18]

The new regime also created the first institutionalized military treasury dedicated to paying soldiers' salaries and discharge payments. Augustus boasts in the *Res Gestae* that he first opened the treasury's account with a massive donation of 170 million sestertii from his own private funds—yet another way of reminding the legions who was the ultimate guarantor of their well-being.[19] Two new taxes were subsequently introduced and imposed on Romans in order to finance the armed forces—a 5 percent tax on inheritances and a 1 percent tax on auction sales. These taxes, though reportedly deeply unpopular at the time, only covered a small portion of the empire's military expenditure. The vast majority of the imperium's revenue was collected in the provinces, via land and poll taxes. The system of taxation was facilitated by the now regular conduct of empire-wide censuses, which Augustus had revived after decades of abeyance.[20] This practice not only enabled Rome's imperial staff to establish a more systematic and effective fiscal infrastructure, it also allowed for the monitoring of populations in restive provinces and border regions, and, as such, was often deeply resented by Rome's more recalcitrant subject peoples.

In 13 BC, Augustus modified the system of discharge—legionaries were no longer automatically promised land settlements but were offered a cash payment following sixteen years of service and four supplementary years with "veteran" status in the reserves. These veterans, termed *evocati*, served in separate units under their own commander, the *curator*, were excused from engaging in some of the more grueling or tedious physical activities (such as camp and infrastructure development), and were sometimes promoted to the rank of centurion. In AD 5–6, service time was extended to twenty years, with perhaps up to five additional years in the *evocati*.[21] It is unclear why the service period was extended, although some classicists suggest that this may have proven necessary in light of a lack of volunteers.[22]

Over the centuries, historians have commented admiringly on the apparent cost-effectiveness—in terms of manpower, if not financial cost—of Roman primacy in the early imperial era. In addition to the relatively modest size of its standing army, the empire, notes one historian, "as late as the second century AD [...] was run by 150 elite administrators for every 400,000 provincials." In comparison, he adds, "British India in the nineteenth century was governed by around 7,000 administrators, one for every 43,000 natives, while under the Song Dynasty in China, in the twelfth century, there was one official for every 15,000 natives."[23] The reasons behind the success and longevity of this relatively light footprint can be explained by three principal factors: Rome's preference for more indirect forms of domination, the absence of competitors capable of sustained, large-scale expeditionary operations, and the Principate's military effectiveness.

Rome's indirect forms of domination
Wherever possible, Rome preferred to rule through cooperative local elites rather than govern directly. These reigning oligarchies were often urban aristocracies; it would therefore not be inaccurate to venture, as does one German historian, that in many aspects the empire was a "conglomeration of urban self-administrative units" with only loose organizational ties to the imperial government in Rome.[24] Elite co-option was naturally far more effective in regions with a long history of autonomous city-states run by well entrenched, clearly identifiable, and easily corruptible aristocracies, as in Sicily, Greece, and Asia Minor. In more rural, less economically developed areas such as "long haired Gaul," Britannia, and, most importantly, Germania, imperial governance could prove more arduous, with linguistically challenged Roman officials having to gingerly wade through the muddy waters of tribal politics, trying to ally with one clan against another, or pit one seemingly promising warlord against another.[25] The hope, openly confessed by writers such as Tacitus, was that such subject peoples would "retain and perpetuate, if not an affection for

us [Rome] at least an animosity against each other! Since, while the fate of the empire is thus urgent, fortune can bestow no higher benefit upon us, than the discord of our foes."[26]

As we shall see, such age-old strategies of divide and rule were fraught with risk and could easily backfire, either by allowing naive imperial officials freshly arrived from Rome to be callously manipulated by fickle local actors, or by engendering a series of cascading and ultimately damaging security commitments to little-understood proxies. Like the leaders of Native American peoples during the first waves of European colonization, foreign elite actors were not hapless pawns—they had both agency and quarrels of their own, and on many occasions were all too happy to try to leverage the interloper's military might to their temporary advantage.[27] Ultimately, however, these initiatives were to prove self-defeating. As Polybius had already noted in the second century BC, while bearing witness to the incremental subjugation of the Greek world, the narrow self-interest of smaller polities nearly always wound up working in Rome's favor, for the Romans had become adept "at availing themselves with profound policy of the mistakes of others to augment their strength and their own empire, under the guise of granting favors and benefiting those who commit the errors."[28] In some cases, writes one of the finest observers of this period, "there was little need [for Rome] to manipulate people. By seeking the support or approval of Rome, people manipulated and weakened themselves and thereby affirmed that power."[29]

Despite the many challenges inherent to political micromanagement along the more territorially fractured regions of the imperial frontier, such approaches were still viewed by most Romans as the most prudent and cost-effective, and as far preferable to a policy of non-engagement or benign neglect. Indeed, the fear was always that if Rome was not proactive enough in its engagement with less "civilized" peoples, it would eventually have to deal with some powerful coalescence of tribes or petty kingdoms that could threaten the Italian heartland—after all, this had happened many times in its history.[30] As we shall see, these deeply ingrained fears were recurrent throughout the reigns of both Augustus and Tiberius. Thus, any protonationalist or religious movement which aimed to provide a viable, unifying political alternative to the more fragmented tribal and aristocratic structures was viewed by Rome's agents with extreme suspicion, if not downright hostility. This explains, for instance, the violence of Roman exactions against certain Jewish religious movements in Judaea, or the relentlessness of their campaigns of persecution—and ultimate extermination—of druidism in Gaul (during the reign of Tiberius) and Britain (under Claudius).[31]

Much like Chinese Communist Party officials in present-day Tibet or Inner Mongolia, Roman agents actively encouraged the development of nucleated urban settlements and sedentary agricultural lifestyles, both of which they deemed critical to the effective exertion of imperial control.[32] Tacitus recounts how his father-in-law Agricola, governor of Britain in the late first century AD, and whom he presents as a model of Roman administrative efficiency, cynically cajoled local Britons into modifying their lifestyle:

> In order that a population scattered and uncivilized, and proportionately ready for war, might be habituated by comfort to peace and quiet, he would exhort individuals and assist communities to erect temples, market places and houses; he praised the energetic, rebuked the indolent, and the rivalry for his compliments took the place of coercion.[33]

With brutal candor, Tacitus highlights the sly effectiveness of his father-in-law's approach—which, by introducing luxury and incentivizing acculturation, slowly anesthetized willingness to resist foreign rule:

> He began to educate the sons of British chiefs in the liberal arts, praising the superiority of the Britons' natural genius over the industriousness of the Gauls. He proved so successful that they who had previously disdained the Latin language now aspired to its eloquence! Even our Roman dress style became fashionable: the toga was now often worn. And gradually they developed a taste for all those luxuries which lead to vice: colonnades, baths, and elegant banquets.

"This"—the historian concludes in characteristically biting fashion—"they called in their ignorance civilization when in reality it was but part of their slavery."

At the end of the day, provincial governors under the principate were expected to accomplish two basic and closely interrelated tasks: preserve a modicum of internal stability, while maintaining a steady flow of funds and resources toward Rome. In order to better succeed in the latter function, they were aided and seconded by the oft-reviled procurator, the official charged with provincial taxation and financial management. These two missions—internal stabilization and resource appropriation—frequently entered into conflict, and there are countless tales of provincial revolts seeming to suddenly and unexpectedly erupt, only to subsequently be explained by long-simmering resentments over exorbitant levels of taxation.[34] On many occasions, Roman writers do not shy away from attributing individual responsibility to venal governors who shamelessly sought personal enrichment at the expense of the local inhabitants.[35] Such personalized indictments had the added advantage of focusing public opprobrium on a few designated "rotten apples" rather than on the ruthlessly extractive nature of the entire imperial enterprise, and of deflecting direct blame away from the emperor.[36] The emphasis on maintaining public order meant that, in order to be successful, governors also needed, over the course of their tenure, to develop shrewd political instincts. This could be challenging even in more culturally familiar settings, such as Greece, where Roman officials were expected to adjudicate complex legal and territorial matters between rival cities or factions.[37] In certain major cities, riots and pogroms (between Greek and Jewish residents in Alexandria, for instance) were commonplace, and Roman troops, caught between feuding communities, struggled to maintain law and order.[38] Enrolling local elites—and, if possible, their thuggish security forces—made Roman officials' lives easier and allowed for a certain degree of plausible deniability. In the famed words of Pontius Pilate, governor of Judaea under Tiberius, they could then "wash their hands" of certain unpleasant outcomes.

Traditionally, one of Republican Rome's great strengths had been its ability to progressively absorb first Italian then provincial elites into its political system, by extending trans-Mediterranean networks of patronage and recruiting members of formerly hostile ruling classes as advisors, educators, or even—once they had acquired citizenship—into the equestrian or senatorial class.[39] This effort of incorporation continued apace during the Principate—albeit at different speeds depending on the emperor in power—and was complemented by imperial Rome's increased reliance on alien peoples for its own defense, as it subcontracted security across significant swathes of its territories to noncitizen auxiliary forces (a practice which will be properly scrutinized in later sections).

As a means, perhaps, of partially compensating for the lightness of Rome's bureaucratic apparatus, the imperial cult was increasingly encouraged throughout the reign of Augustus.[40] With the ritualized veneration of the emperor as a divine or semidivine figure, the construction of imposing, standardized monuments and infrastructure, and the creation of a shared calendar and ceremonies, along with provincial expressions of gratitude for imperial victories and largesse, the Principate provided potent visual and symbolic reminders of its hegemony.[41] As Richard Miles insightfully notes,

> The (imperial) cult was particularly prevalent in the East; sensible emperors were charier of making more wild and hubristic claims to divinity in the uppity political atmosphere of Rome itself, but in the provinces it was a way of giving the emperor a role in the lives of their citizens. When they paid their respects it was as if they had a one-to-one relationship with him. It exploited the idea of the ruler as the protector of the little people and often disingenuously set the emperor up against the officials who represented him locally. The Cult was a kind of hologram, projecting the emperor into the countless towns and cities of his realm.[42]

And yet many imperial subjects probably had vanishingly little awareness of the happenings at its center and may not even have known the identity of its figurehead. It is revealing that in the Gospels, when the Roman emperor is mentioned by either Jesus or his accusers the discussions revolve primarily around the issue of provincial taxation, and he is referred to by the generic title of Caesar rather than as Augustus or Tiberius.[43] As Neville Morley observes,

> The great advantage for the Empire in its chosen style of domination was indeed that, for the most part, any hostility would be directed against the local elite who had to implement their demands and collect their taxes or who took advantage of their privileged position to oppress and exploit the population. Once the initial disruption of conquest was past, the Romans ceased to be the clear enemy; it seems entirely possible that their domination was effectively invisible to the majority of their population, a matter of regular concern only to the client ruling class.[44]

Last but not least, Rome's security was contingent on the careful supervision of a complex constellation of local allies, client kingdoms and military proxies.[45] These protective belts, composed of often unstable regimes whose rulers' very survival sometimes depended on continued Roman support, were situated all around the empire but especially to the east—in the various buffer zones separating Rome-administered territories from the Parthian Empire. Whereas foreign auxiliary units were salaried soldiers operating under Rome's command, the military forces of allies and client kingdoms were nominally autonomous, although they frequently engaged in jointly coordinated campaigns with their great power patron.

An absence of peer competitors capable of sustained,
large-scale expeditionary operations
Since its final victories over Macedon (148 BC), Carthage (146 BC), and the Kingdom of Pontus (63 BC), Rome's only remaining great power rival was the Parthian Empire, which stretched from the Euphrates to eastern Iran. Ever since the empires had first initiated formal contact in the early 90s BC, their rulers had vied for control over the politically fractured regions of Asia Minor, where their respective spheres of influence overlapped. Most of the time, this rivalry consisted of a classic cold war, with both powers sponsoring proxy wars and seeking to establish coalitions of weaker states, or supporting puppet rulers in places such as Armenia—a kingdom frequently at the epicenter of their regional jostling. It was also a fundamentally two-level game, with Rome quietly meddling in various Parthian aristocratic squabbles, all while aiding and abetting political exiles and dissidents, often hosting them in Rome.[46] Similarly, Parthia did not hesitate to offer military support to different warring factions during Rome's civil wars.[47] On occasion, however, the Rome/Parthia competition did boil over into direct confrontation, and in 53 BC Rome suffered one of its most terrible defeats when a large force led by Crassus deep into Parthian territory was almost utterly destroyed. More than seven legions were either annihilated or severely mauled, both Crassus and his son were killed, and the legions' eagles were taken as trophies. It is estimated that out of an invading army of forty thousand men, only ten thousand managed to make their way back to Roman territory, while twenty thousand were killed and ten thousand taken captive.[48] As we shall see, the catastrophic nature of this defeat, as well as what it taught the Romans

with regard to how better to adapt their tactics and force design to radically different theaters and adversaries (the ten-thousand-strong Parthian army, composed of nine thousand horse archers and one thousand cataphracts, had been entirely mounted), was to leave a lasting mark on the Roman military psyche.[49] This humiliation at Carrhae was compounded by Rome's failure to prevent a series of major Parthian incursions into the eastern empire in the 40s BC, and by Mark Antony's abortive campaigns into Parthia during his rule as eastern triumvir.[50]

For all of Parthia's relative success during this period, however, it remained hobbled by a series of internal weaknesses which prevented it from ever seriously threatening the Roman heartland, whereas Rome's legions could—and ultimately would a century later under Trajan—pose an existential menace to the Parthian capital at Ctesiphon (not far from present-day Baghdad).[51] Led by a king drawn from one of Parthia's aristocratic families, the Parthian Empire had no formalized standing army; instead its system of military mobilization resembled that of early medieval Europe. The most powerful nobles, when called upon, would join the fray in the company of their armored cataphracts, mounted on heavy chargers and equipped with a *kontos*, or two-handed lance, which could have a devastating impact at close quarters. This small core of shock troops was complemented by larger numbers of horse archers, often composed of lesser nobles and their retainers riding smaller steppe ponies, and by levies of farmers and hillsmen.[52] Parthian armies—when well officered, as during the battle of Carrhae—could be highly effective, and the large proportion of mounted troops meant that they were also extremely mobile. Their rapid mobilization, however, demanded close coordination among the king and his bickering nobles, and could prove challenging. From this state of affairs, Rome, with its fully professionalized and permanently forward-deployed armies, could derive certain obvious advantages. Furthermore, Parthia's system of elective monarchy—whereby kings were "selected" from the ranks of their fellow aristocrats—was remarkably unstable, and for much of its history the Parthian Empire was racked by civil wars fought by opposing armies of feuding nobles.[53] In the gilded halls of Ctesiphon, power rhymed with peril and precarity. Their kings, Tacitus drily remarked, led lives of clammy apprehension, circled by ravening, green-eyed magnates whose "love was false, but whose hatred was all too real."[54] The toxicity of Parthia's court politics, with its endless cortège of poisonings, kidnappings, and palace

coups, frequently proved debilitating, and greatly facilitated Roman
political interference. Later in the course of the first century AD, Seneca—
then serving as an advisor to Emperor Nero—pointedly reminded the
Parthian king of the tenuousness of his rule, and of its chronic vulnerability to foreign (i.e. Roman) interference:

> you only hold them [your own subjects] in check by fear; they will
> never allow you to relax your hand on the bow, they are your own
> bitterest enemies, always open to bribes and eager for a new
> master.[55]

As one contemporary classicist observes, Seneca's threatening tone has a
disdainful—and distinctly Roman—undercurrent as he seems to regard
Parthia with the supercilious air of "a modern veteran parliamentarian
facing the members of a military junta ruling a distant country."[56]

For all of these reasons, therefore, a certain conventional wisdom
developed within Roman elite circles: that the Parthians were invincible
on their own soil but otherwise manageable, provided that their sporadic
attempts to extend their influence into Asia Minor and the eastern Mediterranean were monitored. This ethnographic stereotype was most
clearly laid out by Cassius Dio when, in addition to contending that the
Parthians were physically predisposed to better endure heat and thirst
than their Roman adversaries, the Greek chronicler argued that they
were reluctant to project power into unfamiliar terrain:

> The sky above them [...] which is very dry and contains not the least
> moisture, offers them perfect opportunity for archery, except in the
> winter. For that reason, they make no campaigns in any direction
> during the winter season. But the rest of the year they are almost
> invincible in their own country and in any that has similar charac-
> teristics. By long custom they can endure the sun, which is very
> scorching, and they have discovered many remedies for the scanti-
> ness and difficulty of a supply of drink—a fact which is a help for them
> in repelling without difficulty the invaders of their land.[57]

The prevalence of such assumptions did not mean, however, that Parthia
was not deemed a threat to Rome's eastern territories, or that there was
not a lust for vengeance in certain quarters, following the stinging

humiliations of Crassus' and Antony's defeats. Nevertheless, Parthia's chronic inability to aim power at Rome's economic and political center of gravity was undoubtedly something that differentiated it from previous great power rivals such as Carthage, or even Pontus, which during the Mithridatic Wars had overrun all of Anatolia, massacring more than eighty thousand Roman and Italian settlers.[58]

Similarly, the structure of tribal societies in places such as Gaul, Germania, and, later, Britannia, meant that while these mosaics of peoples could occasionally forget their own quarrels to federate under a charismatic leader, and even inflict devastating defeats on Roman armies, they were ill equipped to deal with longer wars of attrition.[59] Germanic war chiefs, for example, would often be surrounded by only a small entourage of well-equipped and trained warriors. The remainder of their forces—the rank and file—was composed of levied farmers. This not only resulted in their troops being less well disciplined and trained than their Roman opponents, but also meant that their forced involvement in any protracted campaign could have severe knock-on effects, as their farms and livestock were left unmanned and undefended.[60]

Rome's unparalleled ability to rapidly support and engage in complex expeditionary operations owed more to the simple professionalization of its armed forces, however. Indeed, it was the unique nature of Rome's force structure and regimental organization, along with its prowess in the fields of engineering and logistics, that provided it with a decisive edge over its adversaries. Under the Marian reforms of the late Republic, the military's organizational apparatus had been completely revamped. Whereas previously, under the so-called Polybian system, troops had been divided into distinct categories of soldiers clustered into their own formations, the Marian legions were designed as self-sufficient fighting forces.[61]

Composed of approximately five and a half to six thousand men, about 75 to 80 percent of these troops were the now newly standardized legionary, equipped with *gladius* (a short sword), *scutum* (large shield), and *pilum* (a heavy javelin), while the remainder were specialists—including mounted scouts, carpenters, and siege warfare technicians. The result, notes one prominent scholar of ancient Roman warfare, was that these self-contained units were no longer as reliant on long supply lines and ponderous baggage trains, making them more mobile and rapidly deployable.[62] Their more modular configuration also enabled multiple legions to be more easily "bolted together" when engaging in operations on a larger scale, while the presence of specialist legionaries—ranging from shipwrights to bow makers, smiths, and ballista makers—within each legion reinforced their capacity for operational autonomy.[63] Each legionary was also equipped with a set of tools, which could be used on large-scale engineering projects. This meant that Roman legions could move with greater ease across challenging terrain—building bridges and tunneling through mountains—and rapidly erect fortified encampments in the heart of hostile territory.[64] In addition to the legions, Roman commanders could draw on *vexillationes*, smaller detachments of troops drawn from one or several legions. These numbered from a few hundred to a thousand men, and could be used for smaller-scale operations or surged to the front lines as temporary reinforcements to other legions.[65] Their more ad hoc nature also allowed for a great degree of flexibility, enabling commanders to "mix and match" and experiment with different ratios of troop types, assembling, for example, task forces of archers or mounted troops. Rome's military strength had always laid on the superb quality of its heavy infantry, and the legions of the early Principate largely reflected this warfighting predilection, with typically only a small number of cavalry or long-range missile infantry.[66] For much of the Republic, the Romans had relied heavily on the *socii*, their Italian military allies, to provide the cavalry, which typically positioned itself on the *alae*, or wings, of Rome-led battle formations.[67] During the imperial period, this role—along with that of specialist missile troops, such as slingers and archers—was increasingly filled by auxiliaries who operated both independently and in tandem with the legions, often providing mobile screening forces for legions on the march.[68] Indeed, one of the main reforms of the Augustan era was the incorporation of at least 120 cavalry (nearly always auxiliaries) into every legion to serve as scouts and messengers.[69]

Roman military effectiveness and adaptability
For contemporaries of Augustus and Tiberius, it was the fighting cohesion and discipline of Roman troops which lay at the heart of their success and distinguished them from the unruly hordes of their adversaries. Time and time again, Roman writers extol the virtues of drill and effective command and control, with authors such as Valerius Maximus even attributing Rome's geopolitical dominance to the military discipline of its legions:

I now come to the particular distinction and the mainstay of Roman rule, preserved safe and sound up to this time due to beneficial perseverance: the most steadfast bond of military discipline, in whose bosom and guardianship rests the serene and tranquil condition of prosperous peace. Military discipline, fiercely upheld, acquired the leadership of Italy for Roman rule; bestowed control over many cities, great kings, most powerful nations; opened the straits of the Pontic Gulf; handed over the overthrown barriers of the Alps and the Taurus mountains; and transformed a beginning from Romulus' tiny hut into the peak of the world.[70]

This view was shared throughout the first century AD by keen-eyed foreign observers such as Joseph Ben Matthias, or Flavius Josephus, an aristocratic Jewish priest who had witnessed the Roman legions in action against his countrymen during the revolt of Galilee in AD 66. Like Polybius many centuries earlier, Josephus was impressed by the legions' tactical prowess, famously attributing it to the quality of their training, ability to operate as a team, and constant state of military readiness:

> Military exercises give the Roman soldiers not only tough bodies but also determined spirits. Their nation does not wait for the outbreak of war to give men their first lesson in arms [...] To the contrary, as though they had been born with weapons in their hands, they never have a truce from training, never wait for emergencies to arise. For their peace maneuvers are no less strenuous than veritable warfare; each soldier daily throws his energy into his drill, as though he were in action. Hence that perfect ease with which they sustain the shock of battle; no confusion breaks their customary formation, no panic paralyzes, no fatigue exhausts them; and as their opponents cannot match these qualities, victory is the invariable and certain consequence. Indeed it would not be far from the truth to call their drills bloodless battle, and their battles bloody drills.[71]

It was widely believed that idle soldiers were dangerous vectors of social disorder, and Rome imposed a relentless drilling regimen on its legionaries.[72] Physical conditioning focused as much on stamina as it did on the cultivation of raw strength (indeed, an inordinate focus on strength over endurance was often viewed as one of the main weaknesses of barbarian

Illustration of a Roman Legionary.

armies) and punishments for perceived laxness or disobedience could be severe.[73] Much was made of the fearsome reputation of centurions—towering figures of authority who had climbed their way up the ranks, and whom the grunt legionaries often respected and resented in equal measure. Complex military maneuvers were sometimes carried out on a legion-wide scale and were occasionally overseen by the emperor himself.[74]

Over the centuries, and largely through trial and error, Rome had developed a way of war which allowed it to field the most brutally effective heavy infantry in the ancient world. Indeed, much of Rome's military prowess could be attributed to its adaptability, its willingness to learn from its most formidable adversaries, and its capacity to experiment with different tactics and types of equipment.[75] This was most famously made evident during the First Punic War, when Rome—a land power with little experience of naval warfare—reverse engineered a captured Carthaginian vessel, built its own first-class navy, and gradually established sea control across the Mediterranean.[76] But perhaps even more consequential was Rome's refinement over the centuries of a distinct, and remarkably successful, set of infantry tactics.

The historically accurate illustration of an early Principate-era Roman legionary (see page 61) can help provide a better understanding of Rome's continuous process of military adaptation, and how every aspect of their legionaries' equipment was geared toward operational efficiency and functionality. The Coolus helmet the legionary is wearing, with its cheek and neck guards, is Gallic in origin, and began to be adopted en masse in the wake of Caesar's Gallic wars.[77] Meanwhile, the gladius that hangs on his right-hand side was originally Iberian, or Spanish, and the large rectangular shield, the scutum, may be a derivation from a Samnite shield design.[78] The gladius was worn on the right so that in the tight melee of close-quarter combat the legionary could keep his heavy shield raised and rapidly unsheathe his gladius without breaking formation— this was accomplished in a smooth gesture by inverting his right hand, grabbing the hilt, and pushing the pommel forward.[79] The legionary is holding a heavy weighted pilum, with a pyramidal iron head and a long, soft iron shank. Legionaries may also have been issued with lighter javelins, which could be thrown a greater distance. Some archeologists believe that the Romans first systematically adopted the use of heavy throwing weapons following their wars against the Celtiberians in Spain

(181–151 BC), but this remains a topic of academic contention.[80] Last but not least, the legionary is wearing the plated armor, or *lorica segmentata*, so ubiquitous in visual representations of this period. This constitutes the only "fully indigenous" piece of the soldier's equipment, and some historians believe it may have been adapted from the armor worn by gladiators, a reflection, once again, of the ingenuity of Roman military craftsmen.[81]

This process of selective emulation and experimentation was not limited to Rome's heavy infantry.[82] Indeed, much of the equestrian equipment issued to the cavalry—such as the four-horned saddle which allowed for more freedom of movement than a modern "pommel and cantle" saddle—was Gallic in origin, as was the spatha, a long slashing sword suited to mounted engagements.[83] Rome's willingness to experiment and selectively adopt equipment and tactics from lesser competitors is fascinating, in that it would appear to validate the arguments of contemporary scholars such as Timothy Hoyt, who has argued that the diffusion and emulation process can occur from the periphery to the center, rather than simply downward from the hegemon toward lesser-ranking military powers.[84]

When engaging in close combat, Roman legionaries would initiate a well-worn sequence of moves, first throwing any lighter javelins (if thus equipped), before awaiting their charge in close formation. When the enemy was only a few feet away, the legionaries would throw their heavy pila. The impact of these shock weapons could prove devastating to the first rank of enemy combatants. Their forward momentum would be further disrupted by the fact that the pila's pyramidal heads were designed to puncture armor, and once lodged in shields could be almost impossible to remove due to the soft iron shanks bending upon impact (this also meant that the pila could not be picked up and thrown back toward the Roman ranks). In his memoir of the Gallic Wars, Julius Caesar recounts how during one battle a wave of incoming Gauls were forced to abandon their javelin-pierced shields and reduced to fighting without protective gear.[85]

Once the volley of pila had been discharged, the legionaries would draw their short swords and shelter behind their scuta, which—with their heavy iron bosses—were viewed as offensive as well as defensive weapons. Indeed, Tacitus describes how Roman legionaries were trained to engage in three sequential movements—first throwing their pila, then

Much of the success of the Roman army on the battlefield lay in the soldier's knowledge of close formation fighting: legionaries were trained to fight as a team, to trust each other, and to remain steady under pressure. It was this difference that gave the legion its decisive tactical edge.

A

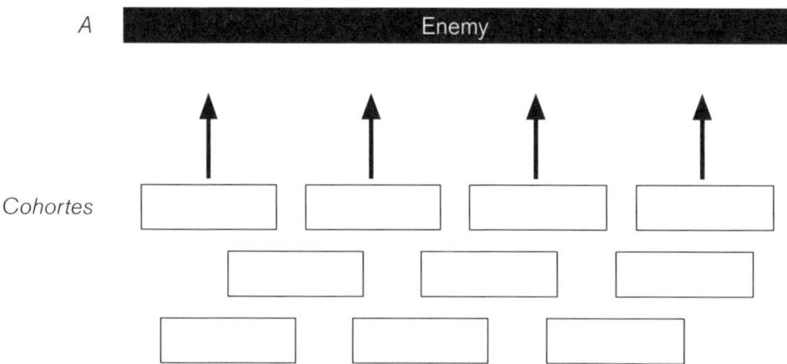

Phase A

A *legio* of ten *cohortes* is deployed for battle into the traditional *triplex acies* formation, with four *cohortes* in the front line and three each in the middle and rear lines. Each *cohors* is arranged *centuria* by *centuria*, each of which is deployed four ranks deep. The *legio* advances steadily and soundlessly into the combat zone.

B

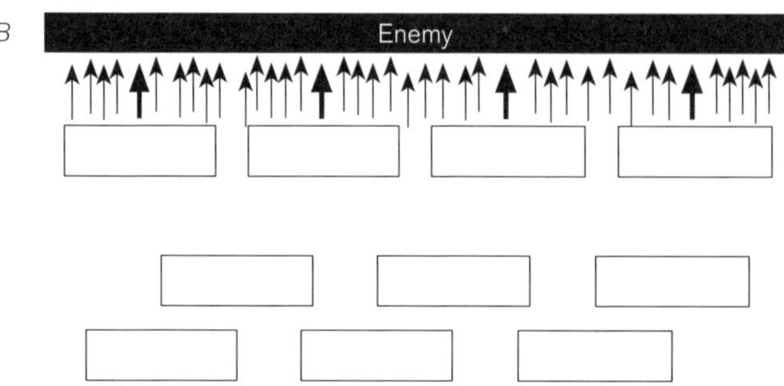

Phase B

Legionaries in the front line *cohortes* discharge their *pila* some 15m or so from the enemy. If the *pila* do not actually hit the enemy, they will often become embedded in their shields, their pyramidal points making them difficult to withdraw. Handicapped by a *pilum*, the shield becomes useless. Additionally, the thin metal shaft buckles and bends on impact, which prevents the weapon from being thrown back.

C

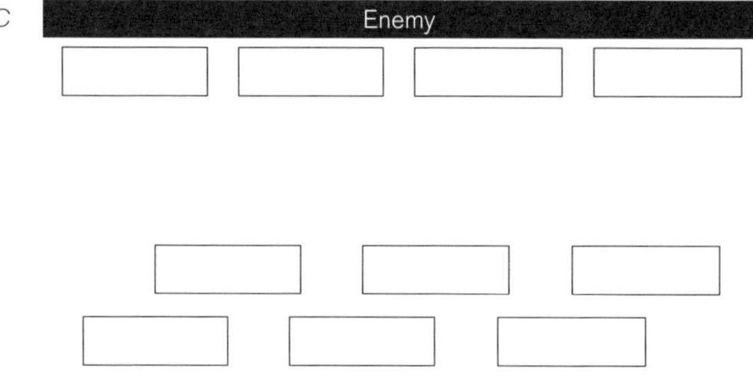

Phase C

During the confusion caused by this hail of *pila*, the advancing legionaries quickly draw their swords and charge at a jog into close contact, yelling their war cries. The standard drill is to punch the shield-boss in the face of the enemy, and jab the sword point in his belly. On breaking the opposition, legionaries are not supposed to break ranks and pursue. On the contrary, their tactical philosophy is to stand their ground. Meanwhile, legionaries of the second-line *cohortes* wait for the order to move forwards to join the fighting line.

Diagram of a Roman cohort's infantry tactics.
Source: Nic Fields, *The Roman Army: the Civil Wars, 88–31 BC* (Oxford, UK: Osprey Publishing, 2008) p. 41.

using the weight of their shields to knock their enemies back or "mangle their faces," before stabbing upward with their gladius.[86] In one prebattle speech, a Roman commander is cited as addressing his legionaries and instructing the following: "Throw your pila and then carry on: use your shield-bosses to fell them, then your swords to kill them."[87] Roman infantry tactics were therefore of a ruthless simplicity, heavily reliant on practice, discipline, and unit cohesion. The relentless focus on combat efficacy is perhaps best epitomized by the infantry's preference for short, thrusting fencing techniques—harder to anticipate and parry—over the wilder, slashing movements frequently adopted by their Celtic or Germanian foes.[88] Such performative modes of combat were those of their barbarian foes, who privileged heroic displays and brute strength over cold lethality:

> For the Romans not only made a jest of those who fought with the edge of that weapon, but always found them an easy conquest. A stroke with the edges, though made with ever so much force, seldom kills, as the vital parts of the body are defended both by the bones and armor. On the contrary, a stab, though it penetrates but two inches, is generally fatal. Besides in the attitude of striking, it is impossible to avoid exposing the right arm and side; but on the other hand, the body is covered while a thrust is given, and the adversary receives the point before he sees the sword.[89]

It was no doubt this rugged efficiency, ruthless pragmatism, and sense of fraternal discipline which Tiberius would later find so appealing. The young blue blood, grandson of a defeated senator, son of a degraded refugee, and stepson of a powerful emperor, was to be raised in a world transformed—under a regime which sat awkwardly in between tyranny and constitutional monarchy, and within a society which clamored for lasting peace while pining for past glories. For the conservatively minded and socially awkward scion of a grand republican family—never Augustus' first choice but always his first defender—the legions of the early Principate were to provide both a precious sanctuary from viperous court rivalries and a crash course in the risks and rewards of imperial primacy.

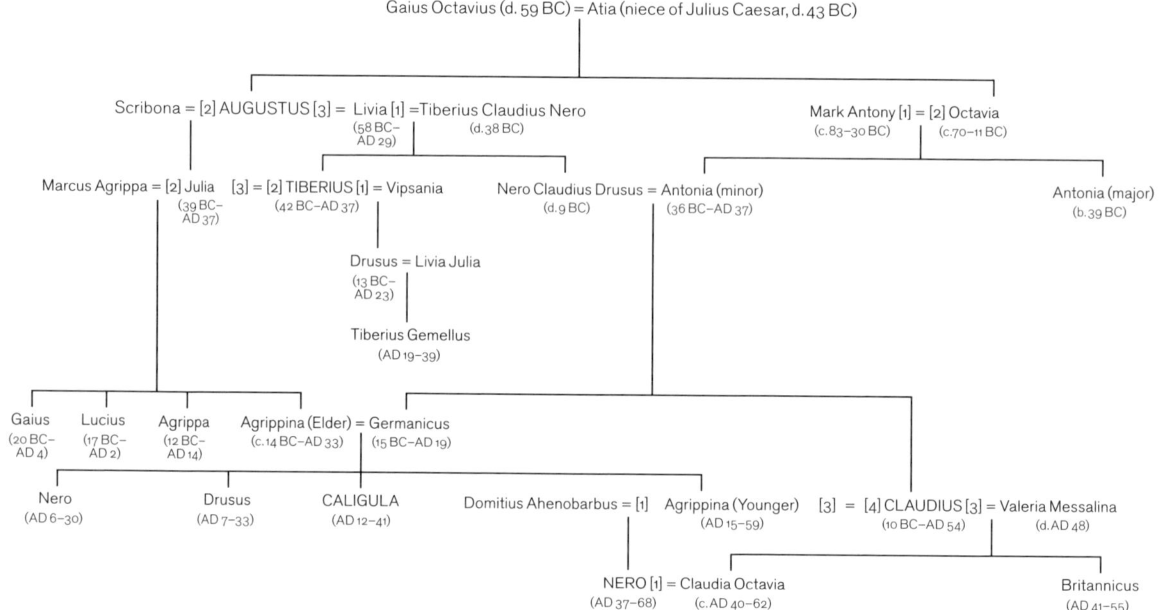

The Julio-Claudian Dynasty.
Source: Antony Kamm, *Julius Caesar: a Life*
(New York: Routledge, 2006).

FROM POLITICAL REFUGEE TO PRINCEPS: TIBERIUS' SLOW RISE TO PREEMINENCE

Barring the mention of the oration given at his father's funeral, little is known of Tiberius' childhood. We know that he and his younger brother, Drusus, were raised and educated at the imperial palace, where their young minds were molded by some of the finest grammarians and philosophers in Rome. As a young boy, Tiberius may have received lessons in public speaking from the elder statesman and poet Messalla Corvinus, as well as from one of the more renowned Greek rhetoricians of the era, Theodorus of Gadara.[1] Both were known for their fastidiously ornate oratory, and some historians have since ventured that certain key elements of Tiberius' governing style—in particular his complex, labyrinthine, and sometimes impenetrable speeches—were a result of this early training.[2] While these theories remain largely speculative, there is no question that Tiberius was exceedingly well educated, and that from his early years he was animated by a passion for learning, with an erudition that could seem to apply itself to the most obscure of topics, from recondite aspects of Greek mythology to astrology and horticulture.[3] Indeed, Tiberius may well have been the most philhellene of the Julio-Claudian emperors, something that would become evident not only in his love of Greek culture and in his later self-imposed exile to the island of Rhodes, but also in the composition of his close entourage, which contained a number of Greek confidants and advisors. Famously, one of Tiberius' most trusted *amici* was Thrasyllus of Mendes, a Ptolemaic Greek grammarian and astrologer the emperor first befriended on Rhodes.[4] Somewhat revealingly, Tiberius' tastes for antiquated Latin, archaizing rhetoric, and hyperformalized Alexandrine lyrical poetry were viewed as archly conservative—at times even superannuated—and thus at odds with the more exuberant literary renaissance of the Augustan age.[5] In ancient Rome, the art of rhetoric—i.e. the association of artfully calibrated public speech with an equally well-choreographed set of physical gestures—was taken extremely seriously, and its mastery was considered a prerequisite to effective statesmanship.[6] It would appear that Tiberius, despite his deep reservoir of knowledge, was not a natural, and that this was a source of some irritation for his more charismatic stepfather. Suetonius describes how the taciturn young Tiberius

> strode along with his neck stiff and bent forward, usually with a stern countenance and for the most part in silence, never or very rarely conversing with his companions, and then with great deliberation and with a kind of supple movement of his fingers. All of these mannerisms of his, which were disagreeable and signs of arrogance, were remarked by Augustus, who often tried to excuse them to the Senate and people by declaring that they were natural failings, and not intentional.[7]

Tacitus famously noted that "the diction of Tiberius, by habit or by nature, was always indirect and obscure, even when he had no wish to conceal his thought," and believed it to be indicative of deeper moral inconsistencies.[8] Yet for all his limitations as a politician and formal orator, Tiberius was not always ineffective as a public speaker, and later, as emperor, is recorded as sometimes providing clear and well-articulated directives—that is, when he eschewed laborious preparation and spoke off the cuff. In striking contrast to Drusus, and to his amiable cousin, Marcellus, Tiberius was of a gruff, reclusive nature, and it was only once he reached manhood that his more deliberate form of intelligence—which applied itself exceedingly well to both administrative and military matters—was to become more immediately apparent.

In the spring of 27 BC, at the age of fifteen, Tiberius formally assumed the *toga virilis*—the garment traditionally associated with entry into adulthood. Only a year later, and despite his young age, he and Marcellus accompanied Augustus to northern Spain, where Roman legions had been waging a savage war of attrition against the fortified hilltop communities of the Cantabrians and Asturians. Both Tiberius and Marcellus were appointed military tribunes for a period of one year, vaulting them onto the *cursus honorum*, or "sequence of offices," at an exceptionally young age, and allowing them to gain valuable military experience.[9]

As Adrian Goldsworthy has noted, commentators have sometimes erroneously dismissed mountain warfare in Spain during this period as little more than a series of nasty skirmishes—or as a form of protracted

1st Century AD Marble Statue of Tiberius,
Louvre, Paris.

guerrilla warfare.[10] Both the historical testimonials and the archeological evidence would suggest otherwise. Involving the deployment of eight Roman legions and a sizable number of auxiliaries, the Cantabrian Wars were fought on a large scale, and the locals presented fierce resistance to the Roman occupying forces, "refusing to yield, because of confidence in their position on the heights," and "always seizing the higher ground in advance and placing ambuscades in depressions and in wooded spots."[11] According to Cassius Dio, the slow, grinding nature of this war, along with the continued "unsettled nature of affairs in Gaul," caused Augustus such angst that his health faltered, and he was forced to indefinitely postpone his plans to invade Britain.[12] The second-century historian Publius Annius Florus describes how the Roman army was forced to erect a "continuous earthwork extending over eighteen miles" around one mountain stronghold until its warriors finally committed collective suicide.[13] This campaign would have provided the youthful Tiberius with an invaluable first set of insights into the conduct of military operations; whether in terms of coordinating substantial forces composed of mixed legionary and auxiliary forces, or in mass logistics, along with mobile siege warfare across mountainous terrain. The unexpectedly challenging and resource-intensive nature of the Cantabrian conflict—and the formidable pugnacity of the local inhabitants—would no doubt have also taught him the value of military prudence, and of engaging in slow, meticulous preparations before launching carefully coordinated, multipronged assaults.[14] Indeed, according to Suetonius, it was at this moment that Augustus famously made the following comments to his subordinates:

> He thought nothing less appropriate in a competent leader than haste and recklessness, and so some of his favorite slogans were: "Hurry Slowly," "Better a safe commander than a bold," and "That is done fast which is done well enough." He used to say that neither battle nor war should be initiated carelessly, but only when the promise of gain clearly outweighed the cost of failure. For he compared those who risked heavy loss for slight gain to a man fishing with a gold hook, the loss of which could not be matched by any possible catch.[15]

Accompanying his stepfather and cousin back to Rome, Tiberius was soon granted the position of quaestor, even though, once again, this was

the result of an Augustan *fait du prince*, for under normal circumstances—
i.e. under the Republic—he would have been considered far too young
and inexperienced.[16] While it was clear that Augustus was grooming his
stepson for a role of some considerable future importance, it was equally
evident that priority was being given to Marcellus, Augustus' direct
nephew and closest blood relative. The latter was granted the higher rank
of *aedile* that same year, and married Augustus' daughter and sole biological child, Julia. Of a sickly disposition, Augustus' acute awareness of
his own physical frailty lent additional urgency to his efforts to forge his
own Julian dynasty, even if that meant engineering the betrothal of two
first cousins—something that was relatively rare even in Roman aristocratic families. Little did the Principate's founding father know that he
would continue to live and rule for almost four decades, and that in that
interval no fewer than three of his designated successors would die in the
flower of their youth. Tiberius, the dour but capable stepson, would liter-
ally be the last man standing.

As quaestor, Tiberius was immediately charged with a series of important administrative missions, tasks which, by all accounts, he accomplished with skill and alacrity. First entrusted with remedying shortages
in the corn supply, he then tackled various issues of law and order, ranging from the prosecution of army deserters to the eradication of the illicit
human trafficking networks that had flourished during the chaos of the
civil wars, whereby freedmen and Roman citizens had been abducted
and pressed into slavery.[17] Shortly after bringing these affairs to a close
the young man was also involved in two high-profile legal cases, successfully defending a Roman client king, Archelaus of Cappadocia, from
charges put forward by his fellow citizens, and arguing in favor of disaster
funds for several Greek cities that had recently been devastated by an
earthquake. These experiences would have served multiple purposes,
acquainting the budding official with the complex political realities
undergirding Rome's network of vassal kingdoms while allowing him to
reinforce his public visibility and prestige in the eyes of the Senate. At the
same time, notes one biographer, it was perhaps not a coincidence that for
some reason Tiberius' most high-profile court cases all seemed to involve
the provinces that, under the Augustan settlement of 27 BC, did not fall
under the emperor's direct remit.[18] His advancement, like that of his fellow family members, was being shrewdly harnessed to consolidate the
new regime and Augustan rule.

In 20 BC, Tiberius was entrusted with his first important overseas military mission, to Armenia. In the years leading up to the expedition, Augustus had been involved in a series of complex negotiations with Phraates IV, the king of Parthia. Ever since the disaster of the Battle of Carrhae in 53 BC, hawkish voices in Rome had called for vengeance, and—most importantly—for the recovery of the captured legionary standards.[19] The nonretrieval of these standards, which had been displayed as trophies in Parthian temples, was viewed as a permanent reminder of Rome's military humiliation, along with the fact that, more than three decades later, ten thousand Roman prisoners of war had yet to be released. Acutely aware of the risks inherent in the launching of another major offensive into Parthia, Augustus opted to pursue a policy of forceful diplomacy, first offering to return the king's son, who had been kidnapped by a rebellious Parthian noble and brought to Rome, in exchange for the eagles and surviving Roman prisoners. When these negotiations foundered, Augustus seized the opportunity provided by a renewed civil conflict in Armenia, where the Parthia-friendly monarch, Artaxes, was being challenged by a rival faction that had coalesced around his younger brother, Tigranes. The latter had been living in Rome for the past decade, and eagerly guaranteed his future cooperation in exchange for Roman military support. Tiberius was thus dispatched at the head of an army with the aim of ejecting Artaxes and replacing him with his brother, who would supposedly be far more amenable to Rome's interests. This act of coercive brinkmanship was wholly successful—Phraates IV, intimidated by such a display of military might so close to Parthia's borders, agreed, following a series of extended negotiations, to return the prisoners and standards in a public ceremony held on the banks of the Euphrates, and Rome's new client king was installed on the throne in Armenia. It seems evident that the wily Phraates must have also received something in return—most probably assurances of Roman noninterference in Parthian territory.

Nevertheless, this was a huge diplomatic triumph and symbolic victory for Augustus—he had succeeded in erasing one of the most indelible stains on Rome's honor—and he had accomplished his aims without embroiling his freshly professionalized military in a grueling campaign against its most formidable peer competitor. The standards were prominently displayed in a newly erected temple in the Augustan Forum, dedicated to *Mars Ultor*, or Mars the Avenger, and imagery of Parthians submissively presenting the standards to Augustus became a common theme in the iconography of his reign, appearing on coins, monuments, and even on the cuirass of the famous *Prima Porta* sculpture of the emperor (see page 76). As the great classicist Erich Gruen perceptively notes, the optics-obsessed princeps had transformed a mere round of coercive diplomacy into something far grander, deeply suffused with "the glow of military mastery."[20] In an elaborate public relations exercise, the princep's bloodless victory was feted like the great military triumphs of old, with the emperor—never one to miss an opportunity for self-congratulation—later crowing in the *Res Gestae*,

> In the case of Greater Armenia, though I might have made it a province after the assassination of its King Artaxes, I preferred, following the precedent of our fathers, to hand that kingdom over to Tigranes, the son of King Artavasdes, and grandson of King Tigranes, through Tiberius Nero, who was then my stepson. [...] The Parthians I compelled to restore to me the spoils and standards of three armies and to seek as supplicants the friendship of the Roman people.[21]

Perhaps most importantly, as one contemporary classicist notes,

> by deposing these [Armenian] monarchs when and how he did, Augustus established an important precedent in Armenia that all future Julio-Claudian emperors would strive to imitate. Henceforth, every Armenian monarch would first have to be vetted by Rome, not just because the kingdom was a strategic buffer zone against Parthian aggression, but because it had quickly evolved into a tangible symbol of the emperor's domestic peace. Under Augustus, Armenia became the barometer by which Romans, especially eastern Romans, measured the effectiveness of the Pax Romana.[22]

Tiberius had proven his worth, and for much of the next two decades he would be fighting Augustus' wars across the ragged edges of the empire. The pace and scale of his military activity during this period was such that historians have occasionally struggled to accurately catalogue his movements.[23] For purposes of clarity, Tiberius' confirmed major campaigns during the Augustan period are listed below:

Statue and breastplate details of Augustus from Prima Porta, depicting the return of the Parthian standards (1st century AD), Vatican Museums, Rome.

During the first half of Augustus' reign a certain pattern developed, whereby the emperor would remain positioned at the periphery, or in a neighboring province to the main theater of operations, while younger members of the imperial household such as Tiberius or Drusus, operating as his *legati*, did the actual hard fighting on the front lines. This became a regular practice during the Principate: emperors were expected to behave in a circumspect fashion during military campaigns—they could travel abroad to oversee and coordinate military operations, but risking their lives in battles was deemed unwise. Imperial princes, on the other hand, were expected to "win their spurs" through the displays of personal bravery and sacrifice that had traditionally formed part of the Roman aristocratic ethos, and by showing their proximity to the troops on the ground.[24] Both Tiberius and Drusus fast gained a reputation as fearsome warriors, fighting side by side during the pacification of the Alps and Raetia, a difficult campaign that was of critical importance to securing Rome's main terrestrial thoroughfare to southern Gaul and to consolidating Rome's possessions in the southeastern European theater.[25] The military historian Lindsay Powell provides the following cogent summary of the campaign's importance to the advancement of Rome's imperial interests:

> The security of Gaul did not exist in isolation. It was only one piece of a larger problem. Studying the maps available to him, Augustus would have seen an obvious gap in the land frontier of Roman territory in the north. The Romans did not yet control the Rhine for its entire length. Additionally the wide strip of land between the Alpine passes of northern Italy and the banks of the River Danube extending eastwards as far as the shores of the Black Sea was also outside Roman control. To move men and materiel, Roman armies had to march through northern Italia then take the coast road to Provincia [Provence] and head north or run the gauntlet through the Alps. The solution arrived at was to annex the entire sweep of Alpine lands and the lowlands down to the Rhine and Danube rivers. This became the immediate strategic imperative, the necessary prerequisite before embarking on a longer-range campaign to address the problem of Germania Magna. That would mean subjugating at least forty-six tribal nations across some of the most difficult terrain in Europe.[26]

Tiberius and Drusus seemed to have shared a particularly close bond, and to have been equally effective military commanders, each conducting a series of ambitious campaigns deep into strongly contested regions such as Illyricum and Germania. The brothers' talents and temperaments also appear to have been somewhat complementary, for while Tiberius was acquiring a reputation for stolid competence, Drusus was renowned for his gallantry and derring-do—as epitomized by his reported habit of singling out enemy commanders and challenging them to duels.[27] Over the course of their furious campaigning, they forged alliances with new tribes, built long roads and great canals, and projected power across vast tracts of uncharted territory, including in the Germanian lands that stretched from the Rhine to the Elbe (see page 82–83).[28] For a few heady years, as both brothers won victory after victory across multiple fronts, it may well have seemed that the Roman empire would continue its irreversible expansion until it encompassed the whole of northern Europe. The vicissitudes of human fortune in the pre-antibiotic era, however, would soon bring an abrupt end to this uninterrupted sequence of triumphs. In 9 BC, a devastated Tiberius lost his younger brother, who died on campaign along the Elbe after a wound he sustained falling off his horse became gangrenous. When he first heard that Drusus was at death's door, Tiberius rode day and night from Pavia, in Lombardy, covering over two hundred miles through hostile territory to be at his side.[29] Narrating Tiberius' frantic journey, Valerius Maximus compares their brotherly affection to that of the mythological twins Castor and Pollux, a symbolic association which would later be encouraged by Tiberius himself, when as emperor he rebuilt the temple of Castor in his brother's honor.[30] Following Drusus's slow and agonizing death, Tiberius accompanied his body back to Rome, insisting on walking at the head of the funeral procession the entire way.

Tiberius' grief at the loss of his closest family member was no doubt compounded by the lingering bitterness he felt after Augustus' dynastic whims had repeatedly wreaked havoc on his personal life. Indeed, in 23 BC, Claudius Marcellus, the emperor's golden boy and heir designate, had suddenly died of fever, plunging Augustus' plans for succession into disarray. Julia had then been married off to his most senior general, Marcus Agrippa, to whom she bore three sons, Gaius, Lucius, and Agrippa (more commonly known as Agrippa Postumus). His daughter's fecundity meant that, for a time, Augustus' plans for a Julian dynasty

Drusus and Tiberius,
Augustus' stepsons, present him with the
laurel of victory, in a symbolic representation of
the conquest of the province of Raetia in 15 BC.
Reverse of a denarius, around 15–12 BC.

seemed ironclad—he had three direct male descendants and Agrippa could act as both their guardian and de facto regent if the emperor were to succumb to one of his many ailments before Gaius, the eldest, was fully mature. In 12 BC, however, it was the usually robust Agrippa who unexpectedly fell ill and perished at the age of fifty-one. Gaius still only being eight years old, he was urgently in need of an adoptive father. Tiberius was thus strong-armed into divorcing his beloved wife, Agrippa's daughter Vipsania—with whom he already had a son, Drusus the Younger—and marrying Julia and formally adopting the children she had conceived with his own former father-in-law. The expectation was that Tiberius would help fill the void occasioned after Agrippa's demise.[31]

It was an uncomfortable situation, to say the least, and one that apparently caused Tiberius much anguish. Whereas he had been happily married to Vipsania, his relationship with the fiery, promiscuous Julia was execrable. According to Cassius Dio, his relations with his adopted sons were not much better.[32] Famously, Suetonius describes how on one occasion Tiberius ran into his ex-wife in Rome (she had by then been forcibly remarried) and followed her through the streets with tears in his eyes. After this embarrassing incident, the all-controlling Augustus ensured that "care was taken that she should never again come in his sight."[33]

It was perhaps the cumulative effect of these familial slights and personal tragedies—along with an exhaustion after years spent campaigning across the empire—that prompted Tiberius to refuse Augustus' orders for the first time and enter his long period of self-imposed exile in 6 BC.

Shortly after having been granted tribunician powers for a period of five years, Tiberius was ordered to head once again to the troublesome kingdom of Armenia, in order to reestablish order between competing factions following the death of Rome's puppet ruler, Tigranes II. To the emperor's bafflement, Tiberius flat-out refused and, turning his back on his adopted family in Rome and his newly elevated responsibilities, withdrew to the island of Rhodes. There he remained for more than seven years, strolling through the markets in casual garb, debating local philosophers, and seeming to lead the quixotic existence of a retired scholar. Ever since, historians have vigorously debated the motivations undergirding this surprising move, one that in many ways seemed to foreshadow his later decision, as emperor, to retire to Capri.[34] In addition to the potential sources of resentment mentioned above, some believe that this may have been a move of self-preservation—getting out of the way of the young princes Gaius and Lucius, so as not to be perceived as a potential rival for the succession.[35] Indeed, some have noted that Agrippa had behaved similarly in 23 BC while Marcellus was still alive, departing on a long journey to the East and thus temporarily extricating himself from the treacherous arena of imperial politics. There is some evidence that, even in Rhodes, Tiberius continued to be viewed by the partisans of Gaius as a threat—during one particularly raucous dinner party Marcus Lollius, an old enemy of Tiberius and a member of Gaius' entourage, drunkenly volunteered to head to Rhodes to "bring back the exile's head."[36]

As the years went by, Augustus' frustration at Tiberius' extended sabbatical began to curdle into a deeper form of resentment, and it seemed as though the now middle-aged former general had durably fallen out of favor. In AD 2, however, Julia's scandalous private behavior finally caught up with her, and Tiberius was allowed to return to Rome to officially divorce her before she was cast into exile. The same year, Lucius died of a sudden illness in Marseilles. Only two years later, his elder brother and heir designate Gaius died in Lycia (present-day Turkey), after a stab wound inflicted by an Armenian insurgent during an earlier diplomatic mission became infected. Of the original line of succession, only Julia's third son, the twelve-year-old Agrippa Postumus, remained. Both he and Tiberius were formally adopted as Augustus' sons—and Tiberius would come to be known as Tiberius Julius Caesar. In exchange, as part of this new dynastic "package deal," Tiberius was required to adopt his nephew (and Augustus' great-nephew) Germanicus, with the understanding that he would privilege him, as being of Julian blood, in the line of succession over his own son.

Following Tiberius' return from Rhodes, he was almost immediately plunged back into a storm of military activity, heading back to the Germanian front, where his former soldiers reportedly cheered at the sight of their old commander.[37] One of the most valuable accounts we possess of Tiberius' decades on the front lines is provided by one such soldier, Velleius Paterculus. Velleius was a military officer of the equestrian class who served directly under the future emperor, first as prefect of the horse, then as *legatus*, taking part in Tiberius' Germanian and Pannonian campaigns. He came from a family of dependable military men—most notably, his paternal grandfather had served as a bodyguard to Tiberius' own father, Tiberius Nero. When the latter and his young family was compelled to flee from Naples in 41 BC, Velleius' grandfather, too frail to follow them, dutifully committed suicide. For many centuries, historians

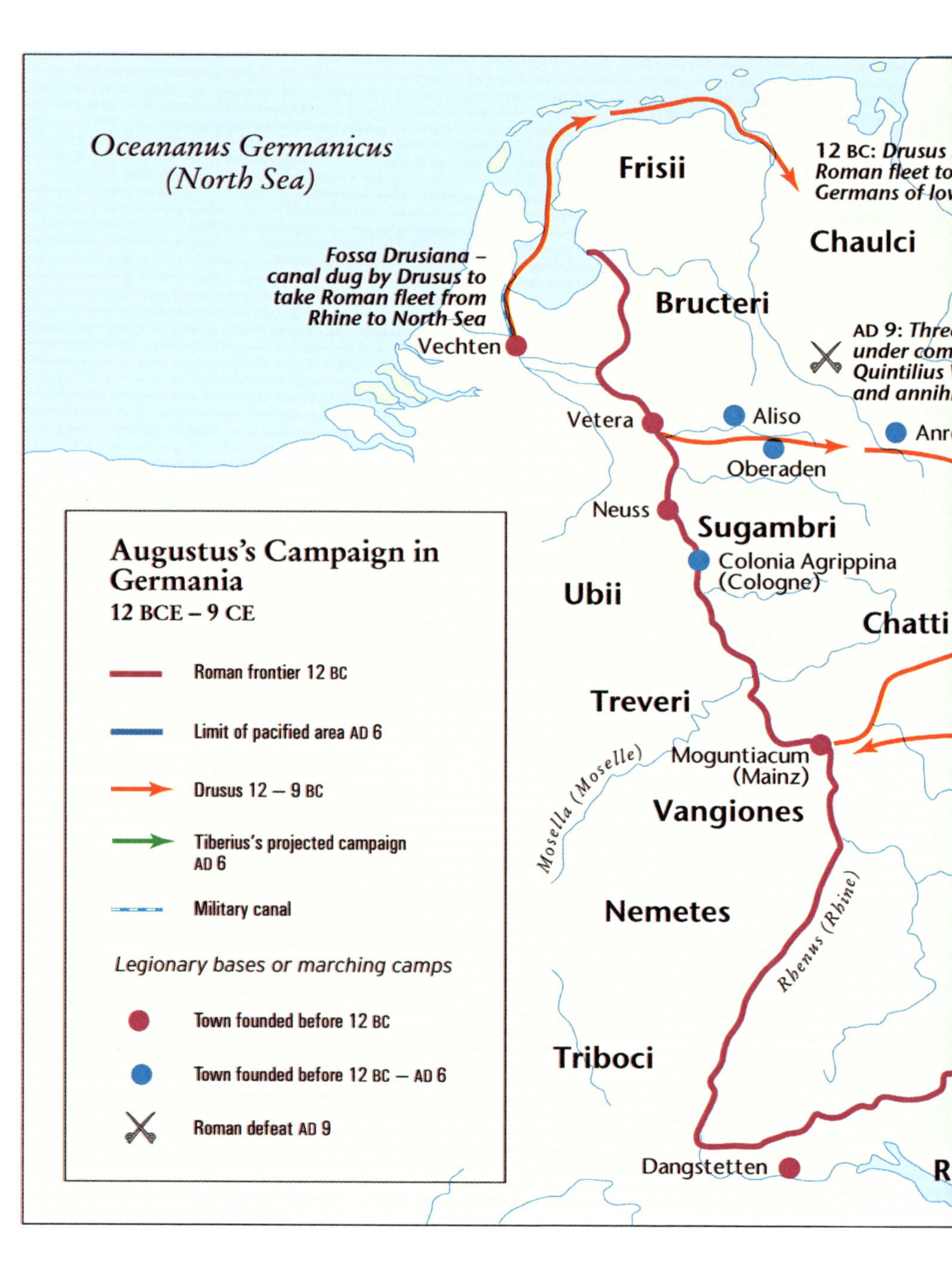

Oceananus Germanicus
(North Sea)
Frisii
12 BC: Drusus l
Roman fleet to
Germans of low
Chaulci
Fossa Drusiana –
canal dug by Drusus to
take Roman fleet from
Rhine to North Sea
Bructeri
AD 9: Three
under com
Quintilius
and annihi
Vechten
Vetera
Aliso
Anre
Oberaden
Neuss
Sugambri
Colonia Agrippina
(Cologne)
Ubii
Chatti
Augustus's Campaign in
Germania
12 BCE – 9 CE
Roman frontier 12 BC
Limit of pacified area AD 6
Drusus 12 – 9 BC
Tiberius's projected campaign
AD 6
Military canal
Legionary bases or marching camps
Town founded before 12 BC
Town founded before 12 BC – AD 6
Roman defeat AD 9
Treveri
Mosella (Moselle)
Moguntiacum
(Mainz)
Vangiones
Nemetes
Rhenus (Rhine)
Triboci
Dangstetten
R

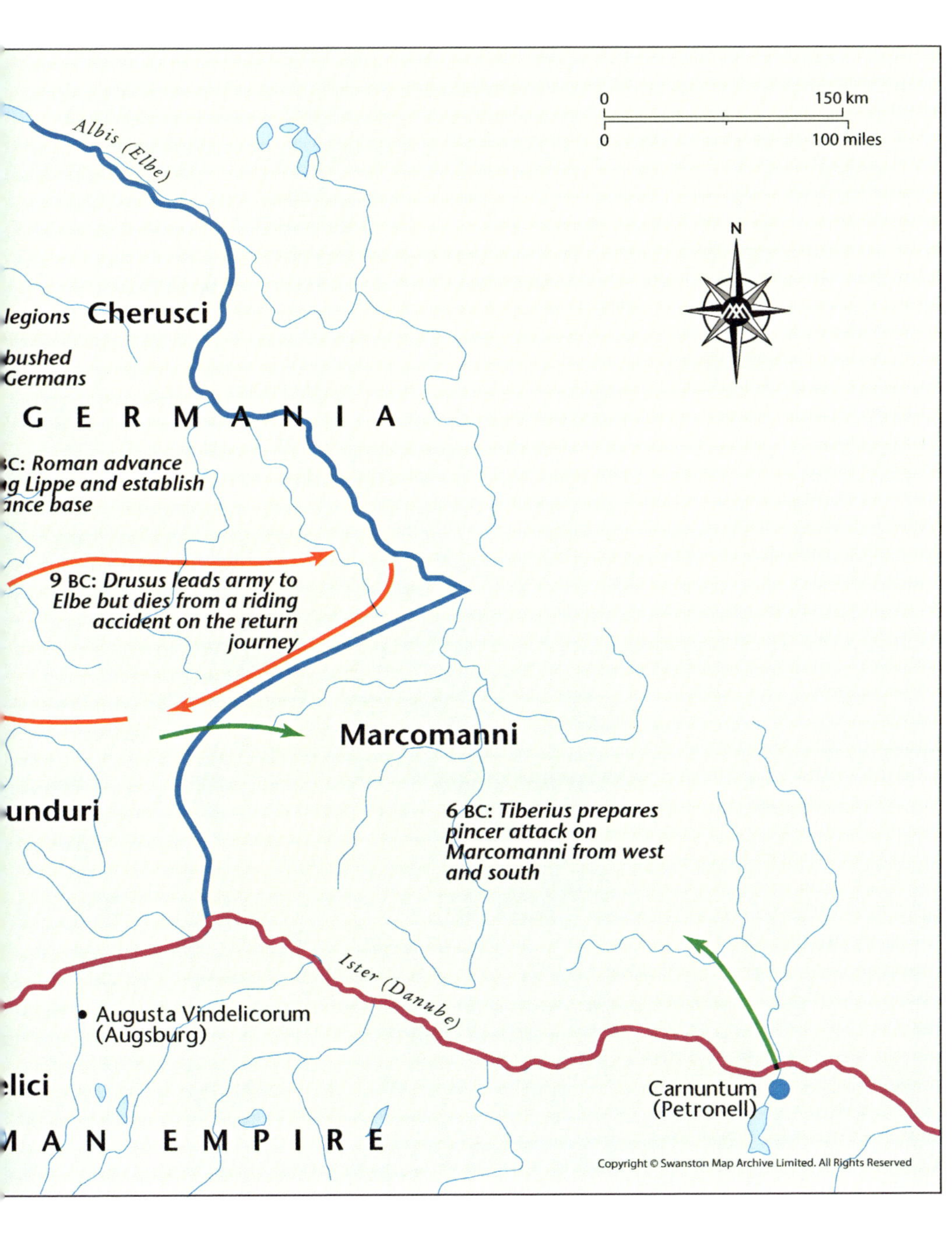
0 150 km
0 100 miles
N
legions Cherusci
bushed
Germans
G E R M A N I A
BC: Roman advance
g Lippe and establish
nce base
9 BC: Drusus leads army to
Elbe but dies from a riding
accident on the return
journey
Albis (Elbe)
Marcomanni
unduri
6 BC: Tiberius prepares
pincer attack on
Marcomanni from west
and south
Ister (Danube)
Augusta Vindelicorum
(Augsburg)
lici
MAN EMPIRE
Carnuntum
(Petronell)

and classicists largely dismissed Velleius' writings, pointing to the rather uninspiring quality of the middle-class officer's prose and the cloyingly sycophantic nature of certain passages on Tiberius. While it is evident that there is a clear bias to Velleius' account—his *Compendium of Roman History* was, after all, most probably published in the course of Tiberius' reign—historians have, over the course of the past century, begun to revise some of the prevailing conventional wisdom surrounding its worth.[38] Frederick Shipley remarks that—by the very nature of the historian's social and military background—the *Compendium* possesses an inherent value:

> Even in the treatment of Tiberius, in spite of its tone of adulation which historians have so generally condemned, we have a document which must be considered [...] as representing the psychological attitude toward the new empire of the group of administrative officers of the equestrian order who ardently supported it without any of the yearnings felt by the senatorial class for the old regime as it existed in the days before the empire had shorn them of their former governmental powers. [...] In fact, his attitude is rather that of the journalist than of the historian. There is little evidence, however, of deliberate falsification. Even his extravagant eulogy of Tiberius for which he has been so severely censured may be explained at least in part as an example of the soldier's uncritical, but loyal and enthusiastic devotion to his old commander, which reflects the attitude toward the emperor of the military and official, as opposed to that of the senatorial class and of the sympathizers of the old republic.[39]

The portrait painted by Velleius is indeed a highly flattering one—the general is depicted as someone close to his men, who willingly partakes in the hardships of life on the front, taking care of the sick and the wounded, and sharing his various perks of office—whether his physicians, luxurious carriages, private kitchens, or bathtubs—with his mud-caked legionaries.[40] As one classicist notes, there is something of the "old-fashioned generals of the Republic in Tiberius' way of conducting wars," something that people had seen in the granite-faced yet deeply humane commanders described in the works of Livy "and that they had liked."[41] Tiberius is depicted as stern but fair, and as more concerned with the preservation of the life of his men than with the pursuit of individual glory, with Velleius claiming that

Engraving of Tiberius from *Roman Emperors on Horseback*, by Adriaen Collaert, c. 1587–9, The Metropolitan Museum of Art, New York.

No chance of winning a victory ever seemed to him timely, which he would have to purchase by the sacrifice of his soldiers; the safest course was always regarded by him as the best; he consulted his conscience first and then his reputation, and finally the plans of the commander were never governed by the opinion of the army, but rather the army by the wisdom of its leader.

One should note that even a later, habitually more hostile source such as Suetonius largely shares Velleius' assessment of Tiberius' military leadership. Thus Suetonius, who also makes much of Tiberius' strength and physical prowess—he memorably wrote that the emperor could "bore a fresh, sound apple through with his finger"—also depicts him as something of an abstemious and punctilious disciplinarian:

> Beyond the Rhine, such was his way of living, that he took his meals sitting on the bare ground, and often passed the night without a tent; and his regular orders for the day, as well as those upon sudden emergencies, he gave in writing, with this injunction, that in case of any doubt as to the meaning of them, they should apply to him for satisfaction, even at any hour of the night. He maintained the strictest discipline among the troops; reviving many old customs relative to punishing and degrading offenders, setting a mark of disgrace even upon the commander of a legion, for sending a few soldiers with one of his freedmen across the river for the purpose of hunting.[42]

Velleius' narrative is perhaps most richly informative, and therefore worthy of deep examination, when it delves into Tiberius' military deployments during the critical period of AD 6–9. The sweeping campaigns that unfolded over the course of these three years were of momentous strategic import. They placed the Augustan Principate's finite military resources under severe strain, to the extent that it appeared to contemporaries that, for a brief moment, Rome's very survival was at stake. Tiberius, now Augustus' most senior general, was to play a leading role in the operations that helped safeguard the future of the empire. In AD 6, the grizzled commander, now in his mid-forties, was stationed in the Middle Danube region, poised for a major military operation "across opposite directions" against the armies of Maroboduus.

Maroboduus was a Germanic noble of the Marcomanni tribe who had migrated from the war-ravaged frontier to establish a new power base or "kingdom" across a broad swathe of present-day Bohemia. It is unclear why Maroboduus decided, in the words of Velleius, to "retire into the interior" to build his new state. He seems to imply it was a personal decision—likewise, Strabo claims that he embarked on this ambitious program of state-building after his "return from Rome," adding that Maroboduus had been either a client ruler or hostage of Augustus before deciding to turn against his former host.[43] Velleius, for his part, describes him as a "man of noble family, strong in body and courageous in mind, a barbarian by birth but not in intelligence," who had "conceived in his mind the idea of a definite empire and royal powers," and "resolved to remove his own race far away from the Romans and to migrate to a place where, inasmuch as he had fled before the strength of more powerful arms, he might make his own all powerful."[44]

Once securely ensconced within a land of "plains surrounded by forests," he had "proceeded to reduce all the neighboring races by war, or to bring them under his sovereignty by treaty."[45] Reading Roman accounts of his perceived menace to the empire's interests, it rapidly becomes evident that the otherwise mysterious figure of Maroboduus is an archetype, one that can perhaps be best described as the "Promethean proxy"—the former ally armed with perilous knowledge who has silently absorbed far too much from his routinized military interactions with the distracted Olympian hegemon—and who is suddenly willing to harness this familiarity with regard to Roman tactics, techniques, and procedures to devastating effect. The episodic spawning of such figures—the Frankenstein creations of Rome's delegative approach to imperial management—was to become one of the defining characteristics of the era. During the reigns of both Augustus and Tiberius, they would seem to suddenly erupt from silently smoldering provinces across the empire, and then go on to lead some of the most effective military efforts to challenge and disrupt the Pax Romana.

In the case of Maroboduus, Velleius describes how the Germanic potentate's forces had been trained "by constant drill to an almost Roman standard of discipline," therefore neutralizing what Romans had always viewed as their key competitive advantage—their superior military organization and readiness—and "placing him [Maroboduus] in a position of power that was dreaded even by our empire."[46] For students of the politics of empire, the figure of Maroboduus presents certain striking similarities with that of the nineteenth-century Sikh ruler Maharajah Ranjit Singh. Like Maroboduus, Ranjit Singh was a unifier and modernizer who imported European imperial tactics to develop his own formidable, well-drilled fighting force.[47] And, like the actions of Maroboduus, these consolidatory efforts triggered unease in imperial circles, ultimately leading to armed conflict in the form of the Anglo-Sikh wars.[48] Indeed, even though it would seem that Maroboduus' attitude toward Rome was one of cautious neutrality, his growing military strength, latent capacity to unify the Germanic tribes, and relative proximity to the mineral-rich province of Regnum Noricum (comprising portions of contemporary Austria and Slovenia) were all sources of anxiety for Rome's security establishment.[49] Velleius' commentary is revealing in its adumbration of the sheer extensiveness of Rome's desired forward defense perimeter. The warrior scholar thus feverishly relays the collective concern that "the summits of the Alps which mark her Rome's boundary were not more than two hundred miles distant from his boundary line."[50] Even though the infant kingdom was more than ten days' march from northern Italy, its relative rise in power was still perceived as a potential threat, and one that required preemptive neutralization.[51]

Only a few days before the planned war, however, a massive revolt flared up in Pannonia and Dalmatia, a vast region stretching from western Hungary and eastern Austria to the Balkans. This was to prove one of the most serious challenges to Roman rule in over a century, and both the scale of the uprising and the rapidity with which the conflagration spread triggered widespread panic in Rome.[52] The severity of the threat was such that a massive recruitment drive was initiated, "veterans were recalled to the standards," and Roman citizens were forced to provide slaves from their households, who were then freed, hastily granted citizenship, and sent to swell the depleted ranks of the legions.[53] As Susan Mattern notes, "this was the Principate's first lesson in how far imperialism can go without increasing the size of the army."[54] Tiberius had to cobble together a hasty truce with a relieved Maroboduus and redirect his legions southward toward Pannonia. The resulting campaign dragged on for over three years, and, involving at least ten legions, an equal number of auxiliaries, and ten thousand recalled veterans—more than a third of Rome's entire military apparatus—constituted the largest concentration of Roman military manpower since the civil wars. Velleius describes how Tiberius, later joined by his nephew Germanicus, was a shrewd, if unconventional, commander, one who employed Fabian strategies against the larger hosts of Pannonian rebels, "evading their untied forces and routing them in separate divisions," and methodically besieging their cities one by one.[55] Desirous of maintaining a degree of tactical agility, he did not hesitate to disaggregate his forces if he felt that their combined mass impeded effective command and control. In so doing, Velleius suggests that Tiberius was operating against conventional wisdom while depriving himself of the prestige of leading the largest imperial army to ever take to the field:

> There were now gathered in one camp ten legions, more than seventy cohorts, fourteen troops of cavalry and more than ten thousand veterans, and in addition to a large number of volunteers and the numerous cavalry of the king—in a word a greater army than had ever been assembled in one place since the civil wars—all were finding comfort and satisfaction in this fact and rested their greatest hope of victory in these numbers. But the general, who was the best judge of the course he pursued, preferring efficiency to show, and, as we have so often seen him doing in all his wars, following the course which deserved approval rather than that which was currently approved, after keeping the army which had newly arrived for only a few days in order to allow it to recover from the march, decided to send it away, since he saw was that it was too large to be managed in battle and was not well adapted to effective control.[56]

Tiberius' methods—laborious and unglamorous, but effective—eventually bore fruit, but only a few days after the rebellion had finally been subdued, news came of a major catastrophe in Germania. While southeastern Europe had gone up in flames, a new Roman governor, Publius Quinctilius Varus, had been working to extend the empire's writ across freshly conquered territories in Trans-Rhenal Germany. Even though the suppression of the Pannonian revolt had drawn upon a large chunk of Rome's military resources, it had still retained a sizable military presence (five legions and several auxiliary units) in Germania. The severity of the defeat Rome suffered under Varus' watch, and the deeply personal nature of his responsibility in the disaster, have led to some unduly harsh historical assessments of his moral character and strategic acumen. Nevertheless, it is fair to say that Varus made a number of serious blunders, and that he was a well-connected but largely ineffectual official who antagonized locals through ill-conceived policies and ultimately made the fatal mistake of placing his trust in the wrong man. The individual in question was Arminius, a chieftain of the Cherusci tribe, who had served as a cavalry prefect (probably at the head of an auxiliary cavalry unit) alongside the Roman army, and who was part of Varus' council of military advisors. Arminius had been educated in Rome, given Roman citizenship, and admitted into the equestrian class. It is unclear why he decided to turn against his imperial overlords, although most historians believe Varus' ham-fisted approach to governance may have played a pivotal role.

Indeed, Roman accounts repeatedly lambasted the counterproductive nature of Varus' efforts to cement Roman control over the restive border regions, accusing him of unnecessary displays of cruelty and of a certain complacency—moving too soon and too fast to register local inhabitants and extend taxation.[57] Velleius, who knew Varus personally, is perhaps the most scathing:

> Varus Quinctilius, descended from a famous rather than a high-born family, was a man of mild character and of a quiet disposition, somewhat slow in mind as he was in body, and more accustomed to the leisure of the camp than to actual service in war. That he was no despiser of money is demonstrated by his governorship of Syria: he entered the rich province a poor man, but left it a rich man and the province poor. When placed in charge of the army in Germany, he entertained the notion that the Germans were a people who were men only in limbs and voice, and that they, who could not be subdued by the sword, could be soothed by the law. With this purpose in mind he entered the heart of Germany as though he was going among a people enjoying the blessings of peace, and sitting on his tribunal he wasted the time of a summer campaign in holding court and observing the proper details of legal procedure.[58]

A century later, this explanation—that Varus had behaved both rashly and cruelly—had calcified into one of the great cautionary metanarratives of Roman statecraft, with Florus writing in his *Epitome of History*,

> It is more difficult to retain than to create provinces; they are won by force, they are secured by justice. Therefore our joy was short-lived; for the Germans had been defeated rather than subdued, and under

the rule of Drusus they respected our moral qualities rather than our arms. After his death they began to detest licentiousness and pride not less than the cruelty of Quinctilius Varus. He had the temerity to hold an assembly and had issued an edict against the tribe of the Catthi, just as though he could restrain the violence of barbarians by the rod of a lictor and the proclamation of a herald. But the Germans who had long been regretting that their swords were rusty and their horses idle, as soon as they saw the toga and experienced laws more cruel than arms, snatched up their weapons under the leadership of Arminius.[59]

In the early autumn of AD 9, Varus was preparing to settle his troops back into their winter camps on the Rhine when Arminius brought him news of a (fictitious) rebellion brewing in the hinterland, and offered to escort Varus and his troops to the area in which the alleged rebel tribesmen were gathering. According to some Roman historians, another allied Germanian noble, Segestes, had repeatedly warned Varus of Arminius' looming perfidy, only for his accusations to be dismissed out of hand.[60] These warnings unheeded, Varus and his three legions followed Arminius deep into the dark, gloomy forests, where they lost their way and eventually found themselves caught in a narrow defile pressed between woody ravines and deep bogs. Expecting to encounter only feeble resistance once they had arrived at their destination, they were encumbered by baggage and large numbers of civilian camp followers, and unable to deploy in good order due to the terrain. Whooping tribesmen, flashing spears and throwing javelins, darted in and out of the dense underbrush, subjecting the column to a series of devastating hit-and-run attacks over the course of several days. Howling winds and heavy rainfall further impeded the legions' progress as they tried to fight their way back to safety, weighing down their shields and armor, slackening the cords of their bows, and preventing them from clearing a path through the trees. Cassius Dio provides perhaps the most vivid description of the chaos and carnage:

The mountains had an uneven surface broken by ravines, and the trees grew close together and very high. Hence the Romans, even before the enemy assailed them, were having a hard time of it felling trees, building roads, and bridging places that required it. They had with them many wagons and many beasts of burden as in times of peace; moreover, not a few women and children and a large retinue of servants [...] Meanwhile a violent rain and wind came up that separated them still further, while the ground, that had become slippery around the roots and logs, made walking very treacherous for them, and the tops of the trees kept breaking off and falling down, causing great confusion. While the Romans faced such difficulties, the barbarians suddenly surrounded them on all sides at once. [...] At first they hurled their volleys from a distance; then, as no one defended himself and many were wounded, they approached closer to them.[61]

After several days of harrowing flight through waterlogged woodland trails, the battered legionaries hastily erected an encampment in a clearing and made their final stand. The Romans were massacred, and Varus and his remaining fellow officers fell on their swords. Arminius subsequently sent the governor's severed head to Maroboduus, hoping to incite him to join forces, but the Marcomanni king cautiously refused, instead choosing to forward the grisly package to Augustus.[62] News of the sudden annihilation of three entire legions—almost eighteen thousand men—and the loss of their eagles hit the aging emperor like a sledgehammer. Suetonius, with his customary flair for the dramatic, describes how the disconsolate ruler roamed the marble corridors of the imperial palace, unkempt and unshaven, banging his head against doorposts and crying out, "O Quinctilius Varus! Give me back my legions!"[63] For a few days, the climate in Rome was one of confusion and panic; after all, this had been the most crushing defeat suffered at enemy hands since the loss of Crassus' legions in Parthia.[64] Foreign residents—and Gauls and Germanians in particular—were kept under close surveillance or expelled from the city, for fear that they might be incited to rebellion, and Augustus abruptly dismissed his unit of Germanian bodyguards. Dire warnings were issued about how Arminius was surely planning to lead a huge army of barbarians into Gaul, and then across the Alps into Italy.[65] The numbers of the three destroyed legions—XVII, XIIX, and XIX—were, by imperial decree, forever expunged from the army list.[66]

Tiberius was once again dispatched to shore up Rome's defenses, and over the course of the next few months an additional six legions would be surged from across the empire. In Germania, Suetonius tells us, he behaved with his customary deliberateness, for after finding that the defeat of Varus was occasioned by the rashness and negligence of the commander, he thought proper to be guided in everything by the advice of a council of war; whereas at other times, he followed the dictates of his own judgment, and considered himself alone as sufficiently qualified for the direction of affairs. He likewise used more cautions than usual. Having to pass the Rhine, he restricted the whole convoy within certain limits, and stationing himself on the bank of the river, would not permit the wagons to cross until he had searched them at the water-side to see that they carried nothing but what was allowed or necessary. [...] He set a mark of disgrace even upon the commander of a legion, for sending a few soldiers with one of his freedmen across the river for the purpose of hunting.[67]

Velleius describes how Tiberius, once he had carefully consolidated Rome's defensive positions and "strengthened the garrison towns," then launched a series of punitive expeditions into Germania, "penetrating deep into the heart of the country," and "opening up military roads, devastating fields and burning houses."[68] As the military archeologist Peter S. Wells has observed, it is unclear how effective such scorched-earth tactics were—for the time being Arminius, having melted back into the interior, remained a frustratingly elusive target—but they had the benefit of "showing the flag" and of reassuring a jittery Roman populace.[69] It soon became apparent that, following Tiberius' actions and the rapid and massive redeployment of force to Germania, Rome's territories were no longer genuinely at risk, and that the fears of Arminius morphing into a Brennus 2.0 and traversing Europe to ravage Rome were overblown.

Nevertheless, there is little doubt that the Teutoburg massacre, occurring so soon after the devastating revolt in Pannonia, constituted something of a watershed moment for Augustus and his policies of imperial expansion.[70] Indeed, shortly before his passing in AD 14, the Empire's founding father is said to have bequeathed a set of documents to be read in the Senate after his death. Three of those documents—his instructions for his funeral, the *Res Gestae*, and a detailed roster of imperial revenue and military dispositions—are mentioned across several sources. Cassius Dio and Suetonius, however, both refer to a fourth document—the so-called political testament—which purportedly laid out several key policy directives, one of which advised against any further territorial expansion.[71] It is unclear whether such a memorandum actually existed, or whether this advice may have been passed on to Tiberius in a more informal manner.[72] Tacitus writes that the clause "advising the restriction of the empire within its present frontiers" was a simple addendum to the breviary of figures. Notwithstanding the current state of academic uncertainty surrounding the precise medium of this directive, it seems clear that the final tumultuous years of Augustus' reign had a decisive effect on Roman grand strategy. As we shall see in the following section, Tiberius—already naturally inclined toward prudence—was to take this final piece of advice to heart, systematically privileging consolidation over expansion, even at the expense of his own popularity.[73]

II.

THE RELUCTANT RULER
Tiberius as princeps

Italy, which has frequently been torn by civil war even since it came under the dominion of the Romans, nay, even since Rome was founded itself, has restrained itself from rushing headlong into confusion and destruction by the excellence of her present form of government and the ability of her emperors. Indeed, it is too challenging to administer so great a dominion other than by turning it over to one man, as to a father. Never have the Romans and their allies thrived in such peace and plenty as that afforded them by Augustus Caesar, from the time he assumed the absolute authority, and is now being afforded them by his son and successor, Tiberius. He is making Augustus the model of his administration and decrees, as are his children, Germanicus and Drusus, who are assisting their father.

Strabo, *Geography*, VI.4.2

No more the happy Golden Age we see;
The Iron's come, and sure to last with thee,
Instead of wine he thirsted for before,
He wallows now in floods of human gore.

Satirical verses allegedly published during
the second half of Tiberius' reign, quoted by Suetonius,
"Tiberius Nero Caesar," *The Twelve Caesars*, 59.1

Engraving by Jan Groenee,
*Works that Exist of Cornelius Tacitus
from the Recension of James Gronovius*,
1721, The Peace Palace Library, The Hague.

AN UNEASY TRANSITION

When Augustus finally died in AD 14, at the ripe old age of seventy-five, he had ruled for more than forty-five years. Over the course of those decades, Rome's system of government had been profoundly transformed. Few remained who remembered the troubled years before the establishment of the Principate, let alone the twilight years of the Republic before it had collapsed into civil war. At the time of his accession, Tiberius was—by ancient standards—already an old man, and twenty-eight of his fifty-six years had been spent waging war across the empire. Although he was never his stepfather's first choice, during the last decade of Augustus' rule it had become increasingly clear to all of Rome's senatorial establishment that Tiberius had been anointed as the princep's successor. Indeed, Tiberius had been granted tribunician and proconsular powers, thus placing him on a quasi-equal footing with Augustus, and in many ways had spent the final years of his predecessor's rule acting as a co-regent, surrounded by his own coterie of advisors.[1] Roman writers, always eager to establish clear contrasts between their different rulers, frequently intimated that relations between the men had been fraught, and that Augustus had only very grudgingly accepted his replacement. Suetonius famously recounted how, upon watching Tiberius leave his chambers, an aged and fatalistic Augustus wistfully sighed, "Ah—unhappy Roman people, whose fate is to be ground up by this slow devourer's jaws!"[2] At the same time, however, Suetonius, who appears to have had access to their correspondence, notes how their private exchanges were often marked by mutual respect, and even a certain degree of affection, and that they seemed to have worked well together. This is the view of most modern historians, who, while recognizing some of the tensions in the two men's relationship, along with the marked differences in their characters, also acknowledge that their professional interactions were altogether quite smooth and effective.[3]

Yet despite the intricate groundwork that had been laid for an orderly succession, the mood following Augustus' death was one of uncertainty. Nobody knew whether the system that Rome's first emperor had erected would survive its architect's demise, and as Velleius vividly relayed in his account of this period of transition, there was a widespread fear that Rome would slide back into civil war.

> Of the misgivings of mankind at this time, the trepidation of the Senate, the confusion of the people, the fears of the city, of the narrow margin between safety and ruin on which we then found ourselves, I have no time to tell as I hasten on my way, nor could he tell who had the time.[4]

This lingering trepidation—and tacit recognition of the wafer-thinness of the institutions dividing "safety" from "ruin"—was exacerbated by several factors. The first, as one classicist rightly notes, was that whereas Augustus had faced no potential rivals within his immediate family, the same could not be said for Tiberius.[5] Indeed, one of the three biological grandsons of Augustus, Agrippa Postumus, still lived, and although he had fallen into disrepute in the final years of his grandfather's reign, there had been whispers of a last-minute reconciliation.[6] More significantly, there was Tiberius' adopted son Germanicus, who had been given powers to command no less than eight legions along the Rhine, and who, as the son of the much-loved Drusus and Augustus' niece Antonia, was the darling of the people of Rome.

Secondly, much of the new political dispensation had been characterized by custom, precedent, and a managed ambiguity with regard to where the role of the Senate ended and that of the princeps began. Augustus, with his unique personality and set of political skills, had by virtue of his *auctoritas*—a nebulous Latin term that falls somewhere between influence and charisma—been the ultimate arbiter and point of reference at the heart of this informal system. Tiberius, as everyone was well aware, was an altogether different beast. As Antonio Garzetti eloquently states, it was always to be expected that Rome's supine senatorial elites would struggle to adapt to his morose and taciturn temperament:

> For a man so outwardly different from Augustus—whose affability, used with such tact and attention, had managed to conciliate and

Marble bust of Germanicus,
Musée Saint-Raymond, Toulouse.

transform into props of the system created by all elements of the system created by himself by all elements of Roman society, from the most illustrious patricians to obscure quartermasters—there was no alternative way of neutralizing the starkness of the difference impressed upon his contemporaries.[7]

Last but not least, there was the seeming reluctance of the man himself, who, in the words of Velleius, had appeared to "refuse the principate for a longer time, almost, than others had fought to secure it," and who—as evidenced from his flight to Rhodes—had always appeared uncomfortable with some of the burdens of power.[8]

Any concerns Romans might have had regarding a devastating internecine struggle among the Julio-Claudians, however, were unwarranted. Augustus' body was not yet cold when, on the Tyrrhenian island where Agrippa Postumus was residing, a centurion accosted the youth and, after a frantic struggle during which the officer was nearly overpowered, slit his throat. The elimination of Agrippa Postumus was later viewed as the Tiberian era's original sin, and sources have traditionally been divided over who ordered the execution—whether it was Augustus who issued a sealed set of orders before dying, Tiberius' ambitious mother, the Empress Livia, or Tiberius himself.[9] Tiberius, for his part, vigorously denied it, even ordering, to his aides' bewilderment, an official investigation into the murder. Meanwhile Germanicus continued to play the part of the loyal son, confounding any early misgivings his stepfather may have had.[10]

The tale of what happened next, during Tiberius' official accession, has been an object of fascination for centuries. Tacitus, ever the cynic, provides us with a masterful description of the disingenuous, fear-laced performativity that characterizes public events in all authoritarian regimes, describing how, at Augustus' funeral, the senators struggled to calibrate their facial expressions as they "rushed into slavery."

> The higher the rank, the greater the hypocrisy and the haste. With expressions composed to show neither pleasure at the passing of one emperor nor too much gloom at another's inauguration, they blended tears and joy, grief and sycophancy.[11]

There followed a series of discussions, held over the course of several days, about the future of the system of government. In his initial address to the Senate, Tiberius, pointing to his age and general state of fatigue, expressed an unwillingness to play as dominant a role as Augustus, and argued in favor of a greater division of labor:

> Only the mind of the deified Augustus was equal to such a burden: he himself had found, when called upon the sovereign to share his anxieties, how arduous, how dependent upon fortune, was the task of ruling a world! He thought, then, that in a state which had the support of so many eminent men, they ought not to devolve the entire duties on any one person; the business of government would be more easily carried out by the joint efforts of a number.[12]

Famously, Tiberius then suggested that state responsibilities should be divided up into three different categories or "parts," one of which he offered to oversee himself, while the remainder would be entrusted to the Senate. The new princeps offered to separate areas of responsibility into roughly concentric circles, with one portfolio comprising Rome and the rest of Italy, the second of the legions stationed abroad, and the third consisting of the "subject peoples outside." The senators, apparently thrown off guard or—if one believes the accounts of Tacitus and Cassius Dio, who both believed Tiberius was a scheming hypocrite—fearful of being later accused of disloyalty, strenuously rebuffed his proposals, earnestly exhorting him to follow his predecessor's autocratic template.[13] Things reportedly became even more awkward when Asinius Gallus—a man whom Tiberius detested, as he was married to his beloved ex-wife Vipsania—asked him to "choose whichever part he wished." This attempt to ingratiate himself with the new ruler apparently backfired, with a peeved Tiberius snapping, "how it is feasible for the same man both to make the division and to choose?"[14]

Tiberius' efforts to convince his audience of his sincerity were hampered by his physical aloofness, rhetorical abstruseness, and general lack of political skills—all of which made Rome's establishment doubt his sincerity. Cassius Dio thus remarks that although the proud Claudian was a "patrician of good education, he had a most peculiar nature, for he never let what he desired appear in his conversation, and what he said he wanted he usually did not desire at all," and that he "was administering in reality all the business of the empire while declaring that he did not want it all."[15] Meanwhile, Suetonius describes how certain senators grew irritated with what they saw as little more than a charade and a protracted exercise in moral self-indulgence:

> He made no scruple to assume and exercise the imperial authorities, by giving orders that he should be attended by the guards, who were the security and badge of supreme power; yet still he affected, by a most impudent piece of acting, to refuse it for a long time; once while reprehending his friends who entreated him to accept it, by claiming they knew little of what a monster the government was; another time by keeping in suspense the Senate, when they implored him and threw themselves at his feet, by ambiguous answers, and a crafty kind of dissimulation; insomuch that some were out of patience, and one cried out, during the confusion, "Either let him accept it, or decline it at once," and a second told him to his face, "Others are slow to perform what they promise, but you are slow to promise what you actually perform." At last, as if forced to it, and complaining of the miserable and burdensome service imposed upon him, he accepted the government; not, however, without giving hopes of his resigning it some time or other.[16]

Over the centuries, commentators, in their great majority, subscribed to the Tacitean depiction of events, viewing Tiberius as sanctimonious and duplicitous.[17] This interpretation has traditionally been reinforced by juxtaposition with the second half of Tiberius' reign, when the regime spiraled into the worst kind of despotism.

Many modern historians, however, are not quite so sure, with some venturing that there may have been a fair degree of sincerity behind Tiberius' initial desire to redefine the nature of the Principate, and his unwillingness to take on full powers, a responsibility which he once memorably described as akin to "holding a wolf by the ears"—something that he may not have wanted, but that he felt he could not afford to safely relinquish.[18] While continuously mindful of the need to follow Augustan precedent, Tiberius was more of a traditionalist than his maverick stepfather. Descending from a long line of prominent statesmen of the Republic, he had always been discomfited by certain aspects of the Principate, while his brother had been suspected of secretly harboring more democratic sympathies.[19] While it is probably excessive to suggest that Tiberius himself might have been a "closeted republican," it does not seem far-fetched to assume that he genuinely wished to establish a healthier equilibrium with the Senate.[20] By the time he came to power, however, it was too late: the authoritarian rot had set in too deep, and the memory of past liberties was too vague.

As contemporary scholarship has shown, illiberal governments spawn self-replicating patterns of corruption and mutually reinforcing networks of patronage that only serve to entrench authoritarian norms and practices.[21] The steady atrophy of Rome's domestic political vitality appears clearly in the accounts of the early reign of Tiberius, where he is portrayed as expressing dismay, and even revulsion, at the excruciatingly sycophantic behavior of senators. Thus one widely shared anecdote recounts how, when walking through the forum, he was startled by a man of consular rank who rushed to prostrate himself at the bewildered emperor's feet, causing Tiberius to trip and fall.[22] Although Tacitus can be a harsh critic of Tiberius' character, he is equally, if not more, contemptuous of the city's fawning elites, famously relaying Tiberius' reaction to their groveling:

> So tainted was that age, so vile its sycophancy, that not only the great personages of the state, who had to shield their magnificence by their servility, but all senators of consular rank, a large proportion of the ex-praetors, many ordinary members even, vied with one another in rising to move the most repulsive and extravagant resolutions. The tradition runs that Tiberius, on leaving the senate house, had a habit of exclaiming in Greek, "These men! How fit they are for slavery!" Even he, it was manifest, objecting though he did to public liberty, grew weary of such self-debasement in his slaves.[23]

Despite Tiberius' frustrations, and the early souring of his relationship with the senatorial elite, most Roman observers—ranging from Tacitus to Seneca—have concurred that the first half of his reign was largely positive.[24] Indeed, notwithstanding his personal distaste for some of its members, these years were characterized by relatively free and vivid senatorial debates, and decrees were sometimes passed that ran contrary to the emperor's own opinion.[25] The Senate's power was strengthened almost as soon as Tiberius came into office, when he transferred to it the right to elect magistrates from the popular assemblies, and numerous accounts testify to the relatively smooth functioning of law courts in the early years of his reign.[26] When the emperor was called upon to pronounce certain judgments, he could display both moderation and clemency, two virtues that he seemed eager to have publicly associated with his personality—indeed, both *clementia* and *moderatio* appear prominently on the imperial coinage of the era.[27]

Despite these developments, individual senators' tendency toward reactivity and the shirking of responsibility—often out of fear that they might offend or jeopardize their standing with the imperial palace—remained profoundly ingrained. As Robin Seager caustically observes, "however much Tiberius tried to be impartial and to force responsibility upon the Senate, the Senate's inclination to servility still found expression."[28] Tiberius' own inscrutability and tendency toward gnomic utterances aggravated this tendency, leading to a number of confusing situations in which the Senate, unsure of the exact extent of its prerogatives, dithered and prevaricated—which, in turn, only served to exacerbate imperial irritability. [29]

Meanwhile, Tiberius personally discouraged the more egregious displays of flattery—such as new honors or titles—and was reluctant to promote the imperial cult, as Augustus had so zealously done, across the empire. When questioned on the issue, he memorably responded that the respect of his peers was his only concern, and that enjoying such a good reputation would be like building a "temple in the hearts of those who admired him."[30] This, along with other displays of modesty and moderation, were not always viewed sympathetically, however, by a Roman audience reared on the notion that the pursuit of excellence was closely tied to the quest for fame and glory.[31] Nevertheless, this period of Tiberius' reign was widely applauded, and Cassius Dio provides perhaps the most succinct overview of what were commonly viewed as its most praiseworthy aspects:

> In the Forum a platform had been erected on which he sat in public to transact business, and he always gathered about him advisers, after the manner of Augustus. Moreover, he did not take any step of consequence without making it known to the rest. He stated his own opinion openly and not only granted everyone the right to oppose it freely in speech, but sometimes even endured to have some vote directly against it. [...] In all other matters, too, he behaved in this same way. He would not allow himself to be called "master" by the

freedmen, nor "imperator" except by the soldiers; the title of Pater Patriae he put away from him entirely: that of Augustus he did not assume (for he never permitted the question to be put to vote), but endured to hear it spoken and to read it when written. And he was so democratic in all circumstances he did not permit any unusual demonstrations, and he did not give people the right to swear by his Fortune nor did he prosecute anyone who after swearing it incurred the charge of perjury. [...] He put in good condition all buildings that had fallen into decay (not constructing anything new at all himself, except the temple of Augustus), and appropriated none of them, but restored to all of them the same names, names of the original builders. While expending extremely little for himself he laid out very great sums for the common good, either building over or adorning practically all the public works. He assisted many cities and individuals and enriched numerous senators who were poor and on that account were no longer willing to be members of the senate. However, he did not do this promiscuously and even expunged the names of some for licentiousness and of others for poverty when they could give no adequate reason for it.[32]

Unfortunately, this period of relative domestic tranquility was not to last. Tiberius' gradual descent into tyranny has been a topic of fascination for political theorists for centuries: early Baroque writers in France, Spain, and England sought to tease lessons on the enduring nature of tyranny from their Tacitean readings of the Tiberian era, while modern commentators have drawn parallels between the climate of fear of this period, with its informers and treason trials, and East Germany under the Stasi.[33] There is not space to do this tortured epoch full justice here, but suffice to say that over the course of the year a combination of factors resulted in the advent of what Suetonius would satirically dub the Principate's "age of iron," in contrast to the golden age that characterized the earlier reign of Augustus. As Theodor Mommsen writes, the second half of Tiberius' reign—for all the emperor's administrative brilliance—was one in which "the leaden fear in which his world was steeped meets us on all sides."[34]

Internal repression—with its cortège of treason trials and executions—reached a bloody crescendo with the rise of Sejanus, the malevolent head of the Praetorian Guard, who painstakingly earned the trust of the increasingly isolated, embittered, and paranoid Tiberius, gradually becoming his right-hand man.[35] Sejanus then began to to position himself to take over as Tiberius' successor, instrumentalizing his function and Rome's newly expanded treason laws to hunt down his enemies and rivals.[36] Writing only fifteen years after these events took place, Seneca described their bleak atmospherics in the following terms:

> there was a common and almost universal frenzy for informing, which was more ruinous to these citizens of Rome than the whole civil war; the talk of drunkards, the frankness of jesters, was alike reported to the government; nothing was safe; every opportunity of ferocious punishment was seized, and men no longer waited to hear the fate of accused persons, since it was always the same.[37]

Unbeknownst to Tiberius, Sejanus also slowly poisoned the imperial son and heir, Drusus the Younger, who died in AD 23 after succumbing to what appeared to be months of agonizing illness.[38] With the devastated emperor's retirement to Capri three years later, Sejanus was even freer to slake his thirst for power, and he and his minions reaped a ghastly whirlwind through a terrified Roman nobility. It was only in AD 31 that Sejanus' campaign of terror came to an end, after Tiberius was alerted to his impending treachery, and—in a meticulously planned set of moves—commanded his execution from afar. The satirist Juvenal would later pen a scathing set of lines on the fickle mob's reaction to Sejanus' sudden downfall, implying that they would have reacted equally joyously if he had succeeded in his coup and it was Tiberius' mangled cadaver that had been cast down the Capitoline steps.

> Some men are hurled headlong by a surplus of power and the envy to which it exposes them; they are wrecked by the long and illustrious roll of their honors: down come their statues, obedient to the rope; the axe hews in pieces their chariot wheels and the legs of the unoffending horses. [...] Sejanus is being dragged along by a hook, as a show and joy to all! "What a lip the fellow had! What a face!"—"Believe me, I never liked the man!"—"But on what charge was he condemned? Who informed against him? What was the evidence, who the witnesses, who made good the case?"—"Nothing of the sort; a great and wordy letter came from Capri." [...] And what does the mob of Remus say? It follows fortune as it always does, and rails

against the condemned. That same rabble, if fate had smiled upon the Etruscan [Sejanus], if the aged Emperor had been struck down unawares, would in that very hour have conferred upon Sejanus the title of Augustus.[39]

The revelation of Sejanus' treachery, of the apparent depth of his support, and of his role in Drusus' murder seems to have had a profound effect on Tiberius, driving him into an orgy of retributive violence against anyone he perceived, rightly or wrongly, as having participated in the attempted coup.[40] The once noble war hero and paragon of republican virtue had come to seem, "in his old age, a ghoulish figure of dread: embittered, paranoid, and murderous."[41] This blood-spattered era would only come to a close with the dictator's death, at the age of seventy-seven, in AD 37. By that time, the withered ogre of Capri was a universally reviled figure, and the people of Rome openly cheered at the news of his demise.[42]

And yet, despite the oppressive horror that had characterized life in the capital during the final years of his rule, the empire had—relatively speaking—rarely known such an extended period of prosperity and peace. Indeed, the stark contrast between the effectiveness of Tiberius' foreign policy and the grim tragedy of his personal political transformation is perhaps fated to remain one of the great enigmas of antiquity. The remainder of this book will not consist, therefore, of an investigation into the root causes of this disconnect (although the degree to which political developments in Rome may have affected Roman grand strategy will, should the need arise, certainly be addressed). Rather, the following section will focus on the independent and individual aspects of Tiberian foreign policy that might have ultimately contributed to its lasting success.

1st Century AD Sardonyx Cameo,
the so-called "Great Cameo of France."
Acquired by King Louis IX of France in 1247,
and depicting Tiberius surrounded by other
imperial family members. Musée de la
Bibliothèque Nationale de France, Paris.

TIBERIUS' MODE OF IMPERIAL MANAGEMENT

In the months following Augustus' death, Tiberius faced an immediate crisis in the form of mutinies among the legions stationed in Rome's most unsettled frontier zones: Pannonia and Germania. There is no evidence that the insurrections were connected or coordinated, and little to suggest that they were initially framed as rejections of Tiberius himself—after all, one must assume that the new princeps, with his decades of service, remained widely respected across the Roman officer corps. Rather, it seems that these movements of insurrection were both opportunistic attempts by agitators to exploit the political uncertainties surrounding the succession, and the result of legitimate dissatisfaction among the rank and file with regard to deteriorating service conditions. Tacitus' accounts of both mutinies are somewhat revealing in their apparent contradictions. On the one hand, when discussing the Pannonian revolt, the historian dismisses the mutiny as a simple act of unprincipled acquisitiveness, facilitated by a breakdown in camp routine and discipline following the death of Augustus. This interpretation was in line with the opinion of most elite Roman commentators regarding the risks that an idle military posed to public order. Thus Tacitus offhandedly comments that

There were no fresh grievances; only the change of sovereigns had excited a vision of licensed anarchy and a hope of the emoluments of civil war. Three legions were stationed together in summer quarters [in Pannonia] under the command of Junius and Blaesus. News had come of the end of Augustus and the accession of Tiberius; and Blaesus, to allow the proper interval for mourning or festivity, had suspended the normal round of duty. With this the mischief began. The ranks grew insubordinate and quarrelsome—gave a hearing to any glib agitator—became eager, in short, for luxury and ease, disdainful of discipline and work.[1]

HEBERNIA
BRITANNIA
Londinium
Oceanus Germanicus
Mare Suebicum
GERMANIA
50°
OCEANUS ALTANTICUS
BELGICA
Lugdunensis
GALLIA
AQUITANIA
NARBONENIS
NORICUM
PANNONIA
D
DALMATIA
Mare Aegeum
40°
HISPANIA
CORSICA
ITALIA
Roma
Neapolis
SARDINIA
Sicilia
MAURETANIA
NUMIDIA
Mare Ir
AFRICA PROCONSULARIS
30°
N
0   200 km
0   200 miles
0°
10°

Roman Empire under Emperor Tiberius
14–37 CE
Territory acquired by Rome by 14 CE
Annexed and conquered by 14–37 CE
Client states of Rome in 37 CE
Legionary fortresses
Major cities
Mare Caspium
Pontus Euxinus
ARMENIA
MAEDIA
ASSYRIA
REGNUM PARTHORUM
MESOPOTAMIA
SOPHENE
MOESIA
THRACIA
PONTUS
BITHINIA
GALITIA
CAPPADOCIA
Commagene
CILICIA
SYRIA
PALMYRENE
ASIA
PANPHILIA
Athenae
AIA
Rhodus
CRETA
Cyprus
r u m   N o s t r u m
PALESTINA
JUDAEA
NABATAEI
AICA
AEGYPTUS
Sinus Arabicus
30°
40°
50°

However, when the historian begins to relay the more specific grievances of the mutineers—whether in Pannonia or Germania—he appears far more sympathetic to their plight.[2] The reader is treated to richly cinematic descriptions of their state of physical wretchedness and exhaustion, and to harrowing testimonials of the unsparing harshness of a life spent soldiering along the empire's frontiers.

> When would they dare to claim redress, if they shrank from carrying their petitions or their swords, to the still unstable throne of a new prince? Mistakes enough had been made in all the years of inaction, when white-haired men, many of whom had lost a limb by wounds, were making their thirtieth or fortieth campaign. Even after discharge their warfare was not accomplished: still under canvas by the colors they endured the drudgeries under an altered name. And suppose that a man survived this multitude of hazards: he was dragged once more to the ends of the earth to receive under the name of a "farm" some swampy morass or barren mountainside. In fact, the whole trade of war was comfortless and profitless: ten asses a day was the assessment of body and soul: with that they had to buy clothes, weapons and tents, bribe the bullying centurion and purchase a respite from duty! But whip-cut and sword-cut, stern winter and sweltering summer, red war or barren peace—these, by the Gods, were always with them. [...] The crowd shouted approval, as one point or the other was told. Some angrily displayed the marks of the lash, some their grey hairs, most their threadbare garments and bare bodies.[3]

Although both mutinies appear to have initially been focused on revising pay and conditions of service, they rapidly began to radicalize as frustrations grew, and became increasingly political. In his account of the events in Pannonia, Velleius notes that the three legions

> seized at the moment by a form of madness and a deep desire to throw everything into confusion, wanted a new leader, a new order of things, and a new res publica.[4]

The situation was even more alarming in Germania, where certain ringleaders of the revolt suggested that they would be willing to pledge loyalty to Germanicus, who was wildly popular among the people of Rome and was believed to have inherited the republican beliefs of his father Drusus, Tiberius' brother.[5] Cassius Dio attributes Tiberius' initial prevarications during the accession to his concern that the disaffected legions in both Pannonia and Germania might rally behind Germanicus and carry the princeling to the throne.[6] Regardless of whether Tiberius was genuinely animated by such a fear, the question of how to manage the fiery, impulsive Germanicus would, as we shall see, become something of a recurring headache for his more cold-blooded uncle and adoptive father. It is also unclear whether Germanicus truly harbored the republican sympathies later ascribed to him by authors such as Tacitus and Cassius Dio. And indeed throughout the duration of the Principate different figures tried to both draw on and manipulate the memory of the Republic—and "republicanism" could be a vague descriptor, simply referring to the perceived attachment to a set of old social values rather than any coherent political program.[7] In the case of both Drusus the Elder and Germanicus, the wide belief in their "hidden republicanism" could simply have been a function of their popularity, and of the desire of the Roman people to project these qualities onto a different branch of the Julio-Claudian dynasty.[8]

The manner in which Tiberius chose to deal with this unrest—by dispatching Drusus to Pannonia and letting Germanicus deal with the mutiny in Germania—was heavily criticized by those who believed that the emperor should have gone to address the rebellious legionaries in person.

"The panic-stricken capital turned on Tiberius," says Tacitus, with raised voices claiming that

> He ought to have gone in person to confront the rebels with the majesty of the empire: they would have yielded at the sight of a princeps, old in experience, and supreme at once to punish and reward.[9]

Such critiques—of Tiberius' refusal to visit provinces and crisis sites in person—were to become a leitmotiv of his reign. On occasion he seemed to ponder a grand tour of the provinces, and would initiate extensive preparations for travel before finally deciding against it. This wavering earned him the gentle mockery of the senatorial class, who dubbed him Callipedes—a Greek character traditionally depicted as running in place. More serious critics charged that a continuous absence of the emperor's physical presence could be interpreted as a sign of imperial neglect. Moreover, his refusal to visit the more troubled territories under Roman rule could be construed as a cynical attempt to underplay the severity of a local uprising, and the threat it posed to his legacy as guardian of the Pax Romana. Tiberius remained unfazed by these criticisms. For Augustus' successor, the imperial "*dignitas*"—and the massive military and logistical baggage train that invariably accompanied it on missions overseas—was to be deployed sparingly, and not in response to each and every brush fire that flared up across the empire. Thus in response to one objection to his refusal to visit Gaul during an uprising, he is reported to have snarled that

> it would be undignified for the sovereign, whenever there was a commotion in one or two states, to rush away from the capital, which was the center of government for the empire as a whole.[10]

Furthermore, as the great classicist Barbara Levick has rightly pointed out, in many ways Tiberius— by sending out the princes to act in his name and by choosing to remain in Rome—was once again hewing to an Augustan precedent:

> The truth was that Augustus' last visit to Gaul had been undertaken when he was a year younger than Tiberius was in AD 14 [the year of his accession]. After 8 BC he too was never to leave Italy again. Tiberius, then, was adopting the same policy that Augustus had pursued for the last twenty-two years of his principate.[11]

In reaction, therefore, to these first criticisms of his behavior as head of state, Tiberius calmly retorted that for him to personally visit the mutineers would be an injudicious plan of action, for by choosing one military region over the other for his first visit, he would inevitably be perceived as displaying favoritism. By entrusting the management of the concurrent crises to both his adoptive sons, he could "approach both at once," and—here very much in line with his conception of the symbolic nature of his function—"without hazarding the imperial majesty, which is always most venerable at a distance."[12] This hands-off approach would also provide the two youths with the breathing space they needed, both to gain additional experience in the management of men and to (hopefully) showcase their respective talents in two of Rome's most critical theaters of operation. Both princes did indeed succeed in defusing the tensions—albeit in very different ways.

Indeed, whereas Drusus, very much his father's son, swiftly reestablished discipline by executing the ringleaders and displaying, in the words of Velleius, "the severity of the Romans of old," Germanicus' manner of placating the mutineers appeared more problematic.[13] Alternating between fine displays of rhetoric and cruder forms of histrionics, Germanicus seems to have struggled to maintain control over the course of events.[14] The insurrectionary fervor of the revolting legionaries was eventually quelled, but only after a shambolically conducted purge, and sordid demonstrations of mob justice. It also came at the price of significant concessions, some of which Tiberius later quietly withdrew.[15] Germanicus raised eyebrows in Rome by hastily paying the legionaries' donatives (the money they were meant to be gifted following the death of Augustus) with some of his personal funds—something that was considered to be the prerogative of the emperor.[16] Whether out of weakness or genuine conviction, he also appears to have believed that the only way to wash away the army's shame was to steep it in the blood of its barbarian foes across the Rhine, allowing it to—in the words of Tacitus—"expiate itself" by thrusting deep into the wilderness.[17] In their methodical savagery, the initial phases of this propitiatory crusade bear all the hallmarks of an ethnic cleansing campaign:

> To extend the scope of the raid, Germanicus divided his eager legions into four bodies, and, for fifty miles around, wasted the country with sword and flame. Neither age nor sex inspired pity: places sacred and profane were razed indifferently to the ground; among them, the most noted religious center of these tribes, known as the Temple of Tanfana. The troops escaped without a wound: they had been cutting down men half-asleep, unarmed or dispersed.[18]

During the next two years, Germanicus was to lead a series of major expeditions; warring against shifting coalitions of tribes, chasing the elusive figure of Rome's great villain, Arminius, and using northern Europe's network of rivers to project force deep into the wooded fastness of Germania. He racked up victory after victory, and the tales of his many exploits (his battle-scarred legionaries even reached the windswept shores of the North Sea) were the thrill of Rome. Suetonius describes how, during one of Germanicus' trips back to Rome, delirious crowds lined up to cheer the young prince even as he was still seventy miles away from the city's outer limits:

All the praetorian cohorts marched out to meet him, notwithstanding the order that only two were to go; and all the people of Rome,
both men and women of every age, sex and social class, flocked as
far as the twentieth milestone to greet him.[19]

In the course of Germanicus' campaigns, two of the lost eagles were
recovered, and a column of legionaries came upon one of the sites in the
Teutoburg Forest where Varus' men had met their doom. Tacitus' description of the legionaries' long journey through the dark, dripping forest
"hideous to sight and memory," and of their eventual discovery of the
desolate charnel ground has a superbly vivid, almost gothic quality to it,
and later inspired a number of Romantic artists:

> Varus's first camp, with its broad sweep and measured space for
> officers and eagles, advertised the labors of three legions; then a
> half-ruined wall and shallow ditch showed where a broken grouping
> might have taken cover. In the plain between were bleaching bones,
> scattered or in little heaps, as the men had fallen, fleeing or standing
> fast. Hard by lay splintered spears and limbs of horses, while human
> skulls were nailed prominently on tree trunks. In the neighboring
> groves stood the savage altars at which they had slaughtered the trib-
> unes and head centurions. Survivors of the disaster, who had escaped
> the battle or the chains of captivity, described how here the legates fell,
> here the eagles were taken, where the first wound was dealt upon
> Varus, and where he found death by the suicidal stroke of his own
> unhappy hand. They spoke of the tribunal from which Arminius
> made his harangue, all the gibbets and torture pits for prisoners, and
> the arrogance with which he had insulted the standards and the eagles.
> And so, six years after the fatal battle, a Roman army, present on that
> ground, interred the bones of the three legions; and no man knew
> whether he consigned to earth the remains of a stranger or a kinsman,
> but all thought of all as friends and members of one family, and, with
> anger rising against the enemy, both mourned and hated their foes.[20]

Tiberius was evidently irritated by Germanicus' decision to bring his
troops—some of whom were survivors of the Teutoburg massacre—to the
site, deeming it potentially damaging to their discipline and morale.
Germanicus had also violated religious decorum by participating in a

funeral ceremony while being a commander vested with the sacred status of the *augur*—something which may at first sight seem a relatively minor infraction, but which would have undoubtedly been a source of aggravation for the hyperconservative Tiberius.[21] For some time now, the emperor had been expressing some broader misgivings about the rationale and conduct of the revived Germanian campaigns. Conscious of his adoptive son's extreme popularity, and of public desire to avenge the Teutoburg massacre, he had given him operational freedom and showered him with honors. Rome had always relied on brutal terror tactics as a form of deterrence by punishment and—for a Roman general culturally conditioned to overlook the moral abhorrence of such methods—Germanicus' genocidal forays had temporarily served a useful function.[22] His amphibious assaults on riverine communities had wreaked havoc, and by laying waste to belts of tribal villages in the vicinity of the frontier zone, he had traced a new sanitary cordon around Rome's embryonic network of border outposts.[23] At the same time, and perhaps most importantly, the campaigns had taken on a symbolic importance, as the Germanian legions, through their actions—and most notably their retrieval of the eagles—had helped to publicly expunge the terrible humiliation suffered in AD 6.

These campaigns had not been without cost, however, and the attrition rate among the troops had been high, with many falling in bloody skirmishes, or drowning in ill-conceived naval operations along the treacherous tidal flats off the North Sea. Despite Germanicus' string of high-profile victories, his had been a war of plunder and devastation, not of durable conquest, and his supply lines were dangerously over-extended. In AD 16, the young prince addressed a series of letters to the emperor requesting a troop surge in order to reannex all the lands his father had conquered two decades earlier. Tiberius—first politely, then more firmly—refused. Noting that Germanicus' successes had frequently been married with disasters, his correspondence observed that

there had already been enough successes and enough mischances. He [Germanicus] had won great victories, but he should also remember all the losses that had been inflicted by wind and wave—losses that were not in any way a result of his leadership, but that remained grievous and shocking.

Next spread: Wood Engraving by Hermann Plüddemann, "The Battle of the Teutoburg Forest," in F. Bülau, *German history in Pictures*, Dresden 1855. Sammlung Archiv für Kunst und Geschichte, Berlin.

When confronted with Germanicus' obduracy, Tiberius subtly reminded his nephew of his greater experience, noting that he had been deployed to Germania nine times, and that he "had effected more by policy than by force." His preferred approach, he stated, was the time-old strategy of divide and rule, adding that "rebel tribes, now that enough has been done to satisfy Rome's need for revenge, can safely be left to their intestine strife."

After voicing additional protests and attempting to negotiate another year "in which to finish his work," Germanicus eventually relented, and after having been granted the honor of a triumph and second consulship, was sent to manage affairs in the East.

Both Tiberius and Germanicus' punitive campaigns had allowed Rome's military planners—in addition to surveying unknown territories— better to map out the complex human terrain in the regions spanning from the Rhine to the Elbe. In the words of Strabo, "all these nations had become known to us [Romans] through their wars with Rome."[24] Armed with this more granular expertise, Rome's second emperor was convinced that the future of the imperium's security in this troubled region lay in sound intelligence work, shrewd diplomacy, and the careful cultivation of proxies. The tribal coalitions the legions faced in northwestern Europe were bound first and foremost by charismatic individuals in the vein of Arminius of the Cherusci and Maroboduus of the Marcomanni—and such individuals could be wooed, co-opted or manipulated by Roman representatives. While Arminius had been markedly successful in the years immediately following the Teutoburg massacre, his heady ambitions had eventually come to alienate a number of influential family members, and in antagonize fellow Germanian tribal chieftains.[25] Both his brother and father-in-law were Roman allies, and his powerful uncle was later enticed to fight for Rome. Tacitus recounts how an embassy from the Chatti tribe—which up to that point had been allied to the Cherusci—secretly contacted the Roman Senate offering to poison the troublesome insurgent in exchange for a promise of future clemency. The emperor reportedly responded himself, imperiously retorting:

> It was not by treason nor in the dark but openly and in arms that the
> Roman people took vengeance on their foes.[26]

Notwithstanding this proud rejoinder, Tiberius surely felt a measure of satisfaction upon learning, in AD 19, that the former Roman auxiliary commander had been killed in a vicious bout of tribal infighting. The threat posed by Maroboduus—which many in Rome had considered far more serious than that embodied by Arminius—had also been neutralized.[27] Indeed, just as the emperor had predicted, in the wake of the power vacuum occasioned by Germanicus' withdrawal, Arminius and Maroboduus had turned on each other. Maroboduus, who under the terms of the peace treaty signed with Tiberius in AD 6 benefited from the quasi-imprimatur of a head of an allied state, had opened formal diplomatic channels with Rome and requested military assistance in the war against Arminius. All too happy to see Germania's two most deadly wolves devour themselves, the wily old man had demurred, coldly reminding the Marcomanni leader that he had chosen to remain neutral during Rome's earlier campaigns in Germania, and that "to demand Rome's military assistance against the Cherusci was hardly appropriate from a man who had brought no help to Rome when she herself was engaged against the same enemy."[28] Meanwhile, Drusus the Younger was dispatched to Germania and "earned considerable credit by tempting the Germanians to revive their feuds and, as the power of Maroboduus was already shattered, to press on his complete destruction."[29] A broken Maroboduus fled across the Danube to seek shelter in the Roman province of Noricum, and was subsequently granted asylum by the emperor. Indeed, Tiberius had always seemed to derive a certain pleasure from highly publicized demonstrations of clemency toward "honorable" barbarian foes.[30] The former Marcomanni king was safely sequestered in Ravenna, where he was to eke out a quiet and solitary existence until his death eighteen years later, in the same year as Tiberius. The emperor's Germanian policy—a combination of masterly inactivity and shrewd proxy management—was thus largely successful, even though it did not enflame hearts in the manner of his adoptive son's ferocious rampage across the edges of the known world.

Tiberius' foreign policy challenges were not confined to the Germanian theater, however. As briefly mentioned earlier, he was also forced to confront a relatively large-scale uprising in Gaul in AD 21. The revolt was led by a man with the cognomen of Sacrovir (holy man), which some historians have interpreted as indicating that he was a druid as well as a Gallic aristocrat. (If this is true, it may well have motivated Tiberius to further repress the practice of druidism in Gaul.) Although the rebellion ballooned, alarming many in Rome, the combatants were poorly equipped—brandishing little more than hunting spears—and were relatively easily crushed by a force dispatched from garrisons in Upper Germany, with Sacrovir choosing to commit suicide.[31] Tiberius' unflappability during the crisis, and his decision only to make a public announcement to the Senate once the uprising was quelled, was a topic of frustration for "patriotic" Roman citizens, who criticized his "studied unconcern," and his "maintenance of his wonted behavior through all those days, whether from deep reserve or because he had information that the disturbances were of moderate extent and slighter than reported."[32]

A more enduring problem materialized in the hinterlands of Africa in AD 17, when a Numidian by the name of Tacfarinas assembled an army of seminomadic tribesmen and began to wage a protracted insurgency against Rome and its allies. Tacfarinas appears to have been a commander of superlative military skill, and—like Arminius—had served as an auxiliary officer alongside the Roman legions. Tacitus notes that, like Maroboduus, Tacfarinas inculcated Roman-style discipline and tactics, not only recruiting "gangs of bandits and vagrants," but marshalling some of them into "a body in the military style by companies and troops." Ranging across North Africa, he divided his army into a more irregular force which "disseminated fire, slaughter and terror," but also retained a smaller, more conventional unit "equipped on the Roman model, and inured to discipline and obedience."[33] A number of theories have been advanced to help explain the genesis of one of the more successful—or at least long-lasting—insurgencies of the early Principate. While some historians have advanced the idea that the nomadic revolt may initially have stemmed from unrest within Rome's client kingdom of Mauretania and then "spilled over" into Rome-controlled territories, requiring Roman military intervention, others have suggested that it was a reaction by nomadic pastoralists to Roman infrastructure development and an influx of Italian settlers—changes that threatened to durably transform their way of life.[34] In any event, this would prove the most intractable insurgency of the Tiberian era, lasting more than seven years, and requiring a temporary troop surge in the form of the redeployment of the IX Legio Hispana, along with its attached auxiliary units, from Pannonia to Africa.[35]

As one scholar notes, this was the only case under Tiberius when a rebellion necessitated the deployment of an entire legion from a distant province—otherwise, all crises were handled by local legions or by smaller vexillationes rushed from neighboring provinces (as during the Sacrovir-led uprising). This was in stark contrast to Augustus' reign, when empire-wide legion movements were more common.[36] Using his light-armed horsemen to devastating effect, Tacfarinas raided deep into Roman territory, disrupting the capital's grain supply, then melting back into the deserts or the Atlas Mountains. As we shall see in greater detail in the following section, the challenge posed by such a mobile and fleeting foe forced the African Roman legions to adapt their tactics and force structure. Eventually, these changes were to prove successful, and Tacfarinas was finally cut down in a dawn raid in AD 24.

For the remainder of Tiberius' rule, the provinces seem—in the main—to have been relatively quiescent. Throughout his reign, Tiberius is shown to have been an attentive steward of Rome's overseas territories, closely following issues pertaining to infrastructure development and taxation even during the eleven-year period when he was living in relative seclusion on Capri. Indeed, the assertion by Suetonius that he completely neglected his imperial duties once he had relocated to his island sanctuary does not seem to be borne out by the facts.[37] Shortly after acceding to the throne, in AD 15, Tiberius responded to petitions from cities in Greece and Turkey that had been devastated by an earthquake by pushing forward a senatorial resolution which exempted them from paying taxes for three years.[38] When the Achaeans and Macedonians protested unfair levels of taxation, Tiberius reacted by relieving them of their predatory proconsular governor and unifying the territories into one province under an imperial legate. This was both a means of asserting greater imperial control over provincial finances and a practical move—as one study concludes, this consolidation ultimately proved economically beneficial, substantially reducing administrative costs.[39] Across the empire, the princeps trained his beady eye on the actions of provincial governors and imperial legates, watching for signs of financial mismanagement or corruption. When, during his earlier existence as Augustus' lead general, Tiberius was waging war in the Balkans, he had once asked Bato, the leader of the Pannonian rebels, why he had chosen to take up arms. The captured warlord's response became famous: "The Romans," he said, "were to blame, for they do not send shepherds or even dogs to tend their flocks, but wolves." It was perhaps with this metaphor in mind that Tiberius advised some of his more rapacious governors that Rome's provincial subjects should, like sheep, be shorn but not flayed.[40] Tiberius also began to keep sitting governors in place for much longer periods of time, thus perpetuating a tendency toward prorogation that had already begun

Author's photograph of Villa Jovis,
Capri, May 2022.

under his predecessor.[41] According to the Judaean historian Flavius, this was to discourage graft, for governors rapidly rotating through different provinces had a tendency to focus all their time and energies on self-enrichment. Tiberius reportedly illustrated this line of reasoning with yet another colorful analogy:

> He permitted those governors who had been sent once to their government to stay there for a long while, out of regard for the subjects that were under them; for all governors are naturally disposed to get as much as they can from their time in office, and those that are not truly settled there but only stay a short time, operating under an uncertainty as to when they will be relieved, fleece the people even more vigorously; but if they remain in office a long time, they become satiated with their spoils and become less predatory in their pillaging. [...] He gave them an example to show his meaning: a great number of flies was clustered all over the bleeding sores of a man that had been wounded; upon which a passerby, pitying the man's misfortune [...] offered to drive them away. The wounded man prayed him not to do so [...] explaining, "if you drive these flies away, you will hurt me worse, for these are already gorged with my blood, they do not crowd about me, nor pain me as much as before, but are less active. The fresh ones that come, though, will be famished, and finding me already drained and wounded, will be the cause of my destruction.

Josephus was more disapproving of Tiberius' delays in appointing ambassadors and officials, accusing him of negligence and overly ponderous decision-making, a criticism that was also leveled by Tacitus. And indeed, in many cases important positions did remain unfilled. In other instances, Tiberius preferred that men he trusted manage their provinces "in absentia," from the comforts of Rome.[42] Such gaps in the provincial administrative structure may have also been somewhat unavoidable, considering the sparse number of truly qualified (and uncorrupt) candidates—Tiberius is on record as expressing skepticism as to the wisdom of foisting candidates who, to his mind, lacked "merit and influence" into positions of responsibility.[43] Tiberius' mode of imperial administration was certainly not irreproachable (his appointment of Gnaeus Calpurnius Piso as governor of Syria in AD 17, for example, was a markedly poor choice) yet most historians acknowledge its overarching qualities, especially when benchmarked against that of his successors.[44] Separately, it has been noted that more men were convicted of governmental malpractice in the provinces under Tiberius than under any other emperor from Augustus to Trajan.[45]

Tiberius also revealed himself to be a consummate player of the Romano-Parthian great game, not only solidifying his predecessor's geopolitical advances in the shatter belt stretching from Armenia to Anatolia, but also expanding Rome's own direct sphere of influence. After a short stint in Rome, during which he had been granted a triumph for his victories over the Germanic tribes, Germanicus had been sent east. Granted *maius imperium*, or supreme command, over all other provincial governors in the region, the heir apparent seems to have initially performed relatively well, closely following Tiberius' directives and fulfilling his mission, in the words of Josephus, of "settling the empire's affairs to the east."[46] The first order of business related to managing the fallout of a recent civil war in Parthia. In AD 8, Vonones, a Parthian prince who had been raised in Rome, captured his home country's throne with Roman diplomatic support and the aid of a group of Parthian nobles. Rapidly, however, his Roman ways had aggravated the local aristocracy. Tacitus recounts how his alien habits and seeming excessive subservience to Rome had fostered resentment among his people:

> Their feelings soon gave way to shame, they said that the Parthians had degenerated: they had gone to another continent for a king tainted with the enemy's arts, and now the throne of the Arsacids [the ruling dynasty of Parthia] was held, or given away as one of the provinces of Rome. Where was the glory of the men who slew Crassus and had ejected Antony, if a creature of Caesar, tied to him in bondage through all these years, was to govern Parthians? Their contempt was heightened by the man himself, with his remoteness from his ancestral traditions, his rare appearances in the hunting field, his languid interest in horseflesh, his use of a litter when passing through towns, and his disdain of national banquets. Other subjects for mockery were his Greek retinue and his habit of keeping even the humblest household necessaries under lock and key.[47]

Roman observers soon realized that their backing of Vonones had been ill-judged. As with other émigré rulers initially supported by foreign powers throughout history—Ahmed Chalabi in modern post-invasion Iraq comes to mind—his rise to power had not reinforced his imperial benefactor's influence. To the contrary, it had generated a nationalist backlash vis-à-vis Rome, as well as further instability.[48] Taking note of these developments, Augustus had wisely refused to officially recognize Vonones as ruler—indeed, he had been briefed by his then governor of Syria, Quintus Caecilius Silanus, that the growing unrest in Parthia now meant that there was a genuine risk that Rome could be dragged into a civil war. This proved to be wise counsel, for in AD 11, after only three years of rule, Vonones was ousted by Parthia's aristocracy, who replaced him with another noble by the name of Artabanus, later crowned Artabanus II. Vonones fled to Armenia and, taking advantage of a local power vacuum, seized power there. This new state of affairs put Rome in an exceedingly uncomfortable position. Artabanus was threatening to invade Armenia, to depose his troublesome former rival, and to replace him with his own son. This would have been an unacceptable outcome for Rome, as it would have essentially resulted in Armenia's annexation by Parthia. Germanicus was thus dispatched by Tiberius to negotiate with the Parthians as to a mutually satisfactory solution. Meeting on the banks of the Euphrates, Germanicus and Artabanus II signed a peace treaty, and the irksome Vonones was spirited away to Syria, where he resided with a "toy court" under Roman surveillance. He was replaced in Armenia by Artaxes, a member of the royal family of Pontus, a kingdom sympathetic to Rome. Though pro-Roman, he was eastern in his ways, of a more cautious, conciliatory nature than his predecessor, and thus acceptable to the Parthians. Engineered by Tiberius but ably executed by Germanicus, this had been a diplomatic *coup de maître*.[49] Indeed, as Barbara Levick comments,

> Rome was now in a stronger position than she had been eighteen years before [during the 2 BC negotiations]. It was her candidate and not the Parthians' that was on the throne of Armenia, and there was no need to acknowledge Parthian equality. Tiberius' choice too was astute or fortunate. Artaxes' tastes were those of the Armenians: riding and hunting. [50]

Artaxes was to remain in power until his death seventeen years later, toward the end of Tiberius' reign, in AD 34. Artabanus continued to rule over Parthia and—according to Tacitus—began to feel emboldened as the years rolled by, "disdaining the old age of Tiberius as no longer fit for arms," and "coveting Armenia." After Artaxes' death, he briefly succeeded in putting two of his sons, Arsaces and Orodes, on the Armenian throne (Arsaces was poisoned by his servants after less than a year in power), before Tiberius swung into action. "Faithful to his rule of manipulating foreign affairs by policy and craft without a resort to arms," and working through his envoy Lucius Vitellius, Tiberius sponsored an uprising against Artabanus.[51] The latter eventually triumphed over Rome's proxy, but was considerably weakened, and forced, once again, to grudgingly accept Rome's choice of candidate for Armenia, the Iberian Mithridates. This sequence of events illustrates once again how Tiberius, even toward the end of his life—and despite the bug-eyed paranoia which had come to infect his management of domestic affairs—remained in complete possession of his faculties with regard to foreign policy.

Over the course of his reign, when presented with opportunities for peaceful territorial annexation, Tiberius seems to have run careful cost-benefit analyses, and eschewed undifferentiated expansion. Thus, when the kings of Commagene and Cappadocia died, leaving their respective countries leaderless, Tiberius opted to formally annex their territories. This made sense both militarily—they bordered the Euphrates and Parthia's own traditional sphere of interest—and economically. Both provinces were more than financially self-sufficient, and Cappadocia, in particular, provided a veritable windfall of revenue. Indeed, its absorption subsequently allowed Tiberius to reduce both domestic taxation and the taxes previously levied on the Cappadocians themselves. These shrewd financial policies, note one classicist, contributed greatly to the popularity—and resultant long-term stability—of Roman rule in that portion of Asia Minor.[52] When given the chance to absorb the poor mountainous territory of Thracia—a territory populated by fierce, unruly hillsmen—Tiberius demurred, content to meddle in its murderous clan politics from afar. On one occasion, the wily emperor even tricked one troublesome Thracian king into coming to Rome, where he put him under lock and key and replaced him with a more amenable family member.

It is therefore not surprising that it is Tiberius' able stewardship of Rome's foreign policy that has traditionally garnered the most praise, including from hostile chroniclers such as Suetonius, who, almost grudgingly, acknowledges the soundness of the princeps' grand strategy of war avoidance:

> Disturbances from foreign enemies he quelled by his lieutenants, without ever going against them in person; and he would only employ his lieutenants with much reluctance and when it was absolutely necessary. Princes who were ill-affected toward him, he kept in subjection, more by menaces and remonstrances, than by force of arms. Some of whom he induced to come to him, he would never permit to return home, such as Maroboduus the Germanian, Thrascypolis the Thracian, and Archelaus the Cappadocian, whose kingdom he later even reduced into the form of a province.[53]

It is perhaps fitting that the most effusive praise following Tiberius' death came not from a Roman but from a foreigner, Philo of Alexandria. The Jewish philosopher, after having chafed under Caligula's far more erratic brand of tyranny, reflected wistfully on the provincial stability that had largely characterized the Tiberian era, and blamed his contemporaries for having taken the uncharismatic former emperor's virtues for granted:

> O ye most foolish of all men! [...] why did you never think Tiberius, who was emperor before Gaius, who indeed was the cause that Gaius ever became emperor, who himself enjoyed the supreme power by land and sea for three and twenty years, and who never allowed any seed of war to smolder or to raise its head, either in Greece or in the territory of the barbarians, and who bestowed peace and the blessings of peace up to the end of his life with a rich and most bounteous hand and mind upon the whole empire and the whole world; why, I say, did you not consider him worthy of similar honor? [...] This man, though he was so wise, and so good, and so great, was passed over and disregarded by you![54]

Two auxiliaries present Trajan with the severed heads of Dacian princes as a trophies; two auxiliary soldiers with heads. Plaster cast, 1861, of marble originals on Trajan's Column (113 AD) in Rome. Museo della Civiltà Romana, Rome.

GREAT POWER RETRENCHMENT,
MILITARY ADAPTATION, AND THE
EVOLUTION OF ROME'S WORLDVIEW

As a ruler, Tiberius played a critical role in ensuring the political continuity of the Principate, preventing the resurgence of civil war, and in averting potentially ruinous geopolitical overextension. How did Rome's military and intellectual elites react and adapt to this policy of imperial consolidation and retrenchment? How did the newly professionalized and downsized Roman legions learn from the two greatest defeats they had experienced in the course of a century—Carrhae and the Teutoburg massacre—and how did they tailor their force design and tactics to fight against different adversaries across a broad spectrum of conflict? Why did auxiliaries come to play a greater role in Rome's imperial defense, and what were the benefits and risks of such an increased reliance on noncitizens? Last but not least, how did Rome's intellectual elites rationalize or respond to Tiberius' more prudent brand of statecraft?

Explaining and learning from defeat

Ill-accustomed to witnessing Roman legions suffer severe defeat, ancient commentators had a tendency to fall back on a rote set of explanations. Strabo, for example, attributed the disasters of Carrhae and the Teutoburg Forest to the forbidding, unfamiliar nature of both regions' terrain, which had flummoxed habitually doughty legion commanders and neutralized the famed superiority of Roman heavy infantry on an open field. A clear understanding of geography, the Greek philosopher argued, was "essential to all the transactions of the statesman," for

> a hunter will be more successful in the chase if he knows the character and extent of the forest; and again, only one who knows a region can advantageously pitch camp there, or set an ambush, or direct a march. The utility of geography is even more evident, however, in

great undertakings, in proportion as the prizes of knowledge and ignorance that result from ignorance are greater. [...] I believe that the modern campaign of the Romans against the Parthians is a sufficient proof of what I say, and likewise that against the Germans and the Celts, for in these cases the barbarians carried on a guerrilla warfare in swamps, in pathless forests, and in deserts; and they made the ignorant Romans believe to be far away what was really near at hand, and kept them in ignorance of the roads and of the facilities for procuring provisions and other necessities.[1]

The ignominy of a military rout could also be pinned on the fecklessness of individual commanders (i.e. Crassus and Varus), the treachery of scheming natives (i.e. Arminius), or preferably—as in the case of the Teutoburg massacre—a combination of the two.[2] Roman writers had always been aware that their key competitive advantage lay in conventional, rather than asymmetrical, warfare, and that adversaries would seek to offset their military might by unconventional means. One of the most famous examples is Sertorius, a talented early-first-century-BC Roman commander who turned against his country, and became a leader of a group of Lusitanian insurgents in Spain. In his *Memorable Doings and Sayings*, Valerius Maximus describes how Sertorius advises his new recruits to abandon any hope of prevailing against his former countrymen in open battle, and adopt guerrilla warfare:

> He offered them the following metaphor. Two horses were brought out, one strong, the other weak. Sertorius ordered a weak old man to gradually pluck the tail hairs of the strong horse, and a powerful young man to tear off the tail hairs of the weak horse in one yank. Only the weak old man succeeded. Sertorius told the Lusitanians that the Roman army was like the horse's tail, in that anyone could defeat the Romans if they attacked them bit by bit, rather than all at once. And so the barbarian nation, rough and difficult to rule, and which had been rushing to its own destruction, saw with its own eyes the usefulness of the approach which it had rejected with its own ears.[3]

Tacfarinas, with his hit-and-run tactics, had adopted a similar approach during Tiberius' rule, methods which Tacitus describes with unalloyed disdain, narrating how, by adopting such strategies, the African initially "befooled with impunity the ineffective and footsore Roman."[4] Native treachery, difficult terrain, dishonorable tactics—all of these, in the eyes of the Romans, could provide socially acceptable explanations for unexpected military disasters. On occasion, though, even the staunchest of patriots had to recognize that there was something more enduring and disconcerting in the enemy force's design or strategy that had confounded Roman military operators.

This had clearly been the case with the Parthians at Carrhae, where the superior firepower and mobility of the enemy's mounted force had completely annihilated the more numerous but infantry-dominated Roman army. Clouds of horse archers had surrounded the densely packed cohorts, and Rome's legionaries had, as a result of a series of miscalculations, been forced to contend with two unforeseen factors: the Parthians' unexpectedly large munition stock, and the quality of said munitions. In past conflicts, when offsetting the risks posed by enemy missileers and skirmishers, the Romans had traditionally either pulsed out detachments of allied or auxiliary light cavalry, or waited for the enemy to run out of missiles before advancing to attack, confident that their shields and armor could safely soak up most of the remaining enemy missile fire. When faced with a force structure as unique as that of the Parthian army at Carrhae, however, these tried and tested assumptions were rapidly and brutally shown to be invalid. Rome's small detachment of Gallic cavalry, though it fought valiantly, was qualitatively overmatched by the heavily armored Parthian cataphracts—a troop type the Romans had only infrequently encountered. Meanwhile, Surenas, the highly capable Parthian general, had displayed his capacity for creative thinking by bringing along a mobile supply train of camels laden with large bags of arrows, thus ensuring an almost inexhaustible munitions supply to his nine hundred horse archers. Fired from compound bows—whose draw weight ensured greater velocity and force of impact—the arrows were also barbed, and penetrated Roman armor and shields with ease.

Plutarch provided a harrowing account of how Rome's massed heavy infantry was destroyed by the Parthians' relentless barrage:

But the Parthians now stood at long intervals from one another and began to shoot their arrows from all sides at once, not with any accurate aim, for the dense formation of the Romans would not suffer an archer to miss his man even if he wished it, but making vigorous and powerful shots from bows which were large and mighty and curved so as to discharge their missiles with great force. At once the plight of the Romans was a grievous one; for if they kept their ranks, they were wounded in great numbers, and if they tried to come to close quarters with the enemy they suffered just as much. For the Parthians shot as they fled and it's a very clever thing to seek safety while still fighting and it is a very shrewd tactic to seek safety while still fighting.[5]

As discussed in an earlier section, one of the Roman military's great strengths was its ability to innovate, adapting or emulating new tactics and methods in response to its perceived weaknesses. Marc Antony's invasion of Parthia may ultimately have proved to be a costly failure, but the one signal success of those grueling years of campaigning—the crushing victory of the Roman general Publius Ventidius over Prince Pacorus at the Battle of Mount Gindarus, in 38 BC, was in large part due to one shrewd Roman commander's ability to draw the right lessons from Carrhae. Most notably, he cleverly baited the Parthian cavalry into breaking formation and charging uphill, before counterattacking with his infantry—all while making effective use of large numbers of freshly recruited slingers. As Gareth Sampson notes in his gripping account of Antony's eastern campaigns, the Parthian prince's errors of judgment echoed, in many ways, those of Crassus—as did his grim fate. Cut down while "fighting with great gallantry," his severed head was then triumphantly displayed by Rome's vengeful eastern legions across Syria.[6]

As with Crassus, under normal circumstances Pacorus' army should have defeated a smaller Roman force; one without archers or cataphractii. Yet as with Crassus, he faced an opponent who was a cut above the standard commanders of his day. In 53 BC Surenas had fashioned a Parthian army for the occasion and ensured they fought on his choice of ground, so did Ventidius with slingers and hilly territory. Pacorus was equally guilty of the mistakes which Crassus made a decade and a half earlier, namely overconfidence and a battle plan which assumed his opponents would fight in the traditional way and not have a customized force.[7]

Turning now to the imperium's contested western sectors, we can again see clear signs of operational learning. Indeed, various aspects of Germanicus' extended campaigns displayed Rome's determination to not repeat Varus' mistakes and to master—rather than be mastered by— Germania's immense, thickly forested wilderness. Germanicus relied more heavily on screening forces of mounted auxiliaries to increase his situational awareness, and frequently tasked Roman engineers with building bridges and roads both ahead and behind his forces, to ensure that—if needed—he could stage an organized retreat.[8] He also, much like his father Drusus, relied more heavily on waterways for military transit, thus avoiding situations where his troops could be ambushed in unfavorable terrain. Tacitus relates that, seeking to rally his dispirited legionaries one evening, Germanicus pointed to how the closed terrain could also be used to the legionaries' advantage—provided they used their equipment, discipline, and combat training to good effect:

> He summoned a meeting of the troops and laid before them the measures his knowledge had suggested and the points likely to be of service in the coming struggle—"A plain was not the only battlefield favorable to a Roman soldier: if he used judgment, woods and glades were equally suitable. The barbarians' huge shields, their enormous spears were not as effective amid tree-trunks and undergrowth as the Roman javelins, short swords, and close-fitting armor. [...] Their first line alone carried spears of a fashion, the rest carried only darts, fire-pointed or too short. Their large physiques, while intimidating and powerful enough for short spurts, lacked the stamina to support exhaustion and wounds. They were men who would leave the field and flee with no thought for the disgrace of it, and no concern for their leaders—panic-stricken in adversity and oblivious to any law, human or divine, in their moments of victory."[9]

Similarly, the Romans substantially revised their counterinsurgency tactics in the course of the seven-year war against Tacfarinas. Noticing that the Numidian appeared to take advantage of seasonal lulls in Roman military activity, Rome's commanders organized randomized patrols throughout the winter. A chain of forward outposts was erected and, since it was noticed that the African, overmatched in solid fighting strength but more expert in the petty knaveries of war, operated with a number of bands, first attacking, then vanishing, and always maneuvering for an ambush [...] flying columns of men familiar with the desert [most likely auxiliaries] hounded Tacfarinas from one desert to another.[10]

Ptolemy of Mauretania, a local client king, was asked to provide a large number of highly mobile light cavalry scouts, whom Tacitus also accuses of often acting like "brigands" but who proved highly effective in hunting down Tacfarinas' desert raiders. Last but not least, Tiberius offered a generous policy of amnesty to informers and defectors, slowly peeling away at Tacfarinas' closest entourage until he was eventually betrayed and butchered with the last of his followers in an early-morning raid.

Rome also began to gradually tailor elements of its legionary force structure and equipment to different theaters of operation. Thus to the east, Rome incrementally began to revert to phalanx-type infantry formations that it had fielded in the earliest days of the Republic—such units, with their longer thrusting spears and more densely packed ranks, were better able to act as shock absorbers when countering Parthian cataphract charges.[11] Both Caracalla (AD 198–217) and Severus Alexander (AD 222–35) transformed groupings of eastern legions into *phalangiarii* in preparation for their Parthian campaigns. Meanwhile, eastern legions also began to incorporate higher ratios of missile infantry and light cavalry.[12]

An increased reliance on auxiliaries: The benefits and
drawbacks of such a delegative approach
Indeed, one of the key features of this period is Rome's increased dependence on local allies and auxiliaries. Whereas the Republic had frequently relied on the troops provided by allies and client kings, it was only under Augustus that the *auxilia* was formally incorporated into the Roman military command structure, with auxiliaries receiving a set salary and a promise of citizenship, usually delivered after twenty-five years of service.

As mentioned earlier, it is estimated that there were as many auxiliary soldiers under Augustus and Tiberius as legionaries and praetorians combined. Historians assess that by the time of the Emperor Trajan (AD 98–117) the *auxilia* probably accounted for 220,000 men, as compared to 156,800 legionaries.[13] Somewhat surprisingly, given the importance noncitizen units played in Rome's defense, it is only relatively recently that the *auxilia* has been the object of in-depth scholarship.[14]

Indeed, auxiliary units proved to be essential components of Rome's force structure in a number of ways. Not only could they be "plugged into" legions, serving as cavalry or as missile specialists, they were also frequently deployed in their own military formations, which were of a smaller size than the legions. Infantry units of the *auxilia* were thus either based on a single *quingenary* cohort of 480 men, or a larger *milliary* cohort of 800 men, while cavalry units were organized into quingenary alae of 512 troops, or milliary alae of 768.[15] Units could also be "mixed and matched," combining cavalry and infantry in creative ways. This provided provincial commanders with great flexibility and allowing them to draw on *auxilia* units in the same manner as vexillationes of legionaries. There is certainly evidence that auxiliaries were in many cases treated as more expendable, and as second-class troops—Tacitus, in the *Life of Agricola*, comments approvingly on how a Roman commander let the auxiliaries bear the brunt of the casualties during one particularly bloody battle, sparing the more valuable lives of citizen legionaries—but this was far from always the case.[16] For instance, while auxiliary infantry were paid less than their legionary counterparts, it would appear that auxiliary cavalry were often better compensated than the Roman citizen-soldiers.[17]

Auxiliaries did not solely act, as conventional wisdom once suggested, as appendages to the legions—they often operated relatively autonomously over vast stretches of territory and conducted independent military operations. And whereas in the early days of the Principate there is evidence that some auxiliary units served under Roman or Italian officers—much as foreign legionaries and noncommissioned officers (NCOs) serve under French officers in today's French foreign legion— this does not appear to have been a routinized practice. Indeed, in many cases, auxiliaries served under their own warlords and chieftains, and there are records of Germanian cavalry units stationed along the border with Scotland writing to their "king"—most likely the head officer in the cavalry unit deployed to Britain—requesting more beer.[18]

The sheer variety of auxiliary forces also provided Rome with a rich roster of specialized military capabilities to choose from, capabilities which could then be used to offset Rome's traditional weaknesses in certain areas—in both mounted and missile warfare. With the Marian reforms and adoption of the cohortal legion, citizen units of light infantry and skirmishers—such as the famed *velites*—had been phased out in favor of the legionary, a heavy infantry troop type that, as we have seen, was optimized for force-on-force confrontations in pitched battle and on level terrain. Rome's light infantry was now exclusively drawn from the ranks of the *auxilia*, where their tactical versatility rendered them indispensable in a wide variety of military contingencies, ranging from scouting to intelligence gathering and force protection. Indeed, historical studies have shown that auxiliary skirmishers were frequently deployed as protective screen or "cloud" both ahead and behind marching columns, and that they were also entrusted with the protection of foraging parties.[19] Their lighter equipment and greater agility meant that they were also often tasked with mounting offensives uphill or across challenging terrain.[20]

Over time, certain troop types acquired a mythos of their own. This was the case of Batavian cavalry, for example, who were renowned not only for their temerity in battle, but also for their ability to cross rivers and marshy terrain on horseback. Numidian light cavalry were also held in high esteem, as were Balearic slingers and Cretan archers. While Roman elites may not have subscribed to theories of "martial races" as clearly articulated as those later held by the British administrators of the Raj, there is certainly evidence that their vision of the world was undergirded by a number of strong ethnic stereotypes.[21] Thus, various mountain peoples—from the Thracians to the Alpine tribesmen—were considered unruly, savage, and warlike, and therefore fit for recruitment. The primitive, forest-dwelling Germanians were portrayed by writers such as Tacitus as "noble savages," whose strange diet of milk and meat, Julius Caesar argued, granted them uncustomary strength.[22] For some Parthian aristocrats, service in the *auxilia* provided an opportunity for adventure and renown—or an escape from vicious factional feuds at home—and they would frequently sign up for a lifetime of service under Roman arms in the company of their retainers. Meanwhile, certain peoples had negotiated a distinct status, whereby they were dispensed from paying taxes in exchange for providing men for the *auxilia*. The Batavians, "foremost in valor of all these peoples [living along the Rhine]," Tacitus writes, are not insulted with tribute or worn down by the tax collector: exempt from the burden of taxes and levies, they are set aside for battle and like weapons and arms they are reserved for war.[23]

It is difficult, of course, to ascertain the degree of agency such peoples had in the negotiation of any "special arrangements." In many cases, recently pacified areas were given little choice as to providing troops for the *auxilia*, and forced conscription generated enormous resentment, sparking numerous revolts; whether in Thracia, where in AD 26 Thracians briefly revolted for fear of being forcibly recruited and sent to serve in some remote backwater overseas, or in Pannonia twenty years prior. Indeed, some of the prime instigators of the great revolt of AD 6–9 were apparently Dalmatian auxiliaries who revolted while being assembled for operations in Bohemia. And while auxiliaries were most often stationed in their home provinces, or sent to neighboring territories, there are many records of auxiliaries being deployed to opposite ends of the empire—not only the aforementioned Batavians patrolling the Scottish Highlands, but also Thracians garrisoning remote desert outposts in Egypt.[24] Perhaps the most famous auxiliary revolt occurred in AD 69–70, when a Batavian force led by an auxiliary commander named Julius Civilis led a major uprising, even attracting defecting legionary forces to his cause.[25] In a rousing speech, Civilis lambasted the injustices of Rome's subcontracting of its security, shouting to his troops that it was "by the blood of the provinces that provinces are won."[26]

Roman officials were, of course, fully aware of the dangers of an over-reliance on such a smorgasbord of auxiliary and allied soldiers. This study has shown how, in the early Principate, many of Rome's most redoubtable foes were its "Promethean proxies," men such as Arminius and Tacfarinas. Commenting on the uprising of AD 69–70, one classicist notes the following:

> Led by a man who could operate both with and against Roman armies, the revolt thus exposed the Empire's one great weakness. It was intensely vulnerable to those provincials who, armed and trained to protect its interests, chose instead to pursue their own.[27]

An anonymous second-century treatise on Roman military surveying, *De Munitionibus Castrorum*, provides some measure of insight into Rome's awareness of this persistent vulnerability. The manual provides instructions for the construction of a military camp—and for the stationing of its mixed assortment of troops.[28] The emperor or legate is positioned toward the center, surrounded by his elite guard of praetorians and the commanding officers. Then, in another concentric circle, are garrisoned the auxiliaries. They are then encompassed by a wider concentric circle of allied troops, who are in turn surrounded by the largest circle—which girdles the whole camp—of citizen legionaries. These rings correspond to different levels of reliability. If the foreign allied troops attempt betrayal, they will be wedged between the legionaries and auxiliaries. If the auxiliaries attempt to turn against the Romans, they will be ensnared between the praetorians and the legionaries. Thus, even though the auxiliaries are considered more trustworthy than the foreign allies, they are still not accorded the same level of trust as the legionaries who encircle the entire encampment. This treatise is revealing, as one historian astutely observes, in that

> just as in other Roman depictions of characterizations of auxiliaries, here, too, in a treatise on the proper arrangement of soldiers within a military base, auxiliary troops straddle the nebulous boundary between Roman and foreigner, trustworthy and treacherous, faithful and fickle.[29]

How, then, should one explain Rome's continued reliance on such recruitment practices? Indeed, even after the Batavian revolt, there is no indication that Rome's commanders attempted to reduce their level of dependency on auxiliaries—quite the contrary—or that they significantly modified their practices by, for instance, incurring the costs of systematically transferring ethnically homogenous or tribal units away from their home provinces.[30]

The answer is probably quite simple: the benefits were considered to be worth the risk. Indeed, Rome's emperors may have been afforded little choice in the matter. Evidence shows that by the time of Tiberius it was already becoming increasingly difficult to recruit Italians into the legions, and that the majority of new recruits came from provinces such as Spain and Gaul. As time went on, it even became difficult to entice provincial citizens to sign up, and to maintain stable conventional force levels.[31] Barring a reimposition of the *dilectus*—something which no princeps would view as politically feasible, let alone desirable—or the adoption of emergency measures such as those undertaken during the Pannonian revolt, when slaves were liberated en masse and hastily granted citizenship, it was impossible for Rome to generate manpower in sufficient levels. The legions, notwithstanding their combat prowess and aptitude for military adaptation, could not have survived alone when confronted with such a broad array of adversaries and combat theaters. The specialized skills and local expertise of the auxiliaries and allies were indispensable, and the dangers tied to such a bifurcated military apparatus were the price to pay for continued Roman dominance and a citizenry that was no longer regularly obliged to hammer its plowshares into swords.

Tiberian retrenchment and the evolution of Rome's worldview
Last but not least, how did Rome's elites—many of whom still harbored dreams of further conquest and of *"imperium sine fine"* adjust to the policy of retrenchment and consolidation set in motion by Tiberius? The evidence would suggest that his policies were not always popular. Indeed, in the *Annals*, Tacitus preemptively apologizes for the potential dullness of his narrative—something which he attributes to the unglamorous nature of Tiberian foreign policy—while reminiscing about the halcyon days of old:

> I am not unaware that many of the events I have described, and shall describe, may perhaps seem little things, trifles too slight for record; but no parallel can be drawn between these chronicles of mine and the work of the men who composed the ancient history of the Roman people. Gigantic wars, cities stormed, routed and captive kings, or when they turned by choice to domestic affairs, the feuds of consul and tribune, land and corn laws, the duel of nobles and plebeians— such were the themes on which they dwelt, or digressed at will. Mine is an inglorious labor in a narrow field: for this was an age of peace unbroken or half-heartedly challenged, of an emperor careless to extend the empire.[32]

Prudent foreign policy, it would seem, does not make for entertaining history. Tacitus' objections ran deeper, however. Indeed, the second-century former senator and historian was concerned that future emperors might choose to overly emulate the policies of Tiberius, and in so doing run the risk of projecting an image of irresolution to foreign audiences. Much like contemporary policymakers, Roman security elites placed a great deal of emphasis on the psychological aspects of deterrence, and were convinced of the interconnection of security commitments, as well as of the importance of maintaining a "reputation for action."[33] Writers such as Tacitus, while cognizant of the human costs of military action, were pre-occupied by the potential reputational losses associated with a less aggressive or forward-leaning foreign policy, and by how such a per-ceived shift in Roman attitudes could encourage provincial disorder, invite acts of opportunistic aggression, or encourage the formation of hostile coalitions.

For example, when commenting on Tiberius' decision to withdraw the IX Hispana after its temporary redeployment as part of a troop surge to Africa, Tacitus accused the emperor of having weakened Roman credi-bility and emboldened Tacfarinas—who at that moment in time had yet to be neutralized.

> Caesar, as though no enemies were left in Africa, had ordered the ninth legion back [....] Tacfarinas therefore spread the word that the power of Rome was being torn to shreds by other tribes elsewhere across the empire, and that it was, for that reason, withdrawing from Africa. The Romans remaining behind could be cut off, he said, if all who preferred liberty to slavery simply applied themselves to the task.[34]

Suetonius is often equally critical, and both he and Cassius Dio projected their negative perceptions of Tiberius' personality onto his disagreements with Germanicus over the future of expansion into Germany—attributing his decision to halt the campaigns to personal jealousy or fear over the risks tied to his nephew's ascendancy, rather than to sound judgment. Critiques of Tiberian foreign policy are also perceptible in the writings of Pliny the Younger, a friend and contemporary of Tacitus, who in his *Panegyric to Trajan* accused past rulers of jeopardizing Roman credibility by being too accommodating in their diplomacy, and of diluting military readiness by maintaining the legions in a state of (relative) inactivity:

> During the preceding reigns [i.e. the emperors preceding Trajan] the barbarians had become insolent, and no longer struggled to gain

their liberty, but fought to enslave us. But on your [Trajan's] accession they were again inspired with fear and willingness to obey your commands. For they saw that you were a general of the old stamp—one of those who had earned their title on fields heaped high with slaughter, or on seas resounding with the shouts of victory. The result is that we now accept hostages; we do not buy them. Nor do we now make peace on disadvantageous terms in order to keep up the appearance of success. Our enemies seek and implore peace; we grant or deny according to what the dignity of the empire requires. […] For ours is not a prince who sees preparations against his enemies as a threat directed against himself, after the fashion of his predecessors, who feared to fall victim to their own harsh practices and so were glad to see a falling-off of interest in the soldier's life, slack training, and lowered morale, while swords grew dull and blunted through disuse.[35]

There is a striking parallel between the unpopularity of Tiberius' foreign policy among Roman elites and that of the later emperor Hadrian.[36] Indeed, like Tiberius, Hadrian came to power after a hyperexpansionist and much-loved emperor, Trajan the *"optimus princeps."* And similarly, Hadrian almost immediately initiated a policy of retrenchment, although in his case the actions undertaken were far more drastic, as he decided to formally relinquish large tracts of freshly acquired territory. Hadrian was also a contemplative philhellene, who—in the words of Cassius Dio—"did not stir up wars in any way and terminated those already in progress."[37] Meanwhile, Trajan's wars of conquest, like those of Germanicus, had fired the imaginations of the Roman elites, with Florus writing that

From the time of Caesar Augustus down to our own age there has been a period of not much less than two hundred years […] During that time, owing to the inactivity of emperors, the Roman people grew old and impotent. During the rule of Trajan it again stirred its arms and, contrary to general expectation, again renewed its vigor with youth as if it were restored.[38]

The sedateness of Hadrian's statecraft, like that of Tiberius, came as a disappointment to Rome's intellectual elites, who still occasionally clung to vague dreams of expansion. And interestingly, just like Tiberius, he was accused of objecting to pursue his predecessor's forward-leaning policies for petty personal motives, rather than out of a sincere desire to avoid overextension.[39] Imperial policies that appeared too fixed or static seem to have induced among some Romans a diffuse cultural angst not so remote from Frederick Jackson Turner's later dirgelike ruminations on the closing of the Western frontier, to which, he famously argued, the American intellect "owed its striking characteristics."

> That coarseness and strength combined with acuteness and inquisitiveness; that practical, inventive turn of mind, quick to find expedients; that masterful grasp of material things, lacking in the artistic but powerful to effect great ends; that restless, nervous energy; that dominant individualism, working for good and for evil, and withal that buoyancy and exuberance which comes with freedom—these are the traits of the frontier, or traits called out elsewhere because of the existence of the frontier. [...] He would be a rash prophet who should assert that the expansive character of American life has now entirely ceased. Movement has been its dominant fact, and, unless this training has no effect upon a people, the American energy will continually demand a wider field for its exercise. But never again will such gifts of free land offer themselves. [...] What the Mediterranean Sea was to the Greeks, breaking the bond of custom, offering new experiences, calling out new institutions and activities, that, and more, the ever-retreating frontier has been to the United States.[40]

Like Turner, early imperial historians such as Tacitus fretted over the loss of the restless, roving energy that had accompanied expansion, and over the slow withering of national ambitions in a "quiet world" where "peace maintains on a single level the man of action and the sluggard."[41]

At the same time, however, these same elites proved remarkably adept at intellectually rationalizing the more or less fixed delimitations of the Roman empire. Indeed, over time certain commonly shared concepts began to crystallize. One such notion was that certain peoples or territories were simply not worth conquering. Thus Seneca, writing during Emperor Claudius' reign, painted a lugubrious picture of the portions of the globe that had yet to fall under Rome's writ:

Consider all the races to whom Roman peace does not extend—the Germanians, for example, and whatever nomadic peoples continue to harass us along the Danube. Eternal winter and a gloomy sky smother them: barren ground barely sustains them; they fend off endless rain with mere thatch and leaf roofs; they wander marshes hardened by ice; and they can only capture wild animals for food.[42]

Tacitus had made similarly disparaging observations about the general dreariness of northwestern Europe in the *Germania,* asking his Mediterranean readers who in their right mind would want to trade their crisp blue skies and sun-dappled olive groves for Germania, "with its desolate landscape, harsh climate, barbarous way of life and customs—unless he was born there?"[43] Meanwhile, authors such as Strabo, Philo of Alexandria, and Dionysus of Halicarnassus—provincials writing for an affluent Roman audience—argued that even if Rome did not rule the entire world it could console itself through the knowledge that it ruled "the most essential parts," the "parts truly inhabited by men" (i.e. not by wretched nomads), and all of the major cities.[44]

The continued coexistence of another great power competitor, in the form of the Parthian Empire, presented a more complex form of intellectual challenge. Indeed, alongside the ritualized claims of Roman moral and geopolitical superiority over their decadent, oriental neighbor there existed another literary tradition, according to which Parthia was depicted as an independent and capable "frenemy," with whom Rome had tacitly agreed to a "*divisione orbis,*" or division of the world.[45] And indeed this was occasionally reflected in the two great powers' diplomatic summitry. Velleius provided us with his own memorable eyewitness account of the encounter between the young heir designate Gaius Caesar, then acting as proconsul of the eastern provinces, and King Phraates IV, in AD 1:

He [Gaius] met with the king of the Parthians, a most eminent young man, on an island, around which the river Euphrates passes, with an equal number of each group. This spectacle, of the army of the Romans here, that of the Parthians there, opposite each other, when the two heads of the most prominent empires of mankind came together between each other, an exceedingly remarkable and memorable thing fell to me to see, a military tribune in the first years of my service.[46]

For the dazed, overawed young tribune, this heavily ritualized encounter was clearly one between two evenly balanced regional hegemons, a reality reinforced by the protocolary emphasis on symmetry and on the Euphrates as a clear dividing line; with Phraates first dining with Gaius on *nostra ripa*, "our bank," and the Roman princeling then feasting "with the Parthian king on enemy soil."[47]

Similar views—on the relative equality between the two great powers—were espoused by Strabo and Pompeius Trogus, both of whom lived during the period examined in this study. Whereas Pompeius Trogus seemed to suggest the existence of some kind of informal compact delineating respective spheres of influence, commenting that "today the Parthians rule the East," with "the world being partitioned, as it were, between them and the Romans," Strabo was more forthright in his assessment of Parthia's status as a peer competitor:

> at present they [the Parthians] rule over so much land and so many tribes that in the extent of their empire they have become, in a fashion, rivals of the Romans. The cause of is their mode of life, and also their customs, which contain much that is barbarian and Scythian in character, though more that is conducive to hegemony and success in war.[48]

Both these writers were foreign in origin—Greek in the case of Strabo, Gallic in the case of Pompeius Trogus—and their opinions were not necessarily shared by some of their more jingoistic Roman contemporaries. Livy, his words oozing contempt, dismissed the scribblings of "the most worthless of Greeks [perhaps referring somewhat passive-aggressively to Strabo] who favor the glory of even the Parthians over that of the Roman people."[49] A few decades later, Lucan also lamented that Parthia had yet to be brought to heel:

> Shameful is it that the people of the East shrank more from contact with the phalanx [here he is referring to the Persian campaigns of Alexander in the fourth century BC] than they shrink now from contact with the legion. Though Roman rule extends to the North and home of the West Wind, though we subjugate the lands that lie behind the burning South Wind, yet in the East we still yield precedence to the lord of the Parthians.[50]

What rankled was not so much the fact that Rome did not directly administer Parthian territories (indeed, there seemed to be an almost universal assumption that their sprawling lands were too alien, remote, and parched to be of genuine interest), but rather the lingering sentiment that the Parthians—despite the Augustan Principate's public relations efforts surrounding the return of the standards and prisoners—remained insufficiently submissive.[51] Thus "the ghost of Crassus still wanders unavenged in the literature of the first century AD."[52]

As mentioned earlier, the Roman concept of hegemony was not necessarily consubstantial with territorial control—it simply required a universal recognition of Roman primacy.[53] The mere presence of the Parthian Empire, along with its proven ability to inflict severe defeats on Rome's armed forces, remained, therefore, something of a recurrent source of discomfiture; and this despite the growing perception that it was possible for both powers to more or less coexist within their respective spheres of influence.

Meanwhile, writers such as Strabo questioned the value of absorbing Britain, an impoverished and barbarian-infested region. For centuries after, Roman legionaries, auxiliaries, and officials garrisoned at Hadrian's Wall would send missives home grousing about the rain-sodden climate and questioning the value of their continued presence.[54] Indeed, as one writer notes, there is a timeless quality to many of the letters that archeologists have recently unearthed at Vindolanda, a Roman auxiliary fort just to the south of Hadrian's Wall. With their complaints about the strange customs of the locals, urgent requests for warmer socks and underwear, and ribald expressions of affection directed toward family members and faraway sweethearts, the Vindolanda correspondence appears "indistinguishable from e-mail sent home by American forces in Iraq and Afghanistan."[55]

Florus may be one of the best embodiments of the somewhat schizoid nature of Rome's mindset toward imperial grand strategy. While he waxed lyrical about Trajan's expansionism, he also criticized Augustus's wars in Germania:

Would that Augustus had not thought so highly of conquering Germania. Our losses there have been more shameful by far than our acquisitions glorious.[56]

Similarly, he questioned the value of extending Roman rule into Sarmatia, claiming that the Sarmatians had little to offer except "snow, frost and trees," before contemptuously adding, "Their barbarism is such that they don't even understand the concept of peace."[57] And although Tacitus appears critical of Tiberius' military drawdown from Germania, the bleak imagery and geographical descriptors provided in both the *Annals* and *Germania* convey a forbidding and self-contained world, "shagged with forests or deformed with marshes," far removed from Rome's civilizing light—rather than a lush province-in-waiting.[58]

> All Germania is separated from the Gauls and Pannonians by the Rhine and Danube rivers, and from the Sarmatians and Dacians by shared fear or by mountains; oceans surround the rest, embracing vast peninsulas and an immeasurable expanse of islands, where certain tribes and kings have only recently been made known to us, unveiled by war.[59]

There was therefore an increasingly shared assumption that the Roman Empire had reached its natural perimeter, and that where those vague, porous boundaries slowly dissipated into mysterious, exotic, and primeval lands, there remained little that could—or should—be conquered.[60] The enduring loneliness of Tiberius' genius resides, perhaps, in the fact that he uncovered this uncomfortable truth earlier than most.

Engraving by Giovanni Battista Piranesi,
The Arch of Titus, c. 1760,
The Metropolitan Museum of Art, New York.

CONCLUSION

For centuries, statesmen have plumbed the history of ancient Rome, examining every aspect of its rise and fall in their quest for insights and wisdom. This approach has not always been applauded. Arguing against teleological notions of human progress, while simultaneously warning of the pitfalls of overly cyclical representations of the history of statecraft, Montaigne quipped, "Man does not go in a straight line, we rather ramble and turn this way and that. We retrace our steps."[1] The French humanist was of the opinion that to ignore history was to frustrate experience, but that to expect its systematic replication was almost equally foolish. As the Florentine historian Francesco Guicciardini once noted, rolling his eyes at those who "wrongfully cite the Romans at every turn," the one general truth of history is the inconstancy of human affairs, and any thorough examination of the past must necessarily involve what he termed "discernment," i.e. the ability to make distinctions and exceptions due to differences in circumstances, as well as to tease out striking parallels and shared truths.[2] In short, notes Yale professor John Lewis Gaddis, this is both one of the key challenges and one of the "chief paradoxes," for all modern historians: how to grapple with the contrast between "timefulness—fidelity in narration, to how things were—and timelessness—patterns drawn from the past suggesting how things might in the future be."[3]

Nevertheless, for many anxious stewards of primacy there has always been an almost eerie relevance to many of the dilemmas confronted by the Romans, as they charted their own rise from a small, scrappy monarchy along the Tiber to a powerful trans-Mediterranean republic and then to one of the world's most enduring hegemonies. Certainly for the Victorians, there was a firm conviction that the plot of Roman history was, in many ways, "the recurrent story of the world."[4] Rome's narrative arc and the dense, vibrant, and sophisticated writings of its ancient chroniclers constituted far more than a simple repository of wisdom—they were both a source of imperial inspiration *and* a warning against hegemonic overextension. In 1885, when the British Empire was arguably at its apogee, a famous professor of history at Oxford, Montagu Burrows, advised that

> the danger of our not perceiving our real position is exactly the same as was experienced by the old Roman Empire. The decay of the centre gradually makes its way to the extremities; and these drop off, one by one, till the seat of the empire itself, unprotected and forlorn, goes down in the general crash.[5]

For figures such as Gladstone, on the other hand, it was the very impulse for untrammeled expansion that imperiled British primacy, and he fretted that, like Rome, England, "which has grown so great," could easily "become little; through the effeminate selfishness of luxurious living," and through the neglect of pressing "realities at home to amuse herself everywhere else in stalking phantoms."[6] America's founding fathers were no less alive to these risks, and to read the *Federalist Papers*, notes one writer, is to enter into a "running debate about Roman history, in which the Roman example is one to be alternately emulated and shunned."[7]

It is this author's hope that this study of the Tiberian era, during which a ruling hegemon temporarily succeeded in consolidating its power, husbanding its resources, and arresting imperial overextension, has provided an instructive set of insights—insights and parallels which, if filtered through the intellectual sieve of discernment, could prove useful to both the policymaker and the general reader.[8] After all, many of the issues raised by authors such as Tacitus, Suetonius, Sallust, Strabo, and Velleius—and addressed by figures such as Augustus and Tiberius—remain strikingly relevant.

Consider, for example, the challenge evoked by Posidonius and Sallust—that of Rome, in the wake of its victory in the Punic Wars, struggling to calibrate its grand strategy and maintain its unity of purpose in the context of uncontested unipolarity. For Sallust, as for so many of his intellectual forebears and successors, great-power rivalry was fundamentally a two-level game—and it was impossible to disentangle a state's domestic values from its foreign policy.[9] Actions in one domain inevitably bled into the other. The existential nature of the Carthaginian threat had not only unified the Roman populace in a shared struggle; it had also

Horatio Greenough,
marble statue of George Washington,
1832, National Museum of American History,
Smithsonian Institute, Washington DC.

provided them with a valuable countermodel—a *refractive mirror* against which they could continuously contrast, define, and ultimately perfect their own distinct tradition of republican governance.[10] In the wake of the Punic nemesis' eradication, that energizing focus had been lost, while territorial expansion and a glut of foreign money had encouraged avariciousness, licentiousness, and corruption:

> When our country had grown great through toil and the practice of justice, when great kings had been vanquished in war, savage tribes and mighty peoples subdued by force of arms, when Carthage, the rival of Rome's sway, had perished root and branch, and all seas and lands were open, then Fortune began to grow cruel and bring confusion into all our affairs.[11]

Widening socioeconomic disparities and incessant internecine political feuding had sapped the moral foundations of the Republic, polluted its political vocabulary, and warped its statecraft. Out of this sorry state of affairs had slithered an ouroboros of decay and self-sabotage, as Rome's increasingly dissipated and hubristic foreign policy progressively widened suppurating internal fissures.[12] Sallust's sentiments retained their funereal appeal long after his passing. Centuries later, Florus was still agonizing over "whether it would not have been better for the Roman people to have been content with Sicily or Africa, or even to have been without these and to have held dominion only over their own land of Italy, than to increase to such greatness that they were ruined by their own strength."[13]

How, the reader may ask, do these ancient historians' tortured ruminations pertain to contemporary discussions of American grand strategy? Perhaps in more ways than one. Indeed, the sudden collapse of the Soviet Union left the United States' national security establishment in quest of a unifying sense of purpose. In effect, an awareness of the intellectual challenges inherent to such a precipitate power transition were at the heart of the debates surrounding the U.S. 1992 Defense Planning Guidance and have, more broadly, permeated American discussions over the future of its grand strategy ever since.[14] At a time of extreme political polarization and generalized uncertainty over how the U.S. should balance its variegated security commitments, the Sallustian criticism of late Republican Rome's descent into acrimony and its inability to develop a clear strategic focus can provide a cautionary tale.[15] Indeed, as many analysts have observed, much of the national defense community has yet to move from a clear diagnosis of our era's geopolitical ills—as encapsulated by much of the fretful commentary on the revival of geopolitical competition or on a "new Cold War" with China—to actual prescriptive guidance as to how the United States and its allies should revise and/or adapt grand strategy accordingly.[16] Might the rise of China as a serious peer competitor inject greater clarity, unity, and general intellectual seriousness into American policy and defense planning?

No easy question.[17] Indeed, Sallust's theory remains starkly unforgiving, almost uncomfortably so, for a modern reader. As political scientist Daniel Kapust notes, this creates a dilemma whereby "the coherence of a community may become linked to the existence of a dangerous foreign enemy."[18] Healthy democracies should be able to guarantee the conditions of their own success without fear of a great-power competitor, and no sensible individual would argue in favor of cultivating foreign enmity for its own sake.

And yet Sallust's grim insights, however unsettling, may hold some truth. It is possible to acknowledge that an unwelcome new strategic dispensation—the emergence of China as a redoubtable near-peer competitor—may paradoxically provide a clarifying and restorative sense of purpose to a deeply fractious American democracy. Indeed, since the end of the Cold War, U.S. security managers have frequently struggled to set clear priorities, define an overarching vision, and manage bureaucratic infighting. Meanwhile, intense domestic polarization has rendered U.S. foreign policy more volatile, unpredictable, and—in the eyes of international observers—unreliable.[19]

As contemporary political scientists such as Jennifer Mitzen and Emily Goldman have noted, physical security is not always coterminous with "ontological security," and "relative quiescence in great-power rivalry paradoxically increases uncertainty."[20] Highly diverse threat environments, with little to no ordering of potential adversaries, can complicate strategic assessments and undermine political-military coordination. Threat-based defense planning—particularly if oriented primarily toward only one or two major opponents—is less intellectually burdensome than so-called portfolio planning, which demands consistent adjudication between myriad competing risk assessments and force structure variants.[21] The absence of a major challenger can also cause restless policymakers to elevate, and perhaps even artificially inflate, formerly second-order threats, as John Mueller has sardonically remarked:

> The post-Cold War jungle had snakes whereas the Cold War jungle was inhabited not only by the snakes but by a dragon as well. Some people might consider that a notable improvement and, as jungles go, a palpable reduction in the complexities of daily life. However, when big problems (dragons) go away, small problems (snakes) can be elevated in perceived importance.[22]

The urgency of the China challenge has already led to demonstrations of bipartisanship that have remained more elusive in other areas of foreign policy. Although the U.S. public remains depressingly tribalized, a shared, albeit belated, recognition of the fact that competition with China requires internal as well as external balancing has given birth to some surprising new manifestations of cross-party consensus—such as on the need for the U.S. to devise a more robust industrial policy or revive its moribund infrastructure. It would appear, therefore, that Sallust's assessment of a peer competitor's elucidating function and dampening effect on the "spirit of faction" has proven to be at least partially correct.

That being said, there are also certain key risks tied to rigidly subscribing to the theory of *metus hostilis*. By viewing every geopolitical development through the prism of a bipolar rivalry, American defense planners might neglect or underestimate secondary theaters along with other less formidable, but still consequential, challengers. By construing every regional crisis as a test of national will in a globe-girdling struggle with China, analysts in Washington also risk overly simplifying local conditions and disregarding the value and agency of small and mid-ranking powers. Last but not least, couching the U.S.–China relationship solely in terms of geopolitical enmity risks encouraging less wholesome and more nationally divisive sentiments. During certain periods of the Cold War, for example, thinkers such as Reinhold Niebuhr warned of the "spiritual aberrations which arise in a situation of intense enmity" amid a "public temper of fear and hatred."[23] Niebuhr was, of course, alluding to McCarthyism, but the ugliness of certain current developments, from a recent explosion of anti-Asian xenophobia and violence to misguided attempts, in some quarters of the previous administration, to frame the U.S.–China rivalry in "civilizational" terms, also serve as a valuable reminder that a spirit of knee-jerk hostility toward a foreign competitor can engender its own unique set of domestic perils.[24]

All of which brings us to the final, and most essential, aspect of Sallust: the importance of grounding foreign policy in clear values and of continuously reminding the American people that their nation's struggle lies with the People's Republic of China's ideologically driven revisionism, rather than with the Chinese people or some antiseptically framed Asian great-power rival. Indeed, distinguished Sinologists have repeatedly drawn attention to the ideational drivers behind Beijing's assertiveness and vision, in which "*tianxia* [imperialism with Chinese characteristics] meets Leninism," with the latter's traditional focus on power, cynicism, and subversion.[25] To this mixture one might add an unhealthy dose of Han chauvinism, which is reflected not only China's abhorrent treatment of its own ethnic minorities but also its disdainful attitude toward fellow Asian states.[26] Meanwhile, Chinese officials and spokespeople regularly take to social media to tout the purported superiority of their political system and heap scorn on American democracy. In recent years, the Chinese Communist Party has begun a new campaign of "patriotic education" aimed at purging "Western ideas" from primary and secondary school libraries.[27] As recent Pew polls show, the clearest bipartisan consensus with regard to America's China policy is in the field of values, with over 70 percent of Americans expressing support for promoting human rights in China, even if such support should jeopardize economic relations with Beijing.[28] As Sallust well knew, no great power can muster the will and determination to prevail in a multigenerational struggle without drawing on such inner reservoirs of moral strength.[29] Like the Roman Republic of old, America has its own *"mos maiorum"*—one inextricably bound up with the universalist ideals of its classically educated founding fathers.

A second question is how, in an era characterized by a decline in U.S. relative power, should American defense planners adjudicate force levels in different theaters and tailor force planning constructs? The expenses and recruitment challenges tied to the maintenance of a highly trained, well equipped, and fully professionalized military force meant that the Rome of the early Principate was compelled to adopt a one-war standard—as evidenced, for example, during the Pannonian revolt, when Tiberius was compelled to sign a separate truce with Maroboduus in order to redirect his legions toward the Balkans. Tiberius' operations in Pannonia ultimately proved successful, but Rome's telegraphed inability to address multiple major military challenges in concert may have prompted opportunistic attacks in Germania (the Teutoburg massacre), buoyed the propaganda of insurgents in the vein of Tacfarinas or Sacrovir, and prompted attempts at the formation of countervailing coalitions. What lessons might such incidents hold for current debates over the wisdom and/or necessity of the U.S. adoption of a one-war sizing and shaping construct, as outlined in the 2018 National Defense Strategy (NDS), and more recently reiterated in the 2022 NDS, which calls for prevailing in one conflict while deterring "opportunistic aggression elsewhere"?[30] As one excellent survey of U.S. force planning scenarios since 1945 notes, global interests and commitments have traditionally been so expansive that it has proven almost impossible to design a "fiscally acceptable force," that could "defend all U.S. interests simultaneously."[31] How, then, can the U.S. reorient its efforts toward peer competition without incurring unacceptable levels of risk in so-called "lower priority areas"?[32]

Third, what insights can be derived from Rome's rich experience with surrogate or indirect warfare, particularly at a time of increased gray zone competition and proxy warfare?[33] Can Washington's strong flow of military support to Ukraine in its battle against Russian aggression provide the template for another, more financially sustainable, form of two-war construct—one involving fewer American boots on the ground, but whereby the U.S. "sizes its military to win one war against one major power but sizes its defense industrial base to provide the wherewithal to win two wars simultaneously," thus allowing "the United States to fight one war directly and another by proxy"?[34]

This book has outlined many of the risks and opportunities associated with the Principate's increased dependence on allies, client kingdoms, and auxiliaries, and how Roman security managers were acutely aware of both the advantages and trade-offs associated with the adoption of such delegative security strategies. Tiberius proved to be singularly adept at alliance management and great power competition, consolidating Rome's geopolitical position along its troubled eastern periphery while avoiding being drawn by imprudent allies or clients into potentially debilitating conflicts. The U.S. alliance portfolio is undoubtedly one of Washington's key competitive advantages in its great power competitions with the People's Republic of China, the Russian Federation, and to a lesser extent the Islamic Republic of Iran.[35] Yet, as two former U.S. government officials have noted, "Washington's post-Cold War alliance architecture still reflects arrangements formed during the unipolar era, when the United States needed little help to underwrite the security of its partners."[36] How can America's military alliances be rehauled to better confront the challenges of the twenty-first century?[37] Perhaps it is time to move beyond the traditional—albeit highly necessary—discussions on burden sharing and regional divisions of labor to engage in a more thorough and wide-ranging assessment of the U.S.'s disparate partnerships and alliance networks. Which alliances are worth reprioritizing or upgrading, and obversely, which relationships risk morphing into liabilities? How, for instance, should the U.S. plan for sudden and unexpected deteriorations in its defense relationships with countries such as Turkey or Saudi Arabia, and how can it militate against the possibility of being entangled in partner-initiated conflicts that would be detrimental to its long-term strategic interests?[38] Writing in 1967, in the midst of the Vietnam War, Richard Nixon argued in favor of a more differentiated form of U.S. great power involvement overseas, one which would focus on the development of regional security pacts, on foreign internal defense, and on the shifting of a greater portion of the collective defense burden onto the shoulders of partners and allies:

> If the initial response to a threatened aggression, of whichever type—whether across the border or under it—can be made by lesser powers in the immediate area and thus within the path of aggression, one of two things can be achieved: either they can in fact contain it by themselves, in which case the United States is spared involvement and thus the world is spared the consequences of great-power action; or, if they cannot, the ultimate choice is presented to the U.S. in clear-cut terms, by nations which would automatically become allies in whatever response might prove necessary. To put it in another way, the regional pact becomes a buffer separating the distant power from the immediate threat. Only if the buffer proves insufficient does the great power become involved, and then in terms that make victory more attainable and the enterprise more palatable.[39]

Should such thinking be revived for the twenty-first century, and if so, how? Does Tiberius' shrewd creation of buffer zones in Asia Minor to offset the threat posed by Parthian expansion hold any lessons for contemporary grand strategists? What role can allies with more specialized and terrain-specific sets of capabilities—such as the Mauretanian desert raiders who prosecuted much of the war against Tacfarinas—play in assisting and defraying the costs of U.S. defense operations?[40] Are there any hidden costs—in terms of influence and control—to not exerting the same degree of overwhelming primacy within international alliance structures, and are U.S. security managers fully prepared for what such a transformation in the nature of their relationships with their allied counterparts might entail?[41]

Fourth, Tiberius' actions demonstrate that in some cases, in order to pursue a grand strategy that one deems the most effective, it is necessary to engender certain risks, both in terms of the potential second- or third-order consequences of swift course corrections, and in terms of domestic political capital. As Henry Kissinger famously noted in his study of the Congress of Vienna,

> Those statesmen who have achieved final greatness did not do so through resignation, however well founded. It was given to them not only to maintain the perfection of order, but to have the strength to contemplate chaos, there to find material for fresh creation.[42]

Tiberius was willing to embrace the possibility of chaos by staging a major military withdrawal from Germania and by gambling—ultimately successfully—that the warlords would turn on themselves rather than join forces against Rome. He was also well aware that his actions—in stark contrast to those undertaken by his adulated stepson—were deeply unpopular with traditional Roman national security elites, yet decided to forge ahead regardless. Despite the many criticisms aimed at him, there is little doubt that Tiberius, a dyed-in-the-wool aristocrat wedded to timeworn Roman notions of *dignitas* and *gloria*, was mindful of the need to preserve the vitality of the imperium's deterrent and the strength of its security guarantees. His life experience, however, had rendered him all too aware of how an unchecked, hasty, or ill-managed process of territorial expansion—by fostering provincial instability or sparking an endless cascade of security commitments—could end in violence, disorder, and disaster. A degree of prestige could thus be traded in the short term for the preservation of greater credibility in the long run. At the same time, however, Tiberius' patent inability to gain enduring support or approval for his policies underscores the importance of at least attempting to build a shared consensus around a grand strategy, particularly if that grand strategy is viewed as potentially disruptive or at odds with a nation's self-image.[43] Rome's second emperor was a master strategist, but a dismal politician.

Of course, ill-staged or ill-timed drawdowns can prove almost equally ruinous as hubristic overextension. Unlike in the first century AD, threats in our shrunken, hyperconnected world can rarely be safely quarantined beyond the undulating screen of a vast imperial cordon sanitaire, or behind far-reaching constellations of fortlets and watchtowers. Nor can they easily be compartmentalized to a remote and amorphous corner of the world map. Was the United States' confused and precipitate departure from Afghanistan in the summer of 2021 ultimately, for all the terrible human tragedy and disastrous optics, an act of sound statecraft? Or merely the deferred promise of future chaos—which will necessitate renewed armed intervention, much as in Iraq following the withdrawal of U.S. troops and the subsequent metastasis of ISIS? Perhaps only time can tell. Meanwhile, Washington has shown admirable resolve, diplomatic dexterity, and leadership in its support of Ukraine. How long, however, can it maintain the political will and industrial brawn to support Kyiv in its bloody war of attrition without running up against domestic fatigue or imperiling its military position and commitments in Asia? How severely should the Russian bear be gored before Washington decides to withdraw the twenty thousand additional troops it surged to bolster NATO's eastern flank following Putin's invasion? And how will its jittery eastern and central European allies react when it opts to do so?

When it comes to all such tortuous decisions, much, as in the Tiberian era, will depend on *fortuna*—on the nature of circumstances as they arise, and on the precise sequencing of challenges as they present themselves. It will also rest heavily on how the United States and its allies choose to grapple with the issue of strategic simultaneity, i.e. the adjudication of increasingly finite military and financial resources within a stubbornly multivectored threat environment.[44] These decisions will not be easy—inevitably they will come freighted with enormous political risks and geopolitical costs.

Last but not least, this period in history should be an object of study for all those who view the current state of great power competition as more than just a tussle for resource and positional advantage, but also as an ideological struggle between competing systems of government.[45] For generations, students of authoritarianism studied Roman writings on the early Principate, and on the Tiberian era in particular. Tacitus was viewed as a particularly fine diagnostician of democratic decay and the rise of illiberalism.[46] As Justus Lipsius, the great late Renaissance neo-Stoic thinker, wrote in his annotated study of the *Annals*, the uplifting perorations of Livy may have left him "more moved," but they did not always make him "better equipped to face the vicissitudes of life." In contrast, Tacitus' grim work was an invaluable source of instruction on how to detect, delay, or survive the onset of authoritarianism:

> In his work let each reader consider princes' courts, the inner life of princes, their policies, commands and deeds, and let him anticipate (since the likeness to our own times is obvious) the same results from the same causes. You will find under tyranny flatterers and informers, evils not unknown in our time. You will find nothing honest or candid, not even among friends will you find good faith. You will find executions of distinguished men in heaps and peace more cruel than any war. Most of this is depressing, I admit, and makes for gloomy reading. But let us think that Thrasea's [a Roman senator executed under Nero] dying words were addressed to each one of us, "Observe, young man, and may the gods avert the omen, but you live in such a time that is good to strengthen your resolve by means of such examples and by constancy."[47]

Indeed, the story of Tiberius is above all one of history's great tragedies— it is the story of a capable, honorable man who collapsed under the dull, crushing weight of an entrenched authoritarian system, and in so doing was irredeemably altered and corrupted. It is a tale that showcases both the terrible strengths and abiding weaknesses of illiberal governments: their cancerous roots, once burrowed deep, can be almost impossible to extirpate, but they also destroy talent, devour their own, and debase their best and brightest. Tiberius, expounded one early twentieth century biographer, "has always been, and he remains, the greatest psychological problem in history. He is Hamlet and Lear and Othello rolled into one; and he is more than this."[48] For Roman elites at the time, however, his fall was above all a damning indictment of the abandonment of republican values. As one nervous senator noted in the days leading up to the accession of Tiberius' depraved successor, "If absolute sway had the power to convulse and transform the character of Tiberius after his vast experience of affairs," what hope was there for the young Gaius Caligula?[49]

KEY EVENTS

53 BC: Battle of Carrhae

44 BC: Assassination of Julius Caesar.

42 BC: Battle of Philippi. Deaths of Brutus, Cassius, and of Tiberius' republican grandfather, Marcus Livius Drusus Claudianus. Birth of Tiberius.

39 BC: Pact of Misenum. Tiberius' family is pardoned and allowed to return to Rome. Tiberius' father, Tiberius Claudius Nero, is forced to annul his marriage to his wife Livia Drusilla, who is then betrothed to Gaius Octavius, or Octavian, the future emperor Augustus.

33 BC: Death of Tiberius' father. Tiberius delivers the funeral oration, in his first public appearance.

31 BC: Battle of Actium, defeat of Mark Antony and final triumph of Octavian.

27 BC: The "Augustan settlement" and formation of the Principate. Octavian becomes the "princeps," or "first citizen" Augustus.

26 BC: Tiberius is appointed military tribune and accompanies Augustus and his nephew, Marcellus, to northern Spain during the Cantabrian War.

23 BC: Tiberius is appointed quaestor. Marcellus, until then the heir apparent, dies of a sudden fever.

20 BC: Tiberius is entrusted with his first major military and diplomatic command and sent to the eastern borderlands, where he acquits himself well. Roman client king Tigranes III is installed on the Armenian throne. Following lengthy negotiations, the Parthian king Phraates IV agrees to return the legion standards and surviving Roman prisoners of war from the battle of Carrhae.

15–14 BC: Together with his brother Nero Claudius Drusus (or Drusus the Elder), Tiberius completes the conquest of Raetia and the Alps in a series of superlatively conducted campaigns.

12 BC: With the death of Agrippa, Tiberius is forced to divorce his beloved wife Vipsania, marry Augustus' daughter Julia, and formally adopt her sons (and Augustus' heirs), Gaius, Lucius, and Agrippa Postumus.

9 BC: Death of Tiberius' brother, Drusus the Elder, while on campaign along the Elbe.

6 BC: Tiberius is granted tribunician powers, and ordered to proceed on another mission to Armenia. To Augustus' astonishment and irritation, he refuses and retires to Rhodes, where he will remain for seven years.

AD 2: Tiberius returns to Rome to divorce a now-disgraced Julia. Lucius dies of illness in Marseilles.

AD 4: Gaius is fatally wounded in Armenia. Tiberius is formally adopted as Augustus' son and heir, and becomes Tiberius Caesar. In exchange, he is required to adopt his nephew (and Augustus' great-nephew) Germanicus, with the understanding that he will privilege the latter over his own son, Drusus the Younger, in the imperial line of succession.

AD 6: Tiberius is dispatched to Germania to deal with Maroboduus, king of the Marcomanni. He is subsequently forced to sign a truce with Maroboduus to redirect his forces southward to deal with the Pannonian revolt.

AD 6–9: Tiberius crushes the Pannonian revolt in a grueling war of attrition.

AD 12: Vonones I, the pro-Roman son of Phraates IV and king of Parthia, is deposed and replaced by the more nationalist Artabanus II. Vonones flees to rule over the kingdom of Armenia.

AD 14: Death of Augustus and accession of Tiberius, at the age of fifty-six. Julia's sole remaining son, Agrippa Postumus (exiled under Augustus), is promptly eliminated. Simultaneous mutinies erupt among the legions stationed in Germania and Pannonia and are quelled by Germanicus (in Germania), and Drusus the Younger (in Pannonia).

AD 15: Sejanus becomes the sole commander of the Praetorian Guard and begins to worm his way into Tiberius' closest inner circle.

AD 14–16: Germanicus' campaigns deep into Germania.

AD 17: Recalled to Rome, the wildly popular Germanicus is accorded a triumph.

AD 18: Germanicus is granted *maius imperium* over the eastern provinces of the empire, and dispatched to the east.

AD 18: Following lengthy Romano-Parthian negotiations, Vonones, the king of Armenia, is replaced by a ruler more mutually acceptable to both great powers, Artaxias III. Vonones and his court-in-exile live under surveillance in Roman Syria.

AD 17–18: Annexation of Cappadocia, and of Commagene (which is integrated into the province of Syria).

AD 19: Death of Germanicus.

AD 17–24: Tacfarinas-led insurgency in North Africa, which lasts seven years, and only ends with the targeted killing of Tacfarinas in a dawn raid in 24 AD.

AD 19: Death of Arminius. Maroboduus becomes a political exile/detainee in Italy.

AD 21: Revolt of Sacrovir in Gaul.

AD 23: Drusus the Younger appears to die of natural causes. It is later revealed that he was poisoned by Sejanus.

AD 26: Tiberius retires to Capri, never to return to Rome.

AD 31: Sejanus' dramatic downfall and execution. Tiberius becomes increasingly paranoid, vengeful, and despotic.

AD 34: Following the death of Artaxias III, Artabanus II, maneuvers to put one of his sons on the Armenian throne.

AD 35: Tiberius sponsors a Parthian uprising against Artabanus, which the latter only quashes with great difficulty. Weakened and chastised, Artabanus II is forced to accept the installation of a Roman puppet, Mithridates, as ruler of Armenia.

AD 37: Death of Tiberius.

NOTES

Introduction

1   See Norman Douglas' great classic, first published in 1911, *Siren Land: A Celebration of Life in Southern Italy* (New York, NY: Bloomsbury, 2019).

2   Legend has it that Homer's deadly winged sirens preyed on mariners in the waters between present-day Capri and Sorrento. Aeneas was also believed to have plied these waters, "spreading his sails before the winds before reaching at length the Cumaean shore" not far from Naples and consulting the Cumaean Sibyl. See Virgil, *Aeneid*, VI. Meanwhile, local folklore has long claimed that the Grotta di Matermania, a large natural cave on Capri's eastern edge, was connected with Mithraic mysteries or the worship of Cybele. See Tobias Busen and Andreas Guner, "The Grotta di Matermania on Capri: Construction, Space and Atmosphere of an Imperial Pavilion," *Archäologischer Anzeiger*, 1 (2018), pp. 183–210, James Money, *Capri: Island of Pleasure* (New York, NY: Faber & Faber, 2011), and Amedeo Maiuri, *Capri: Its History and Its Monuments* (Rome, Italy: Istituto Poligrafico e Zecca dello Stato, 1955).

3   Tacitus has left us with a particularly vivid description of Capri: "the isle of Capri, which three miles of strait divide from the extreme point of the Surrentine promontory. The solitude of the place I should suppose to have been its principal commendation, as it is surrounded by a harborless sea, with a few makeshift roadsteads hardly adequate for small-sized vessels, while it is impossible to land unobserved by a sentry. In winter, the climate is gentle, owing to the mountain barrier which intercepts the cold sweep of the winds; its summers catch the western breeze and are made a delight by the circling expanse of open sea; while it overlooked the most beautiful of bays, until the activity of Vesuvius began to change the face of the landscape." Tacitus, *Annals*, IV.67.

4   For "neck stiff and bent forward," see the famous description of Tiberius' somewhat gauche physical demeanor in Suetonius, "Tiberius Nero Caesar," *The Twelve Caesars*, 68.

5   See R.H. Woodman and A.J. Woodman, "Introduction," in *Tacitus: Annals Book IV* (Cambridge, UK: Cambridge University Press, 1989), p. 31.

6   On Tiberius' life and alleged extracurricular activities on Capri, see, for example, Edward Champlin, "Sex on Capri," *Transactions of the American Philological Association*, 141, No. 2 (2011), pp. 315–32, George W. Houston, "Tiberius on Capri," *Greece and Rome*, 32, No. 2 (1985), pp. 179–96, and Rebecca Edwards, "Tacitus, Tiberius and Capri," *Latomus*, 70, No. 4 (2011), pp. 1047–57.

7 According to Suetonius, "in Capri he [Tiberius] arranged a number of nooks of venery where boys and girls disguised as Pans and nymphs solicited outside bowers and grottoes: people openly called this the old goat's island, punning on the island's name." Suetonius, "Tiberius Nero Caesar," *The Twelve Caesars*, 43. (Goat is *caprae* in Latin, hence the waspish effectiveness of the pun.)

8 Tom Holland, *Dynasty: The Rise and Fall of the House of Caesar* (New York, NY: Doubleday, 2015), pp. 251–2.

9 Ibid., p. 254.

10 For examples of modern biographies of Tiberius that grapple with some of these questions, see Robin Seager, *Tiberius* (Oxford, UK: Blackwell, 2005 edn), Barbara Levick, *Tiberius: The Politician* (London, UK: Thames & Hudson, 1976); Gregorio Marañón, *Tiberius: The Resentful Caesar* (New York, NY: Duell, Sloan and Pearce, 1956), and Willemijn Van Dijk, *The Successor: Tiberius and the Triumph of the Roman Empire* (Waco, TX: Baylor University Press, 2019).

11 The fascination with the Janus-faced personality of Tiberius largely coincided with the growth of interest in Tacitus as a theorist of prudence and statecraft in early modern Europe. See, for example, Mark Morford, "Tacitean Prudentia and the Doctrines of Justus Lipsius," in T.J. Luce and A.J. Woodman (eds), *Tacitus and the Tacitean Tradition* (Princeton, NJ: Princeton University Press, 1993), pp. 129–51, and Jacob Soll, "Amelot de la Houssaye and the Tacitean Tradition in France," *Translation and Literature*, 6, No. 2 (1997), pp. 186–202.

12 G.W. Bowersock, "The Roman Emperor as Russian Tsar: Tacitus and Pushkin," *Proceedings of the American Philosophical Society*, 143, No. 1 (March 1999), pp. 130–47.

13 See Baron Gaston de Montesquieu (ed.), *Pensées et fragments inédits de Montesquieu* (Bordeaux, France: Imprimerie de G. Gounouilhou, 1899), available at fr.wiki-source.org/wiki/Pens%C3%A9es_et_Fragments_in%C3%A9dits_de_Montesquieu/V, accessed 14 August 2023, and Adrianna E. Bakos, "Qui Nescit Dissimulare, Nescit Regnare: Louis XI and Raison D'Etat During the Reign of Louis XIII," *Journal of the History of Ideas*, 52, No. 3 (1991), pp. 399–416.

14 Theodor Mommsen, *A History of Rome Under the Emperors: Based on the Lecture Notes of Sebastian and Paul Hensen, 1882–86* (New York, NY: Routledge, 2005 edn), p. 132.

15 There is a vast literature on the battle of the Teutoburg Forest, its ramifications, and the early evolution of Rome's frontier policy. For two excellent recent samplings, see Peter S. Wells, *The Battle That Stopped Rome: Emperor Augustus, Arminius, and the Slaughter of the Legions in the Teutoburg Forest* (New York, NY: W.W. Norton and Company, 2015), and Matthew Symonds, *Protecting the Roman Empire: Fortlets, Frontiers, and the Quest for Post-Conquest Security* (Cambridge, UK: Cambridge University Press, 2018).

16 See Suetonius, "Tiberius Nero Caesar," *The Twelve Caesars*, III.32.

17 On the importance of the ONA in the intellectual history of U.S. defense strategy, see Thomas Mahnken (ed.), *Net Assessment and Military Strategy: Retrospective and Prospective Essays* (Amherst, NY: Cambria Press, 2020), and Andrew F. Krepinevich and Barry D. Watts, *The Last Warrior: Andrew Marshall and the Shaping of Modern American Defense Strategy* (New York, NY: Basic Books, 2015).

18   This is perhaps one of the most workable and succinct definitions of applied his-
      tory, initially provided by Niall Ferguson and Graham Allison in *Applied History
      Manifesto* (Cambridge, MA: Harvard Belfer Center, 2016), available at www.belfer-
      center.org/publication/applied-history-manifesto, accessed 14 August 2023.

19   Robert Crowcroft, "For All Time: History, Statesmanship, and the Primacy of
      Experience," in Robert Crowcroft (ed.), *Applied History and Contemporary Policymaking:
      School of Statecraft* (New York, NY: Bloomsbury, 2022), p. 41. For more on this author's
      perspective on the value of applied history, see Dr Iskander Rehman, "Why Applied
      History Matters," *Engelsberg Ideas*, November 20, 2021, available at engelsbergideas.
      com/essays/why-applied-history-matters/, accessed 14 August 2023.

20   On early imperial Roman grand strategy and rule, see, for example, Susan P.
      Mattern, *Rome and the Enemy: Imperial Strategy in the Principate* (Berkeley, CA:
      University of California Press, 1999), Neville Morley, *The Roman Empire: Roots of
      Imperialism* (London, UK: Pluto Press, 2010), Clifford Ando, *Imperial Ideology and
      Provincial Loyalty in the Roman Empire* (Berkeley, CA: University of California Press,
      2000), P.A. Brunt, "Laus Imperii," in P.D.A. Garnsey and C.R. Whittaker (eds),
      Imperialism in the Ancient World (Cambridge, UK: Cambridge University Press,
      1978), pp. 159–93, and James Lacey, *Rome: Strategy of Empire* (New York, NY:
      Oxford University Press, 2022).

21   For two excellent recent studies of the evolution of the Roman military, see Simon
      Elliott, *Roman Legionaries: Soldiers of Empire* (Oxford, UK: Casemate, 2018), and
      Adrian Goldsworthy, *Pax Romana: War, Peace and Conquest in the Roman World* (New
      Haven, CT: Yale University Press, 2016).

22   On the importance of applied history in statecraft, and on the importance of think-
      ing historically, see Hal Brands and William Inboden, "Wisdom Without Tears:
      Statecraft and the Uses of History," *Journal of Strategic Studies*, 41, No .7 (2018),
      pp. 916–46, Dr Iskander Rehman, "Polybius, Applied History, and Grand
      Strategy in an Interstitial Age," *War on the Rocks*, March 29, 2019, available at
      warontherocks.com/2019/03/polybius-applied-history-and-grand-strategy-in-an-
      interstitial-age/, and Robert Crowcroft, "The Case for Applied History," *History
      Today*, September 9, 2018, available at www.historytoday.com/archive/feature/
      case-applied-history, accessed 14 August 2023.

I. GUARDIAN OF THE EMPIRE – *Tiberius during the reign of Augustus*

Imperial Rome and the birth of a new order

1   On the Roman tradition of honorable suicide as a means of preserving the family
      name, see J.E. Lendon, *Empire of Honor: The Art of Government in the Roman World*
      (Oxford, UK: Oxford University Press, 2002), pp. 252–65, and Yolande Grise, *Le
      suicide dans la Rome antique* (Paris, France: Les Belles Lettres, 1982).

2   On the Claudian family and its role in Roman politics throughout the Republic,
      see George Converse Fiske, "The Politics of the Patrician Claudii," *Harvard Studies
      in Classical Philology*, 13 (1902), pp. 1–59.

3   For a good and succinct overview of the terrain, order of battle, and conditions at
    Philippi (during which dust clouds often obscured entire regiments from view and
    impeded effective maneuver), see Si Shepphard, *Philippi 42 BC: The Death of the
    Roman Republic* (Oxford, UK: Osprey Publishing, 2008). For an excellent study of
    this pivotal period in Roman history more broadly, see Josiah Osgood, *Caesar's
    Legacy: Civil War and the Emergence of the Roman Empire* (Cambridge, UK: Cambridge
    University Press, 2006).

4   Appian, *Civil Wars*, IV.127–8.

5   See Lucan, *Pharsalia*, I. Lucan's epic poem *De Bello Civili* (The Civil War), also
    known as the *Pharsalia*, written during the reign of Nero (circa AD 61) is perhaps the
    most celebrated epic account of the civil wars that marked the end of the Republic.

6   Tiberius' father, Tiberius Nero or Tiberius Senior, was also a member of the *gens
    Claudia*, albeit from a less distinguished branch than Tiberius' mother, Livia.

7   Indeed, after the Ides of March, Tiberius Claudius Nero even went so far as to pro-
    pose honors for the tyrannicides. On the climate of fear surrounding the proscrip-
    tions and purges of the civil wars, see Hannah Cornwell, "The Construction of One's
    Enemies in Civil Wars (49–30 BCE)," *Hermathena*, No. 196/197 (2014), pp. 41–68.

8   See Suetonius, "Tiberius Nero Caesar," *The Twelve Caesars*, VI.

9   Octavian also promptly divorced his first wife, Scribonia, with whom he had his
    only natural child, Julia the Elder.

10 "The woman was given in marriage by her husband himself, as some father might
    do." See Cassius Dio, *Roman History (Romaika)*, XLVIII.44.

11 Naturally, there was an additional, more political rationale behind Octavian's
    marriage to Livia, one that extended beyond mere physical attraction and a latent
    urge to humiliate an erstwhile opponent. Indeed, by marrying into one of Rome's
    most venerable families, the future emperor was reinforcing his ties to the more
    conservative branches of the old republican nobility, along with their extended
    networks of clientele. As Suetonius was later to note, Octavian's (relatively) humble
    aristocratic background had frequently been the subject of mockery by rivals such
    as Mark Antony, who "taunted him with his great-grandfather, saying he was a
    freedman and rope-maker from the country about Thurii, while his grandfather
    was a money-changer." Suetonius, "Augustus," *The Twelve Caesars*, II.3. For a semi-
    nal examination of the importance of patronage in the Late Republic and Early
    Principate, see Richard P. Saller, *Personal Patronage Under the Early Empire*
    (Cambridge, UK: Cambridge University Press, 1982).

12 The son of Octavian's sister, Octavia. See page 66 for a simplified genealogical
    chart of the Julio-Claudian dynasty.

13 For "delicate compromise of supervision and control," see Mason Hammond, "The
    Sincerity of Augustus," *Harvard Studies in Classical Philology*, 69 (1965), p. 150.

14 See Fotini Metaxi-Mitrou, "Violence in the *Contio* during the Ciceronian Age,"
    L'Antiquite Classique, 54 (1985), pp. 180–7, A.N. Sherwin-White, "Violence in Roman
    Politics," *Journal of Roman Studies*, 46 (1956), pp. 1–9, and Mary Beard, *SPQR: A
    History of Ancient Rome* (New York, NY: Liveright, 2015), Chapter 6.

15   See Susan P. Mattern, *Rome and the Enemy: Imperial Strategy in the Principate* (Berkeley, CA: University of California Press, 1999), Chapter 3.

16   The following provinces were put under senatorial control: Sicily, Crete, Asia, Greece (including Epirus), Baetica, Bithynia and Pontus, Illyricum, Numidia, Sardinia, and Corsica. Whereas senatorial provinces were ruled by governors, these imperial provinces were ruled by imperial legates. Augustus continuously accrued power over the course of his reign, essentially acquiring tribunician powers for life (through their automatic renewal) along with "*maius imperium*" (greater imperium) over senatorial provinces—which allowed him to intervene more or less as he saw fit. By the end of his life, all legions save one were under the orders of an Augustan appointee.

17   For two good overviews of this interstitial period in Rome's history, see Richard Alston, *Rome's Revolution: Death of the Republic and Birth of the Empire* (Oxford, UK: Oxford University Press, 2015), Chapters 13–16, and Fred K. Drogula, *Commanders and Command in the Roman Republic and Early Empire* (Chapel Hill, NC: University of North Carolina Press, 2015), Chapter 7.

18   Ronald Syme, *The Roman Revolution* (New York, NY: Oxford University Press, 1939), p. 323.

19   Julius Caesar had antagonized much of the Roman aristocracy with the liberality of his reform agenda, most notably his decision to enlarge the Senate from six hundred to nine hundred members, and his generous extension of Roman citizenship rights to large numbers of Gauls.

20   For a nuanced discussion of Augustus' reforms and political views, see Hammond, "The Sincerity of Augustus," pp. 139–62.

21   Edward Gibbon, *The History of the Decline and Fall of the Roman Empire*, I.3. Available at www.gutenberg.org/ebooks/25717, accessed 14 August 2023.

22   For two excellent recent biographies of Augustus, see Adrian Goldsworthy, *Augustus: First Emperor of Rome* (New Haven, CT: Yale University Press, 2014), and Anthony Everitt, *Augustus: The Life of Rome's First Emperor* (New York, NY: Random House, 2006).

23   For a masterful exposé of the rhetoric and propaganda of the Augustan age, which expressed itself equally in architectural and literary works, see Kathleen S. Lamp, *A City of Marble: The Rhetoric of Augustan Rome* (Columbia, SC: University of South Carolina Press, 2013). On the notion of an Augustan restoration or golden age, see Andrew Wallace-Hadrill, "The Golden Age and Sin in Augustan Ideology," *Past and Present*, 95 (1982), pp. 19–36.

24   For a good recent biography of Maecenas and his role as a cultural advisor, see Peter Mountford, *Maecenas* (New York, NY: Routledge, 2019). On the Augustan age as a "Thermidorian revolution," and reaction to the social and political turmoil during the late Republic and civil wars, see Chester G. Starr, "How Did Augustus Stop the Roman Revolution?", *Classical Journal*, 52, No. 3 (1956), pp. 107–12, in which the author draws an interesting comparison between Augustus and the Tudor king Henry VII, who "ended the protracted agony of the War of the Roses."

25 A clear overview of Augustus' socially conservative agenda is provided in Richard
    I. Frank, "Augustus' Legislation on Marriage and Children," *California Studies in
    Classical Antiquity*, 8 (1975), pp. 41–52.

26 Karl Galinsky, *Augustan Culture: An Interpretive Introduction* (Princeton, NJ: Princeton
    University Press, 1996).

27 Walter Eder, "Augustus and the Power of Tradition: The Augustan Principate as
    Binding Link Between Republic and Empire," in Kurt A. Raaflaub and Mark
    Toher (eds), *Between Republic and Empire: Interpretations of Augustus and his Principate*
    (Berkeley, CA: University of California Press, 1990), p. 75.

28 See Josiah Osgood, *Rome and the Making of a World State 150 BCE–20 CE* (Cambridge,
    UK: Cambridge University Press, 2018), Chapter 2, and Arthur M. Eckstein,
    Moral Vision in the Histories of Polybius (Berkeley, CA: University of California Press,
    1995). For an astute examination of the topos of fear as a source of unity and moral
    energy throughout ancient literature, including in the works of Thucydides, Plato,
    and Aristotle, see Daniel J. Kapust, "On the Ancient Uses of Political Fear and
    Its Modern Implications," *Journal of the History of Ideas*, 69, No. 3 (2008),
    pp. 353–73.

29 For Sallust's arguments on the loss of a "fear-rooted consensus," and their enduring
    influence, see Daniel J. Kapust, *Republicanism, Rhetoric, and Roman Political Thought:
    Sallust, Livy, and Tacitus* (New York, NY: Cambridge University Press, 2011), p. 40,
    and Lukas de Blois, "The Perception of Expansion in the Works of Sallust,"
    Latomus, 47, No. 3 (1988), pp. 604-619.

30 Lucan, *Pharsalia*, I.

31 See, for example, the arguments of Maecenas in Cassius Dio's *Roman History* in
    favor of enlightened monarchy: *Roman History*, LII.16. Maecenas argues that
    Augustus should seize leadership as a means of staving off further chaos: "Be ready
    and eager to assume the leadership of the State, or rather, do not let it slip. For we
    are not deliberating about taking something, but about not losing it and about run-
    ning hazards in addition."

32 *Res Gestae Divi Augusti*, 34.

33 "And by the word himself was called the Roman folk to name. On them I lay no
    bonds of time, no bonds of earthly part; I give them empire without end." Virgil,
    Aeneid, I. Only a few decades later, the Roman naturalist and philosopher Pliny the
    Elder was to provide an even clearer encapsulation of this exceptionalist worldview
    when extolling the spread of the Latin language from the Italian peninsula: "the
    land which is as at once the foster-child and the parent of all lands; chosen by the
    providence of the Gods to render even heaven itself more glorious, to unite the
    scattered empires of the earth, to bestow a polish upon man's manners, to unite the
    discordant and uncouth dialects of so many different nations by the powerful ties of
    one common language, to confer the enjoyments of discourse and of civilization
    upon mankind, to become, in short, the mother-country of all nations of the
    Earth." Pliny the Elder, *Natural History*, VI.5.

34 For a useful and nuanced overview of the history and historiography of Roman imperialism, see Andrew Erskine, *Roman Imperialism* (Edinburgh, UK: University of Edinburgh Press, 2010).

35 "This enemy [the Ligurians] seemed born for the purpose of preserving military discipline among the Romans, during the intervals between important wars; nor was any province better calculated to form a soldier to active valor. For Asia, from the enticing pleasures of its cities, the abundance of every production both of land and sea, the unwarlike temper of the enemy, and the wealth of its princes, made Roman armies rich, rather than brave." Livy, *Histories*, XXXIX.1.

36 On this aspect of Roman thinking, see Donald Earl, *The Moral and Political Tradition of Rome* (Ithaca, NY: Cornell University Press, 1984).

37 Of the squandered opportunities following the Battle of Pharsalus, Lucan writes: "By that bloody day it was brought about that India does not shudder at the Latin fasces, that [...] Parthia always owes delayed penalties to you; and that liberty, fleeing civil crime and never to return, has retreated across the Tigres and the Rhine and, having been sought so often at the price of blood, wanders as a German or Scythian." Lucan, *Pharsalia*, VII.

38 "We believe from his thundering that Jupiter has dominion in the heavens: Augustus shall be esteemed a present deity, the Britons and terrible Parthians being added to the empire." Horace, *Odes*, III.V. Tibullus also openly advocated such aggressive policies. For a good discussion of these writings, see James J. Stewart, "The Geographic Definition of *Ultimus* from Julius Caesar to Domitian," *Acta Classica*, 43 (2000), pp. 129–37.

Strategy and conflict in the Augustan age

1 For an excellent discussion of the concept of *Pax Romana*, see Hannah Cornwell, *Pax and the Politics of Peace: Republic to Principate* (New York, NY: Oxford University Press, 2017).

2 See Brent D. Shaw, "Bandits in the Roman Empire," *Past and Present*, 105 (1984), pp. 3–52.

3 Neville Morley, *The Roman Empire: Roots of Imperialism* (London, UK: Pluto Press, 2010), p. 47.

4 See Christopher J. Fuhrmann, *Policing the Roman Empire: Soldiers, Administration, and Public Order* (New York, NY: Oxford University Press, 2012), and Benjamin Kelly, "Riot Control and Imperial Ideology in the Roman Empire," *Phoenix*, 61, No. 1/2 (2007), pp. 150–76.

5 See Stephen L. Dyson, *The Creation of the Roman Frontier* (Princeton, NJ: Princeton University Press, 1982), and Orietta Dora Cordovana, "Historical Ecosystems: Roman Frontier and Economic Hinterlands in North Africa," *Historia: Zeitschrift für Alte Geschichte*, 61, No. 4 (2012), pp. 458–94.

6 Susan P. Mattern, *Rome and the Enemy: Imperial Strategy in the Principate* (Berkeley, CA: University of California Press, 1999), Chapter 3.

7   Ibid.

8   Suetonius thus recounts how during his period as triumvir, Octavian personally gouged out the eyes of a praetor whom he had (falsely) accused of making an attempt on his life. Suetonius, "Octavius Caesar Augustus," *The Twelve Caesars*, XXVII.

9   On the early years of Rome's imperial navy, see Raffaele D'Amato, *Imperial Roman Naval Forces 31 BC–AD 500* (Oxford, UK: Osprey Publishing, 2009), and Michael Pitassi, *The Roman Navy: Ships, Men and Warfare 350 BC–AD 475* (Barnsley, UK: Seaforth, 2012), Chapters 1–3.

10 See Andrew Erskine, *Roman Imperialism* (Edinburgh, UK: Edinburgh University Press, 2010), pp. 3–11, and R. Morris Coats and Gary M. Pecquet, "The Calculus of Conquests: The Decline and Fall of the Returns to Roman Expansion," *Independent Review*, 17, No.4 (2013), pp. 517–40. Paul Erdkamp puts this figure even higher, estimating it at "three quarters of the annual imperial budget." See Paul Erdkamp, "Introduction," in Paul Erdkamp (ed.), *A Companion to the Roman Army* (Oxford, UK: Blackwell, 2011). Naturally these figures remain somewhat speculative. For a granular overview of the many costs tied to the maintenance of Rome's military machinery during the Principate, see Peter Herz, "Finances and Costs of the Roman Army," in Erdkamp (ed.), *A Companion to the Roman Army*, Chapter 17.

11 Cassius Dio, *Roman History*, LII.27.

12 Ibid., LII.41.

13 On how this applies to the work of Roman historians in particular, see Caitlin Balmaceda, *Virtus Romana: Politics and Morality in the Roman Historians* (Chapel Hill, NC: University of North Carolina Press, 2017). On how many ancient historians viewed history as a subcomponent—like poetry—of rhetoric, and thus superimposed rhetorical narrative devices (such as fictional speeches or dialogue) as an *exaedificatio* or "superstructure" around the hard kernel of historical facts, see A.J. Woodman, *Rhetoric in Classical Historiography: Four Studies* (New York, NY: Routledge, 2003 edn), and Chapter 2 "Theory: Cicero," in particular.

14 These debates are eerily similar to some of the more modern discussions on the effectiveness of conscript vs. standing professional armies, and on the nature of their interactions with different regime types. See, for example, Elizabeth Kier, "Culture and Military Doctrine: France between the Wars," *International Security*, 19, No. 4 (1995), pp. 65–93, Joseph Paul Vasquez III, "Shouldering the Soldiering: Democracy, Conscription, and Military Casualties," *Journal of Conflict Resolution*, 49, No. 6 (2005), pp. 849–73, and George Q. Flynn, *Conscription and Democracy: The Draft in France, Great Britain, and the United States* (Westport, CT: Greenport Press, 2002).

15 See Yann Le Bohec, *The Imperial Roman Army* (London, UK: Routledge, 2001 edn), pp. 92–6. P.A. Brunt notes that "there is at least a correlation between the abandonment of conscription in Italy [...] and the diminution of the Italian proportion in the legions." P.A. Brunt, *Italian Manpower 225 BC–AD 14* (Oxford, UK: Oxford University Press, 1971). Similarly, Andrew Lintott observes that "Even under Augustus, the bulk of Italians came from Cisalpine Gaul, the regions north of the

rivers Arno and Rubicon, which was not completely incorporated into the Roman citizen body until Caesar became master of Rome; the same regions were later the only source of Italian legionaries. Essentially peninsular Italy became the recruiting grounds for the praetorians and urban cohorts alone." Andrew Lintott, *The Romans in the Age of Augustus* (Oxford, UK: Wiley-Blackwell, 2010), p. 161.

16 Ronald Syme, "Some notes on the Legions Under Augustus," *Journal of Roman Studies*, 23 (1933), pp. 140–53.

17 Adrian Goldsworthy, *Augustus: First Emperor of Rome* (New Haven, CT: Yale University Press, 2014), p. 285.

18 On the foundation of veteran colonies as preludes to further consolidation and/or annexation, see Nicola K. Mackie, "Augustan Colonies in Mauretania," *Historia: Zeitschrift für Alte Geschichte*, 32, No. 3 (1983), pp. 332–58, and E.T. Salmon, *Roman Colonization Under the Republic* (Ithaca, NY: Cornell University Press, 1970).

19 *Res Gestae Divi Augusti*, 17.

20 The first census, initiated in 28 BC, registered a grand total of 4,063,000 citizens in the empire. This was four times the number registered in the previous census, completed in 71 BC. New censuses were conducted in AD 8 and AD 14. On how the organization of empire-wide censuses buttressed Roman primacy, see Jochen Martin, "The Roman Empire: Domination and Integration," *Journal of Institutional and Theoretical Economics*, 151, No. 4 (1995), pp. 714–24, and Beatrice Le Teuff, "Les recensements augustéens, aux origines de l'Empire," *Pallas*, 96 (2014), pp. 75–90.

21 See Lawrence Keppie, *The Making of the Roman Empire: From Republic to Empire* (London, UK: Routledge, 1984), pp. 128–9.

22 These reforms occurred the same year that massive war preparations were apace, first against the forces of the Marcomanni led by Maroboduus, then in order to quell the revolt in Pannonia.

23 Morley, *The Roman Empire*, p. 48.

24 For "conglomeration of" see Martin, "The Roman Empire: Domination and Integration,", pp. 714–24. Pointing to the often relatively informal character of Roman primacy, classicists such as C.R. Whittaker have suggested that it can be useful to oppose the ancient Greek term *hegemonia*—which refers to influence or leadership over other states—to that of *arche*, which more explicitly stands for direct rule over administered territories. Thus, some areas both in and surrounding the Roman empire were subjected to *hegemonia*, while others fell under *arche*.
C.R. Whittaker, *Rome and Its Frontiers: The Dynamics of Empire* (New York, NY: Routledge, 2004), pp. 39–40.

25 The Romans distinguished between "long-haired Gaul," or Gallia Comata, the less Romanized area of Gaul, and "toga-wearing Gaul," Gallia Togata.

26 Tacitus, *Germania*, 33.3. Tacitus makes similar observations in *Agricola*, when commenting on the factionalism of the Britons: "The Britons were formerly governed by kings, but at present they are divided in factions and parties among their chiefs; and this want of union for concerting some general plan is the most favorable

circumstance to us, in our designs against so powerful a people. It is seldom that two or three communities concur in repelling the common danger; and thus, while they engage Rome one by one, they are all subdued." Tacitus, *The Life of Agricola*, 12.

27 On the perils of denying indigenous polities their own agency and diplomatic sophistication, and thus representing "American history as having been set in motion by the arrival of European explorers and colonizers," see Neal Salisbury, "The Indians' Old World: Native Americans and the Coming of Europeans," *William and Mary Quarterly*, 53, No.3 (1996), pp. 435–58. For two superlative treatments of Native American diplomacy in the colonial era, see Timothy J. Shannon, *Iroquois Diplomacy on the Early American Frontier* (New York, NY: Penguin Books, 1964), and Richard White, *The Middle Ground: Indians, Empires, and Republics in the Great Lakes Region, 1650–1815* (New York, NY: Cambridge University Press, 1991).

28 Polybius, *The Rise of the Roman Empire*, XXXI.40.

29 Peter Derow, "The Arrival of Rome: From the Illyrian Wars to the Fall of Macedon," in Andrew Erskine and Josephine Crawley Quinn (eds), *Rome, Polybius, and the East* (Oxford, UK: Oxford University Press, 2015), p. 40.

30 The seminal "trauma" burned into every Roman schoolchild's psyche was the sack of Rome by the Gallic war chief Brennus in 390 BC.

31 Some of the most detailed accounts of the role of druids in Celtic societies are provided by Julius Caesar in his *Gallic Wars*, in which he describes their pivotal function as "supra-tribal" figures of authority, acting as religious officiants, philosophers/educators, and judges. See Julius Caesar, *Gallic Wars*, VI.13–14. The existence of a highly organized caste of individuals with such federative potential came to be viewed as a severe menace by Roman authorities. See Miranda Aldhouse-Green, *Caesar's Druids: An Ancient Priesthood* (New Haven, CT: Yale University Press, 2010), and Hugh Last, "Rome and the Druids: A Note," *Journal of Roman Studies*, 39, No. 1 (1949), pp. 1–5.

32 Morley, *The Roman Empire*, p. 57. On the PRC's decades-long campaign to forcibly settle millions of nomadic pastoralists in order to exert greater control, see Andrew Jacobs, "China Fences in Its Nomads, and an Ancient Life Withers," *New York Times*, July 11, 2015, available at www.nytimes.com/2015/07/12/world/asia/china-fences-in-its-nomads-and-an-ancient-life-withers.html. On the imperial antecedents to such relocation strategies, see Pan Yihong, "Early Chinese Settlement Policies Towards the Nomads," *Asia Major*, 5, No. 2 (1992), pp. 41–77.

33 Tacitus, *The Life of Agricola*, 21.

34 For an excellent study of such provincial revolts, see Gil Gambash, *Rome and Provincial Resistance* (New York, NY: Routledge, 2015).

35 Ibid.

36 P.A. Brunt, "Charges of Provincial Maladministration under the Early Principate," *Historia: Zeitschrift für Alte Geschichte*, 10, No. 2 (1961), pp. 189–227. On the challenges and complexities of Roman imperial administration more broadly, see Alan K. Bowman,

"Provincial Administration and Taxation," in Alan K. Bowman et al. (eds), *The Cambridge Ancient History Volume X: The Augustan Empire* (Cambridge, UK: Cambridge University Press, 2008), Chapter 10, and Fergus Millar, *Government, Society, and Culture in the Roman Empire* (Chapel Hill, NC: University of North Carolina Press, 2004).

37   For a detailed examination of one such case, see Martha W. Baldwin Bowsky, "Roman Arbitration in Central Crete: An Augustan Proconsul and a Neronian Procurator," *Classical Journal*, 82, No. 3 (1987), pp. 218–29. For how this was already a recurring pattern in Rome's relations with the eastern Mediterranean during the republican era, see Craige Champion, "Empire by Invitation: Greek Political Strategies and Roman Imperial Interventions in the Second Century B.C.E.," *Transactions of the American Philological Association*, 137, No. 2 (2007), pp. 255–75.

38   See John Atkinson, "Ethnic Cleansing in Alexandria in 38," *Acta Classica*, 49 (2006), pp. 31–54.

39   See Anna Heller, "Domination subie, domination choisie: les cités d'Asie Mineure face au pouvoir romain, de la République à l'Empire," *Pallas*, 96 (2014), pp. 217–32, Saskia T. Roselaar (ed.), *Processes of Cultural Change and Integration in the Roman World* (Leiden, Netherlands: Brill, 2016), and Leonard A. Curchin, *The Romanization of Central Spain: Complexity, Diversity and Change in a Provincial Hinterland* (New York, NY: Routledge, 2004).

40   For a seminal examination of the imperial cult and its impact across the empire, see the compendium of essays contained in Duncan Fishwick, *Cult, Ritual, Divinity and Belief in the Roman World* (New York, NY: Routledge, 2018).

41   On the "universalizing and unifying" aspects of these nonverbal variants of imperial propaganda, see Clifford Ando, *Imperial Ideology and Provincial Loyalty in the Roman Empire* (Berkeley, CA: University of California Press, 2000), and Simon Price, *Rituals and Power: The Roman Imperial Cult in Asia Minor* (Cambridge, UK: Cambridge University Press, 1985 edn).

42   Richard Miles, *Ancient Worlds: The Search for the Origins of Western Civilizations* (London, UK: Penguin, 2011), p. 303.

43   See Luke 20:24–5 and 23:1–2, and John 19:12.

44   Morley, *The Roman Empire*, p. 58.

45   See Fergus Millar, "Government and Diplomacy in Imperial Rome During the First Three Centuries," *International History Review*, 10, No. 3 (1988), pp. 345–77, and David Braund, *Rome and the Friendly King: The Character of Client Kingship* (New York, NY: St Martin's Press, 1984).

46   See, for example, Jacob Theodore Nabel, *The Arsacids of Rome: Royal Hostages and Roman-Parthian Relations in the First Century CE* (Ithaca, NY: Cornell University doctoral dissertation, 2017).

47   For an excellent overview of this complex rivalry, see Jason M. Schlude, *Rome, Parthia, and the Politics of Peace: The Origins of War in the Ancient Middle East* (New York, NY: Routledge, 2020).

48 For a granular analysis of the lead-up and unfolding of this campaign, see Gareth
C. Sampson, *Defeat of Rome in the East : Crassus, the Parthians, and the Disastrous Battle
of Carrhae, 53 BC* (Barnsley, UK: Pen and Sword, 2008).

49 See Susan P. Mattern-Parkes, "The Defeat of Crassus and the Just War," *Classical
World*, 96, No. 4 (2003), pp. 387–96.

50 Mark Antony's Parthian campaigns were memorably described by Plutarch. See
Plutarch, "Antony," in *Parallel Lives*, IV. For a good contemporary discussion of
Antony's campaigns, see Mary Rose Sheldon, *Rome's Wars in Parthia: Blood in the
Sand* (Portland, OR: Vallentine Mitchell, 2010), pp. 65–81.

51 For a good overview of this entire period, see P. Edwell, *Between Rome and Persia:
The Middle Euphrates, Mesopotamia and Palmyra Under Roman Control* (London, UK:
Routledge, 2008).

52 Peter Wilcox, *Rome's Enemies: Parthians and Sassanid Persians* (Oxford, UK: Osprey
Publishing, 1982), p. 24.

53 The Parthian king had to be drawn not only from the aristocracy, but from the
Arsacid clan. The latter—much like today's House of Saud in Saudi Arabia—was
extensive, as it was customary for nobles to have many wives and/or consorts.
Furthermore, candidates for the monarchy could come from lateral as well as verti-
cal branches of the family—thus brothers and uncles could vie with sons of sitting
kings for the succession. On the complexity and fissile nature of each Parthian
succession process, see Malcolm A. R. Colledge, *The Parthians* (New York, NY:
Praeger, 1967), pp. 57–61, and Neilson C. Debevoise, *A Political History of Parthia*
(Chicago, IL: University of Chicago Press, 1998).

54 Tacitus, *Annals*, VI.44.

55 Seneca, *On the Firmness of the Wise Person*, XIII.

56 All of this despite the fact that Nero's reign—as Seneca would eventually learn to
his expense—was not exactly destined to be tranquil, and that it was immediately
followed by a resurgence of civil war. For "a modern veteran parliamentarian"
see Benjamin Isaac, *The Invention of Racism in Classical Antiquity* (Princeton, NJ:
Princeton University Press, 2004), p. 377.

57 Cassius Dio, *Roman History*, XL.15.6.

58 On the challenge posed by Pontus under Mithridates, see Duane Roller, *Empire of
the Black Sea: The Rise and Fall of the Mithridatic World* (Oxford, UK: Oxford
University Press, 2020).

59 Some scholars have argued that through routinized interactions with the Roman
empire, Germanian tribes rapidly changed both their internal governance structures and their external behavior, formalizing their system of military command
(instead of electing temporary military leaders), enhancing the level of their political interactions with neighboring tribes, and moving away from nomadic pastoral-
ism toward more sedentary farming. See, for example, Andrew T. Young, "From
Caesar to Tacitus: Changes in Early Germanic Governance circa 50 BC–50 AD,"
Public Choice, 164, No. 3/4 (2015), pp. 357–78.

60 E.A. Thompson, "Early Germanic Warfare," *Past and Present*, 14 (1958), pp. 2–29,

and Lindsay Powell, *1st Century AD: Roman Soldier Versus Germanic Warrior* (Oxford, UK: Osprey Publishing, 2014).

61 Jonathan Roth, "The Size and Organization of the Imperial Legion," *Historia: Zeitschrift für Alte Geschichte*, 43, No. 3 (1994), pp. 346–62.

62 Interview with Simon Elliott by Dan Snow, *History Hit*, December 5, 2018, available at tv.historyhit.com/watch/34256999, accessed 14 August 2023.

63 These specialists were also known as "immunes," meaning they were "immune" or exempt from other general duties in order to focus on their particular set of skills. Simon Elliott, *Roman Legionaries: Soldiers of Empire* (Oxford, UK: Casemate, 2018), p. 103.

64 Jonathan P. Roth, *The Logistics of the Roman Army at War* (Leiden, Netherlands: Brill, 2012).

65 The vexillationes were named after vexilla—"small sail"—the small square-like flags used to mark out detachments. See Raffaele D'Amato, *Roman Army Units in the Western Provinces* (Oxford, UK: Osprey Publishing, 2012), p. 30.

66 On Rome's historic predilection for heavy infantry, see Philip Sabin, "The Face of Roman Battle," *Journal of Roman Studies*, 90 (2000), pp. 1–17.

67 Primary sources would suggest that during the Punic Wars, the ratio of Italian allied troops to Roman cavalry formations was 3:1. See Donald Water Baronowski, "Roman Military Forces in 225 BC Polybius 2.23–24," *Historia: Zeitschrift für Alte Geschichte*, 42, No. 2, (1993), pp. 181–202.

68 Phyllis Culham, "Imperial Rome at War," in Brian Campbell and Lawrence A. Tritle (eds), *The Oxford Handbook of Warfare in the Classical World* (New York, NY: Oxford University Press, 2013), pp. 236–61.

69 Valerius Maximus, *Memorable Doings and Sayings*, II.7.

70 Ibid. For a sampling of the modern academic literature that views training and professionalism as key components of battlefield effectiveness, see Anthony King, "On Combat Effectiveness in the Infantry Platoon: Beyond the Primary Group Thesis," *Security Studies*, 25, No. 4 (2016), pp. 699–728, Hew Strachan, "Training, Morale and Modern War," *Journal of Contemporary History*, 4, No. 2 (2006), pp. 211–27, and Caitlin Talmadge, *The Dictator's Army: Battlefield Effectiveness in Authoritarian Regimes* (Ithaca, NY: Cornell University Press, 2015).

71 Titus Flavius Josephus, *War of the Jews*, V.1. On eyewitness descriptions of Roman infantry tactics and the importance of teamwork, see Michael J. Taylor, "Visual Evidence for Roman Infantry Tactics," *Memoirs of the American Academy in Rome*, 59/60 (2015), pp. 103–20.

72 For an outstanding examination of the importance of discipline and training in the Roman army of this period, see Sara Elise Phang, *Roman Military Service: Ideologies of Discipline in the Late Republic and Early Principate* (New York, NY: Cambridge University Press, 2008).

73 Vegetius later records that Roman soldiers were expected to march twenty to twenty-four miles in full kit in the space of five hours, before participating in the construction of the evening *castrum*, or fortifications. Flavius Vegetius Renatus, *Of Military*

Matters, I. For a summary of corporal punishment in the Roman army as listed in primary sources, see H.D. Parker, *The Roman Legions* (New York, NY: Oxford University Press, 1928), pp. 232–3.

74 See, for example, Hadrian's address to the Legio III Augusta in Numidia after overseeing a series of complex legion-wide maneuvers. Michael Speidel, *Emperor Hadrian's Speeches to the African Army—A New Text* (Mainz, Germany: Römisch-Germanisches Zentralmuseum, 2007).

75 There is a growing body of literature on the drivers and mechanics of military diffusion and emulation. For some of the more seminal treatments of the issue, see Michael Horowitz, *The Diffusion of Military Power: Causes and Consequences for International Politics* (Princeton, NJ: Princeton University Press, 2010). Emily Goldman and Leslie Eliason (eds), *The Diffusion of Military Technology and Ideas* (Stanford, CA: Stanford University Press, 2003), Theo Farrell and Terry Terriff (eds), *The Sources of Military Change: Culture, Politics, and Technology* (Boulder, CO: Lynne Rienner, 2002), and Kimberly Marten Zisk, *Engaging the Enemy: Organization Theory and Soviet Military Innovation, 1955–1991* (Princeton, NJ: Princeton University Press, 1993).

76 See John Lazenby, *The First Punic War* (New York, NY: Routledge, 2006), Chapter 5, and J.H. Thiel, *A History of Roman Sea-Power Before the Second Punic War* (Amsterdam, Netherlands: North Holland, 1954).

77 Nic Fields, *The Roman Army of the Principate: 27 BC–AD 117* (Oxford, UK: Osprey Publishing, 2009), p. 23.

78 Simon Elliott, "Servius to Severus: How the Roman Legionary's Armor Evolved," *Battles of the Ancients*, February 8, 2018, available at www.historyhit.com/how-did-the-army-of-the-roman-empire-evolve/, accessed 16 August 2023.

79 Fields, *The Roman Army of the Principate*, p. 31.

80 Some battlefield archeologists thus believe that the more heavily weighted pilum was a development of the late Augustan era. See M.C. Bishop and J.C.N. Coulston, *Roman Military Equipment from the Punic Wars to the Fall of Rome* (London, UK: Oxbow, 2006), p. 76.

81 M.C. Bishop, *Lorica Segmentata Volume I: A Handbook of Roman Articulated Plate Armour* (Oxford, UK: Armatura Press, 2003).

82 On military emulation more broadly, see João Resende-Santos, "Anarchy and the Emulation of Military Systems: Military Organization and Technology in South America, 1870–1990," *Security Studies*, 5, No. 3 (1996), pp. 193–260, and Colin Elman, *The Logic of Emulation: The Diffusion of Military Practices in the International System* (New York, NY: Columbia University doctoral dissertation, 1999). Jon Coulston makes the intriguing observation that many of Rome's military and tactical "imports" seem to have come from more rural and less industrialized societies, where Roman artificers and warriors would have had to rely more on experimentation and quick, ad hoc "fixes" during their long years of campaigning; he states the following: "It may be significant that dominant equipment forms were adopted from regions where Roman forces were least supported by an urban infrastructure,

and thus had to rely more on a combination of self-provision and native tradition. Apart from muscled cuirasses for officers, the Hellenistic East contributed little to the Roman infantryman's panoply." J.C.N. Coulston, "How to Arm a Roman Soldier," *Bulletin of the Institute of Classical Studies*, 71 (1998), pp. 167–90.

83   As one military historian notes, "When a rider's weight was lowered onto this type of saddle the four tall horns closed around and gripped his thighs, but they did not inhibit free movement to the same extent as a modern pommel and cantle designed for rider comfort and safety. This was especially important to spear-armed horsemen, whose drill called for some acrobatic changes in position. In an age that did not have the stirrup, the adoption of the four-horned saddle allowed the horseman to launch a missile effectively while skirmishing, or use both hands confidently to wield his shield and spear (or sword) in a whirling melee." Nic Fields, *Roman Auxiliary Cavalryman: AD 14–193* (Oxford, UK: Osprey Publishing, 2006), p. 18. See also Ann Hyland, *Training the Roman Cavalry: From Arrian's* Ars Tactica (Stroud, UK: Sutton, 1993), pp. 45–51.

84   See Timothy Hoyt, "Revolution and Counter-Revolution: The Role of the Periphery in Technological and Conceptual Innovation," in Goldman and Eliason, *The Diffusion of Military Technology and Ideas*, pp. 179–201. On how, traditionally, most polities seek to adopt the military practices of the most successful state in the international system, see Emily Goldman and Richard B. Andres, "Systemic Effects of Military Innovation and Diffusion," *Security Studies*, 8, No. 4 (1999), pp. 79–125.

85   "The Gauls were greatly encumbered for the fight because several of their shields would be pierced and fastened together by a single javelin-cast; and as the iron became bent, they could not pluck it forth, nor fight handily with the left arm encumbered. Therefore many of them preferred, after continued shaking of their arms, to abandon the shield and so fight bare-bodied." Julius Caesar, *Gallic Wars*, I.25.

86   For "mangle their faces," see *The Life of Agricola*, 36. On the use of shields for such offensive purposes, see also Tacitus, *Annals*, IV.51, and Valerius Maximus' description of the exploits of a Roman soldier during Julius Caesar's campaigns in Britain, who with his "right hand threw upon the foe a quantity of javelins" before drawing his sword "and driving off the boldest of his adversaries now by push of the shield-boss, then by stroke of the sword." Valerius Maximus, *Memorable Doings and Sayings*, III.23.

87   Tacitus, *The Life of Agricola*, 36.

88   Elliott, *Roman Legionaries*, p. 36. Tacitus thus notes in *Agricola*, when commenting on a melee between British and Roman soldiers, that the Britons "were armed with long swords [...] these enormous British swords, blunt at the point, are unfit for close grappling, and engaging in a confined space." Tacitus, *The Life of Agricola*, p. 37.

89   Flavius Vegetius Renatus, *Of Military Matters*, I.

From political refugee to princeps: Tiberius' slow rise to preeminence

1   For an excellent examination of Messalla's rhetoric and networks of influence, see Joanna Kenty, "Messalla Corvinus: Augustan Orator, Ciceronian Statesman," *Rhetorica*, 35, No. 4 (2017), pp. 445–74.

2   As well as, perhaps, his later association with certain of the more traditionalist members of the circle of Maecenas. See Robert Turcan, *Tibere* (Paris, France: Les Belles Lettres, 2017), pp. 24–5, and Henri Bardon, *La Littérature latine inconnue, Tome II* (Paris, France: Klincksiek, 1952).

3   On Tiberius' intellectual dispositions and affectations, along with his lifelong passion for seemingly esoteric aspects of Greek culture, see Steven H. Rutledge, "Tiberius' Philhellenism," *Classical World*, 101, No. 4 (2008), pp. 453–67, and Edward Champlin, "Tiberius the Wise," *Historia: Zeitschrift für Alte Geschichte*, 57, No. 4 (2008), pp. 408–25.

4   On the topic of astrology in ancient Rome, Tiberius' singular rapport with astrology and the occult, and his friendship with Thrasyllus, see A.H. Krappe, "Tiberius and Thrasyllus," *American Journal of Philology*, 48, No. 4 (1927), pp. 359–66, Walter M. Hayes, "Tiberius and the Future," *Classical Journal*, 55, No. 1 (1959), pp. 2–8, and Pauline Ripat, "Expelling Misconceptions: Astrologers at Rome," *Classical Philology*, 106, No. 2 (2011), pp. 115–54.

5   Many classicists across the centuries have thus established a link between Tiberius' somewhat anachronistic intellectual pursuits, his "slow, brooding intelligence and fastidiousness," and his discomfort with the new political realities of the Augustan Principate. See, for example, Antonio Garzetti, *From Tiberius to the Antonines: A History of the Roman Empire AD 14–192* (New York, NY: Routledge Revivals, 2014 edn), Chapter 1. For "slow brooding intelligence," see G.P. Baker, *Tiberius Caesar: Emperor of Rome* (New York, NY: Cooper Square, 2001 edn), p. 10.

6   There is a vast literature on the centrality of rhetoric to Roman politics and statecraft. For a good overview, see Joy Connolly, *The State of Speech: Rhetoric and Political Thought in Ancient Rome* (Princeton, NJ: Princeton University Press, 2007 edn).

7   Suetonius, "Tiberius Nero Caesar," *The Twelve Caesars*, 68.

8   Tacitus, *Annals*, I.II.

9   Under the Republic, the minimum age for such an office had been set at twenty.

10   Adrian Goldsworthy, *Augustus: First Emperor of Rome* (New Haven, CT: Yale University Press, 2014), p. 254.

11   Cassius Dio, *Roman History*, LIII.25. On the Augustan subjugation of Spain, which was only really completed toward 19 BC, see Ronald Syme, "The Spanish War of Augustus, 26–25 BC," *American Journal of Philology*, 55, No. 4 (1934), pp. 293–317.

12   Ibid., 53.22. There is a debate among historians over whether, had Augustus not already been bound by a series of military commitments, he would have truly risked an invasion of Britain. There is evidence, however, that he assembled a fleet of transport ships on the Aquitanian coast of Gaul during this period, and that he

may therefore have been considering an expedition, if not a full-scale invasion. On Augustus' military policies during this period, see J.W. Rich, "Augustus, War and Peace," in Jonathan Edmondson (ed.), *Augustus* (Edinburgh, UK: Edinburgh University Press, 2014), pp. 137–64.

13 "The last incident was the siege of Mount Medullus. When it had been surrounded by a continuous earthwork extending over eighteen miles and the Romans were closing in upon it on every side, the barbarians, seeing that their last hour had come, vied with one another in hastening their own deaths in the midst of banquet by fire and the sword and a poison which is there commonly extracted from the yew-tree." Florus, "XXXIII: The War Against the Cantabrians and Asturians," in *Epitome of Roman History*. Strabo also furnishes vivid imagery of the ferociousness of Spanish resistance, describing how certain prisoners sang defiantly even while being crucified. See Strabo, *Geography*, IV.18.

14 For a good discussion of the complexity of Roman military operations during the Cantabrian Wars, see David Magie, "Augustus' War in Spain 26–25 BC," *Classical Philology*, 15, No. 4 (1920), pp. 323–39.

15 Suetonius, "Augustus," *The Twelve Caesars*, XXV.4.

16 For a succinct overview of the evolution of the *cursus honorum* during the early Principate, see Karl Loewenstein, *The Governance of Rome* (The Hague, Netherlands: Martinus Nijhoff, 1973), pp. 255–73.

17 On this phase in Tiberius' career, see Barbara Levick, "The Beginning of Tiberius' Career," *Classical Quarterly*, 21, No. 2 (1971), pp. 478–86.

18 Willemijn Van Dijk, *The Successor: Tiberius and the Triumph of the Roman Empire* (Waco, TX: Baylor University Press, 2019), p. 337. For a good summary of the division of the provinces according to the Augustan settlement, see "The Augustan Settlement of 27 BC Summarized" (Seattle, WA: University of Washington), available at faculty.washington.edu/alain/CLAS.HSTAM330/ AugSettlement27BC.html, accessed 14 August 2023.

19 See Horace, *Odes*, III.5.2–4, and J. Rich, "Augustus, War and Peace," in L. de Blois, P. Erdkamp, O. Hekster, G. De Kleijn, and S. Mols (eds), *The Representation and Perception of Roman Imperial Power: Proceedings of the Third Workshop of the International Network, Impact of Empire: Roman Empire, 200 BC–476 AD* (Rome, 20–23 March 2002), pp. 329–57. Propertius and Virgil also joined the chorus, calling for Augustan campaigns of conquest in Parthia. See Sextus Propertius, *Elegies*, III.4, and Virgil, *Georgics*, VII.81.

20 See Erich S. Gruen, "The Expansion of the Empire Under Augustus," in Alan K. Bowman, Edward Champlin, and Andrew Lintott (eds), *The Cambridge Ancient History, Volume X: The Augustan Empire 43 BC–AD 69* (Cambridge, UK: Cambridge University Press, 1996), pp. 147–97, and Erich S. Gruen, "The Imperial Policy of Augustus," in Kurt A. Raaflaub and Mark Toher (eds), *Between Republic and Empire: Interpretations of Augustus and his Principate* (Berkeley, CA: University of California Press, 1990), pp. 395–417.

21 *Res Gestae Divi Augusti*, 27. As Barbara Levick notes, this is a textbook case of Augustan hyperbole, for "Augustus' implication that the Parthians were 'supplicants' for the friendship of Rome, and so effectively a dependency, was far from true, and his claim to have received all the sons of the Parthian monarch as hostages surely exaggerated, given the number of concubines that the monarch had. […] The Parthians had been in no hurry to return the standards and the two powers reached an agreement on coexistence, with an end to expansion on each other's ground." Barbara Levick, *Augustus: Image and Substance* (London, UK: Routledge, 2010 edn), p. 236.

22 John J. Poirot, *The Romano-Parthian Cold War: Julio-Claudian Foreign Policy in the 1st Century ce and Tacitus' Annals* (Baton Rouge, LO: Louisiana State University doctoral dissertation, 2014), p. 97.

23 Thus it remains unclear whether Tiberius was also operating in Macedonia in 15 BC. See Garzetti, *From Tiberius to the Antonines*, p. 29.

24 See, for example, B. Campbell, *The Emperor and the Roman Army: 31 BC–AD 235* (Oxford, UK: Oxford University Press 1984), p. 65, and N.S. Rosenstein, *Imperatores Victi: Military Defeat and Aristocratic Competition in the Middle and Late Republic* (Berkeley, CA: University of California Press, 1990).

25 For a good discussion of these campaigns, see T.D. Barnes, "The Victories of Augustus," *Journal of Roman Studies*, No. 64, (1974), pp. 21–6.

26 Lindsay Powell, *Eager for Glory: The Untold Story of Drusus the Elder: Conqueror of Germania* (Barnsley, UK: Pen and Sword, 2011), Chapter 2.

27 For an excellent discussion of the heroic mythos that began to surround Drusus and his behavior on the battlefield, see J.W. Rich, "Drusus and the Spolia Opima," *Classical Quarterly*, 49, No. 2 (1999), pp. 544–55.

28 See Powell, *Eager for Glory*, for a detailed examination of Drusus' campaigns in Germania.

29 See Pliny the Elder, *Natural History*, II.1. 20.

30 "When he learned that in Germany Drusus's life hung in the balance from a grievous and dangerous sickness, he at once dashed off in a panic. How swift and headlong his journey, snatched as it were in a single breath, is evident from the fact that after crossing the Alps and the Rhine, traveling day and night and changing horses at intervals, he covered at full stretch two hundred miles through a barbarous country recently conquered, with his guide Antabagius as his sole companion." Valerius Maximus, *Memorable Doings and Sayings*, V.5. On the ritualized association of Tiberius and Drusus with Castor and Pollux, see Edward Champlin, "Tiberius and the Heavenly Twins," *Journal of Roman Studies*, 101 (2011), pp. 73–99.

31 "Tiberius and Drusus belonged to the generation between that of Augustus and Agrippa's and Julia's children (at the time of Agrippa's death they were respectively 29 and 25 years old) but despite their comparative youth they would have to take on at least some part of the role that had previously been Agrippa's. It was too soon for them to be, as Agrippa had been, a virtual co-ruler with Augustus but within the

family and to an extent in the military field they had to fill the gap Agrippa had left." J.S. Richardson, *Augustan Rome 44 BC to AD 14: The Restoration of the Republic and the Establishment of the Empire* (Edinburgh: UK, Edinburgh University Press, 2012), p. 88.

32   Cassius Dio, *Roman History*, LV.5.

33   Suetonius, "Tiberius Nero Caesar," *The Twelve Caesars*, 7.

34   For one good discussion of this period of self-exile, see Barbara Levick, "Tiberius' Retirement to Rhodes in 6 BC," *Latomus*, 31, No. 6 (1972), pp. 779–813.

35   David Magie Jr., "The Mission of Agrippa to the Orient in 23 BC," *Classical Philology*, 3, No. 2 (1908), pp. 145–52.

36   Suetonius, "Tiberius Nero Caesar," *The Twelve Caesars*, 8.

37   Velleius, *Compendium of Roman History*, CIX.

38   As Eleanor Cowan observes, "In a period in which no other contemporary historical narrative survives other than in meagre fragments, Velleius' work is uniquely important. It is a critical counter to the later accounts by Tacitus, Suetonius and Cassius Dio, not simply because it offers a different view of Tiberius, but because Velleius saw continuity where later authors only saw radical change which destroyed the republic and put monarchy in its place. Velleius not only lived through this period and examined it, did not question the continued existence of the res publica, but neither did he question the supremacy of the Caesars." Eleanor Cowan, "Introduction," in Eleanor Cowan (ed.), *Velleius Paterculus: Making History* (Swansea, UK: Classical Press of Wales, 2011). See also the seminal work by Antony J. Woodman, *Velleius Paterculus: The Tiberian Narrative* (Cambridge, UK: Cambridge University Press, 2004 edn).

39   Frederick W. Shipley, "Introduction," in *Velleius Paterculus* (Cambridge, MA: Harvard University Press, 1929), p. xiii.

40   Velleius, *Compendium of Roman History*, CIV.

41   Catalina Balmaceda, "The Virtues of Tiberius In Velleius' *Histories*," *Historia: Zeitschrift für Alte Geschichte*, 63, No. 3 (2014), pp. 340–63.

42   Suetonius, "Tiberius Nero Caesar," *The Twelve Caesars*, XVIII–XIX.

43   Some scholars believe that Maroboduus may in fact have been forcibly displaced to the Middle Danube, during an earlier Roman pacification campaign. See Michael Erdrich, "Maroboduus and the Consolidation of Roman Authority in the Middle Danube Region," in *Boii – Taurisci: Proceedings of the International Seminar, OberleisKlement,* June 14th–15th, 2012 (Vienna, Austria: Austrian Academy of Sciences Press, 2016).

44   Strabo, *Geography*, I.1.

45   Velleius, *Compendium of Roman History*, XIX.

46   Ibid.

47   Most notably, Ranjit Singh hired former French Napoleonic officers as military advisors and adopted the French system of training.

48   Although in the case of the Anglo-Sikh wars, hostilities only broke out in the wake of Ranjit Singh's death, as the Raj used some of the disputes surrounding his

succession as an opportunity for military intervention in the Punjab. On the Anglo-Sikh wars, see David Smith, T*he First Anglo-Sikh War 1845–46: The Betrayal of the Khalsa* (Oxford, UK: Osprey, 2019), Amarpal Singh, *The First Anglo-Sikh War 1845–46* (Stroud, UK: Amberley, 2010), and Amarpal Singh, *The Second Anglo-Sikh War* (Stroud, UK: Amberley, 2016). See also Pradeep Baruah, "Military Developments in India 1750–1850," *Journal of Military History*, 58, No. 4 (1994), pp. 599–616.

49   In effect, this was a classic security dilemma. While Maroboduus retained an outward policy of neutrality, his actions and geostrategic location increased his own security while heightening Rome's perceived vulnerability. For a seminal discussion of the security dilemma, see Robert Jervis, "Cooperation Under the Security Dilemma," *World Politics*, 30, No. 2 (January 1978), pp. 167–214.

50   Velleius, *Compendium of Roman History*, CIV.

51   For discussion of how Rome may have favored "preemptive defense" against emerging threats, deciding to neutralize them before they reached peer competitor status, see A.N. Sherwin-White, "Rome the Aggressor?," *Journal of Roman Studies*, 70 (1980), p. 177, and Jerzy Linderski, "Si vis pacem, para bellum: Concepts of Defensive Imperialism," in William Harris (ed.), *The Imperialism of Mid-Republican Rome* (Ann Arbor, MI: University of Michigan Press), p. 136.

52   Suetonius describes the revolt as "the most serious of all foreign wars since those with Carthage," adding that it was characterized by "great difficulties of every kind and the utmost scarcity of supplies." Suetonius, "Tiberius Nero Caesar," *The Twelve Caesars*, 16.

53   Velleius, *Compendium of Roman History*, CXI.

54   Susan P. Mattern, *Rome and the Enemy: Imperial Strategy in the Principate* (Berkeley, CA: University of California Press, 1999), Chapter 4.

55   Velleius, *Compendium of Roman History*, CXI. On the Fabian strategy of delay, exhaustion, and harassment, named after the famous Roman general of the Punic Wars, Fabius Maximus, see Paul Erdkamp, "Polybius, Livy and the 'Fabian Strategy'," *Ancient Society*, 23 (1992), pp. 127–41. For a detailed discussion of modern applications of such a strategy, see Dr Iskander Rehman, "Lessons from the Winter War: Frozen Grit and Finland's Fabian Defense," *War on the Rocks*, July 20, 2016, available at warontherocks.com/2016/07/lessons-from-the-winter-war-frozen-grit-and-finlands-fabian-defense/, accessed 14 August 2023.

56   Velleius, *Compendium of Roman History*, CXI.

57   These accusations of inordinate cruelty may not have been too far off the mark: Josephus recounts how, when suppressing a revolt in Judaea in 4 BC, he mercilessly crucified over two thousand rebels. See Josephus, *War of the Jews*, II.V.2. On Varus having perhaps rushed the process of provincial consolidation, see Adrian Goldsworthy, *Pax Romana: War, Peace and Conquest in the Roman World* (New Haven, CT: Yale University Press, 2016), p. 198, and Peter S. Wells, *The Battle That Stopped Rome: Emperor Augustus, Arminius, and the Slaughter of the Legions in the Teutoburg Forest* (New York: W.W. Norton, 2003), p. 84.

58   Velleius, *Compendium of Roman History*, CXVII.

59 Florus, "XXX: The German War," *Epitome of Roman History.*

60 "Segestes had repeatedly given warning of projected risings, especially at the last great banquet which preceded the appeal to arms; when he urged Varus to arrest Arminius, himself, and the other chieftains, on the ground that with their leaders out of the way, the mass of the people would venture nothing, while he would have time enough later to discriminate between guilt and innocence." Tacitus, *Annals*, I.55.

61 Cassius Dio, *Roman History*, LVI.

62 This sequence of events is interesting—not only in that it shows how Rome's enemies could occasionally attempt to coordinate their counterhegemonic military efforts, even at a distance of hundreds of miles, but also because it reveals the extent to which even supposedly "barbarian" leaders were aware of the challenges Rome faced across multiple theaters, and how, armed with this knowledge, they might be tempted to act opportunistically whenever Rome's military credibility was severely challenged. As Adrian Goldsworthy notes, "The rebellion in Germany in AD 9 was the most successful revolt against Roman rule under the Principate, and it was no coincidence that it began just was the war against Pannonia came to an end. That it had taken three years, considerable casualties, and more than a third of the entire Roman army to suppress this rising suggested that the Romans were not invincible."Goldsworthy, *Pax Romana*, p.198.

63 Suetonius, "Octavius Caesar Augustus," *The Twelve Caesars*, XXIII.

64 Even Ovid, exiled hundreds of miles away on the shores of the Black Sea, seems to have rapidly become aware of the momentousness of the defeat. See Ovid, *Tristia*, III.25.

65 "At the time, when Augustus heard of the disaster that had befallen Varus, he rent his clothing and mourned greatly over the lost soldiers as also over the fear inspired by the Germans and the Gauls. His grief was especially keen because he expected that they would march upon Italy and Rome itself. [...] And as there were in Rome a number of Gauls and Germans, sojourning there for various purposes, and some of them serving in the praetorian guard, he feared that they might commit some acts of insurrection: therefore he sent such as were in his guard off to the islands and ordered the unarmed class to leave the city." Cassius Dio, *Roman History*, LVI.23.

66 Michael McNally, *Teutoburg Forest AD 9: The Destruction of Varus and his Legions* (Oxford, UK: Osprey Publishing, 2011), p. 88.

67 Suetonius, "Tiberius Nero Caesar," *The Twelve Caesars*, XVIII.

68 Velleius, *Compendium of Roman History*, CXX.

69 Wells, *The Battle that Stopped Rome*, p. 202.

70 For a good discussion of the aftereffects of the defeat, see David J. Breeze, *The Frontiers of Imperial Rome* (Barnsley, UK: Pen and Sword, 2011), Chapter 8.

71 "The Roman Empire, in the time of Augustus, had attained to a prodigious magnitude; and in his testament, he recommended to his successors never to exceed the limits which he had prescribed to its extent." Suetonius, "Octavius Caesar Augustus," *The Twelve Caesars*, 155.

72   See Josiah Ober, "Tiberius and the Political Testament of Augustus," *Historia: Zeitschrift für Alte Geschichte*, 31, No. 3 (1982), pp. 306–28.

73   As Josiah Ober observes, Tiberius' policies were probably motivated by more than a simple desire to respect Augustus' dying wishes: "Tiberius' refusal to expand the empire by military force has been traditionally imputed to his respect for Augustus's consilium; it is more probable, however, that the general who had actually fought in the long hard wars on the frontiers for most of his adult life had a clearer view of the problems inherent to the unending imperialism than the aging emperor who spent most of his later life in Italy." Ibid., p. 326. There is also a heated debate among historians as to whether Augustan foreign policy genuinely took a turn toward retrenchment in its final years, or whether the aging monarch was still entertaining hopes of expansion in places such as Germania (where Germanicus had been deployed with an ambitious mandate and a large force) or Africa, where in 14 AD roads were still being built for African expansion. See C.R. Whittaker, *Frontiers of the Roman Empire: A Social and Economic Study* (Baltimore, MD: Johns Hopkins University Press, 1994), and Wolfgang Orth, *Die Provinzialpolitik des Tiberius* (Munich, Germany: Ludwig Maximilian University of Munich doctoral dissertation, 1970), Introduction.

II. THE RELUCTANT RULER – *Tiberius as princeps*

An uneasy transition

1   On Tiberius' "government-in-waiting" in the final years of Augustus' reign, see Barbara Levick, *Tiberius: The Politician* (London, UK: Thames & Hudson, 1976), pp. 31–48, and Ronald Syme, *The Roman Revolution* (New York, NY: Oxford University Press, 1939), p. 437.

2   Suetonius, "Tiberius Nero Caesar," *The Twelve Caesars*, XXI.

3   See Mason Hammond, "The Sincerity of Augustus," *Harvard Studies in Classical Philology,* 69 (1965), pp. 139–62, and Eleanor Cowan, "Tiberius and Augustus in Tiberian Sources," *Historia: Zeitschrift für Alte Geschichte*, 58, No. 4 (2009), pp. 468–85.

4   Velleius, *Compendium of Roman History*, CXXIV.

5   David Shotter, *Tiberius Caesar* (New York, NY: Routledge, 1992), p. 18.

6   For a good overview of this complex relationship, see Shelagh Jameson, "Augustus and Agrippa Postumus," *Historia: Zeitschrift für Alte Geschichte*, 24, No. 2 (1975), pp. 287–314.

7   Albino Garzetti, *From Tiberius to the Antonines: A History of the Roman Empire AD 14–192* (New York, NY: Routledge Revivals, 2014 edn), pp. 9–10.

8   Velleius, *Compendium of Roman History*, CXXIV.

9   Naturally, Tacitus was convinced that Tiberius had ordered the execution, writing, "The opening crime of the principate was the murder of Agrippa Postumus; who, though off his guard and unarmed, was with difficulty dispatched by a resolute centurion. In the Senate Tiberius made no mention of the subject: his pretense was an argument from his father, instructing the tribune in charge to lose no time in neutralizing his prisoner, once he himself should have looked his last on the world." Tacitus, *Annals*, I.61.

10   Tiberius' alleged concerns over the possibility of an early coup led by Germanicus are given credence by Cassius Dio, Suetonius, and Tacitus, but there is little actual evidence to suggest that Germanicus contemplated betrayal at that time.

11   Tacitus, *Annals*, I.71.

12   Ibid., I.111.

13   Ibid.

14   Cassius Dio, *Roman History*, LVII.2. Years later, Asinius Gallus was to perish in solitary confinement under Tiberius' orders. On their bitterly hostile relationship, see D.C.A. Shotter, "Tiberius and Asinius Gallus," *Historia: Zeitschrift für Alte Geschichte*, 20, No. 4 (1971), pp. 443–57.

15   Cassius Dio, *Roman History*, LVII.1.

16   Suetonius, "Tiberius Nero Caesar," *The Twelve Caesars*, XXIV.

17   See, for example, the classic biography by John Charles Tarver, *Tiberius the Tyrant* (Cambridge, MA: Harvard University Press, 1902).

18   For "wolf by the ears," see Suetonius, "Tiberius Nero Caesar," *The Twelve Caesars*, XXV. For a nuanced discussion of Tiberius' apparent reluctance to rule, see Robin Seager, *Tiberius* (Oxford, UK: Blackwell, 2005 edn), pp. 46–7.

19   On the debate over Drusus' republicanism, see J.W. Rich, "Drusus and the *Spolia Optima*," *Classical Quarterly*, 49, No. 2 (1999), pp. 544–55, and Sam Wilkinson, *Republicanism During the Early Roman Empire* (London, UK: Continuum, 2012).

20   David Shotter notes that "the conduct of the princeps at least during the first half of his reign appears to have been directed towards securing a cooperation in govern- ment with the Senate which was based on his traditional respect for them and on their fair-minded independence of spirit." See Shotter, *Tiberius Caesar*, p. 29.

21   There is a vast literature on the self-perpetuating practices of authoritarian regimes, and how these same practices can impede or corrupt movements of demo- cratic reform. For one superb study of the perduring nature of "authoritarian rot," see Rasma Karklins, *The System Made Me Do It: Corruption in Post-Communist Societies* (New York, NY: Routledge, 2005).

22   This incident is mentioned by both Suetonius and Tacitus, Suetonius writing, "He had such an aversion to flattery that he would never suffer any senator to approach his litter, as he passed the streets in it, either to pay him civility or upon business. And when a man of consular rank, in begging his pardon for some offence he had given him, he recoiled from him in such haste, that he stumbled and fell." Suetonius, "Tiberius Nero Caesar," *The Twelve Caesars*, XXVII.

23 Tacitus, *Annals*, III.65.

24 Seneca thus equates "the first years of Tiberius' reign," with the "good years of Emperor Augustus." See Seneca, "On Clemency," *Essays*, I.1.

25 See Peter Burgers, "The Role and Function of Senatorial Debate: The Case of the Reign of Tiberius AD 14–37," *Latomus*, 58, No. 3 (1999), pp. 564–73.

26 Velleius, as expected, was especially laudatory: "Credit has been restored in the forum, strife has been banished from the forum, canvassing for office from the Campus Martius, discord from the senate-house; justice, equity, and industry, long buried in oblivion have been restored to the state; the magistrates have regained their authority, the senate its majesty, the courts their dignity; rioting in the theater has been suppressed; all citizens have been impressed with the wish to do right, or have been forced to do so by necessity." Velleius, *Compendium of Roman History*, CXXVI. On the election of magistrates under Tiberius, see A.J. Holladay, "The Election of Magistrates in the Early Principate," *Latomus*, 37, No. 4 (1978), pp. 874–93.

27 C.H.V. Sutherland, "Two Virtues of Tiberius: A Numismatic Contribution to the History of his Reign," *Journal of Roman Studies*, 28, No. 2 (1938), pp. 129–40. On how moderation was framed as Tiberius' "peculiar and distinctive virtue," see Robert Samuel Rogers, *Some Imperial Virtues of Tiberius and Drusus Julius Caesar* (Baltimore, MD: Johns Hopkins University Press, 1943).

28 Seager, *Tiberius*, p. 109.

29 See, for example, the misunderstanding over the nomination of the governor of Africa in AD 21, with Tiberius' expression of frustration over the Senate's inability to select a suitable candidate. Ibid., pp. 110–11.

30 "To have my statue worshipped among the gods in every province would be presumptuous and arrogant, and the honor paid to Augustus will soon be a mockery, if it is vulgarized by promiscuous experiments in flattery." Tacitus, *Annals*, IV.37–8.

31 Tacitus thus writes that Tiberius' continued rejection of divine honors was "an attitude by some interpreted as modesty, by many as self-distrust, by a few as degeneracy of the soul—The best men, they argued, desired the greatest heights […] for in the scorn of fame was implied the scorn of virtue!" Ibid., IV.38.

32 Cassius Dio, *Roman History*, LVII.8–11.

33 See, for example, J.H.M. Salmon, "Stoicism and the Roman Example: Seneca and Tacitus in Jacobean England," *Journal of the History of Ideas*, 50, No. 2 (1989), pp. 199–225, and T.J. Luce and A.J. Woodman (eds), *Tacitus and the Tacitean Tradition* (Princeton, NJ: Princeton University Press, 1993). For the comparison with the climate of fear in East Germany, see Anthony Woodman, "Introduction," in *Tacitus: The Annals: An Annotated Translation* (London, UK: Hackett, 2004), pp. xxvii–xxviii.

34 Theodor Mommsen, *A History of Rome Under the Emperors* (New York, NY: Routledge, 1992 edn), p. 402.

35 On the gradual expansion of the interpretation of treason under the reign of

Tiberius and the corrosive role played by "*delatores*," or private informers with vested interests, see W.W. Flint, "The Delatores in the Reign of Tiberius: As Described by Tacitus," *Classical Journal*, 8, No. 1 (1912), pp. 37–42, and Steven H. Rutledge, *Imperial Inquisitions: Prosecutors and Informants from Tiberius to Domitian* (New York, NY: Routledge, 2002), pp. 89–103.

36 For a good overview of Sejanus' career, see H.W. Bird, "Laelius Sejanus and His Political Significance," *Latomus*, 28, No. 1 (1969), pp. 61–98.

37 Seneca, "On Benefits," *Essays*, XXVI.

38 As with many such purported assassination plots, there is not absolute certainty as to its accuracy. Nevertheless, most historians deem it possible, and even likely, that Sejanus would employ such methods to covertly eliminate his only genuine rival. For a discussion of the alleged poisoning of Drusus the Younger, see Millo L. G. Shaw, *Drusus Caesar: The Son of Tiberius* (Vancouver, Canada: University of British Columbia doctoral dissertation, 1990), pp. 279–88.

39 Juvenal, "Satire 10: The Vanity of Human Wishes," *The Satires,* pp. 54–81.

40 There has been a lot of discussion over when the turning point in Tiberius' reign occurred. For a sampling of these academic debates, see A.J. Woodman, "Tacitus' Obituary of Tiberius," *Classical Quarterly*, 39, No. 1 (1989), pp. 197–205, Sir Ronald Syme, "The Year 33 in Tacitus and Dio," *Athenaeum*, 61 (1983), pp. 3–23, and A.J. Woodman, "Tiberius and the Taste of Power: The Year 33 in Tacitus," *Classical Quarterly*, 56, No. 1 (2006), pp. 175–99. For Millo Shaw, it was the death of Drusus the Younger that marked the beginning of a clear deterioration of Tiberius' reign: "So far, his rule had been characterized, in general, by moderation, prudent and effective administration and justice. Drusus, thought by many to have had a moderating influence on his father, may have contributed significantly to his success. He had probably curbed Sejanus's dangerously strong influence upon Tiberius and the state and had forced him to behave with circumspection and propriety." Shaw, *Drusus Caesar*, p. 301. For others, it was the revelation of Sejanus' perfidy that triggered the most repressive period in Tiberius' reign.

41 Tom Holland, *Dynasty: The Rise and Fall of the House of Caesar* (New York, NY: Doubleday, 2015), p. 251.

42 "The people were so much elated at his death, that when they first heard the news, they ran up and down the city, some crying out, Away with Tiberius to the Tiber; others exclaiming, May the earth, the common mother of mankind, and the infernal gods, allow him no abode in death, but amongst the wicked." Suetonius, "Tiberius Nero Caesar," *The Twelve Caesars*, LXXV.

Tiberius' mode of imperial management

1   Tacitus, *Annals*, I.16–18.

2   For a superb discussion of Tacitus' treatment of the mutinies, see A.J. Woodman, "Mutiny and Madness: Tacitus Annals 1:16–1:49," *Arethusa*, 39, No. 2 (2006), pp. 303–29.

3   Ibid.

4   Velleius, *Compendium of Roman History*, LVI.

5   "The army in Germany absolutely refused to acknowledge a prince who was not their own choice; and urged, with all possible importunity, Germanicus, who commanded them, to take the government on himself, though he obstinately refused it." Suetonius, *The Twelve Caesars*, XXV.

6   "Tiberius acted in this way at that time chiefly because it was his nature and he had determined upon that policy, but partly also because he was suspicious of the Pannonian and Germanic legions and feared Germanicus, the ruler of Germany of that day and a favorite of theirs. He had previously made sure of the loyalty of the soldiers in Italy (the praetorians) by means of the same oaths already established by Augustus; but as he was suspicious of the others he waited for either possible outcome, intending to save himself by retiring to private life in case the legions should revolt and prevail. For his reason, he often feigned sickness and remained at home, so as not to be compelled to say or do anything definite." Cassius Dio, *Roman History*, LVII.3.

7   A.M. Gowing, *Empire and Memory: The Representation of the Roman Republic in Imperial Culture* (Cambridge, UK: Cambridge University Press, 2005).

8   Sam Wilkinson, *Republicanism During the Early Roman Empire* (London, UK: Continuum, 2012), Chapter 1.

9   Tacitus, *Annals*, I.46.

10   Ibid., III.47.

11   Barbara Levick, *Tiberius: The Politician* (London, UK: Thames & Hudson, 1976), p. 167.

12   Tacitus, *Annals*, III.47.

13   On how Germanicus' handling of the mutinies was revelatory of his inexperience and impulsiveness, see D.C.A. Shotter, "Tacitus, Tiberius and Germanicus," *Historia: Zeitschrift für Alte Geschichte*, 17, No. 2 (1968), pp. 194–214. On the ambiguous character of Tacitus' portrayal of Germanicus, see Christopher Pelling, "Tacitus and Germanicus," in T.J. Luce and A.J. Woodman (eds), *Tacitus and the Tacitean Tradition* (Princeton, NJ: Princeton University Press, 1993).

14   As one historian commented on the different methods employed by both imperial princelings to resolve the crisis, "Tiberius may [...] have had a natural degree of partiality for his natural son. Nevertheless, in this particular instance, whatever his dislike of Germanicus, the Emperor had sound, objective reasons for showing greater appreciation of Drusus. Drusus had saved the empire from humiliation, military expense and logistical difficulties; Germanicus had burdened the Empire

and brought shame on its government. Drusus had controlled events; Germanicus
has merely reacted to them." Millo L.G. Shaw, *Drusus Caesar: The Son of Tiberius*
(Vancouver, Canada: University of British Columbia doctoral dissertation, 1990),
p. 108.

15 Thus barely a year later Tiberius found himself compelled to reverse Germanicus'
decision to grant a sixteen-year discharge. Tacitus, *Annals*, 1.78.

16 See Ramsay MacMullen, "The Emperor's Largesses," *Latomus*, 21, No. 1 (1962), pp.
156–62.

17 Tacitus, *Annals*, I.49.

18 Ibid., I.50.

19 Suetonius, "Caius Caesar Caligula," *The Twelve Caesars*, 4.

20 Tacitus, *Annals*, I.60–2.

21 For an excellent and nuanced discussion of the Tiberius/Germanicus relationship,
and of this episode in particular, see Shotter, "Tacitus, Tiberius and Germanicus,"
pp. 194–214.

22 On Rome's predilection for deterrence by punishment, see Susan P. Mattern, *Rome
and the Enemy: Imperial Strategy in the Principate* (Berkeley, CA: University of
California Press, 1999), Chapters 3–4.

23 On how Rome sometimes sought to "empty" frontier areas and create vast neutral
zones in the vicinity of its most outward military installations, either by mass
demographic relocation or by establishing mutually agreed "no man's lands" with
neighboring tribes, see David Potter, "Empty Areas and Roman Frontier Policy,"
American Journal of Philology, 113, No. 2 (1992), pp. 269–74.

24 Strabo, *Geography*, VII.4.

25 According to Tacitus, he "began to aim at kingship, and found himself in conflict
with his kinsmen." Tacitus, *Annals*, II.88.

26 Ibid. There is an interesting parallel here with an earlier episode in Roman history,
when two Roman consuls warned their foe King Pyrrhus of Epirus of a plot to
poison him, stating that "we do not give you this information out of regard for you,
but in order that your ruin may not bring infamy upon us, and that men may not
say of us that we brought the war to an end by treachery because we were unable to
do so by valor." See Plutarch, "Pyrrhus 4," *Parallel Lives,* Vol. II. It is entirely possible that the erudite and fiercely traditionalistic Tiberius modeled his response on
this example of Roman *dignitas*, or that Tacitus sought, for greater effect, to establish a subtle linkage with this past instance of Roman honorable behavior.

27 Velleius provides us with a vivid description of this diplomatic feat, comparing
Maroboduus to a "serpent who clung to the limits of his territory he had seized as a
serpent to its hole," and lauding "the effective diplomacy, carried out through the
help and agency of his son Drusus," via which Tiberius forced the great barbarian
ruler "to come forth like the serpent under his salutary charms." Velleius,
Compendium of Roman History, CXXIX.

28 Tacitus, *Annals*, II.90.

29 Ibid., II.91.

30 According to Velleius, Tiberius also demonstrated clemency toward Bato, a chief
    of the Pannonian rebels, for having fought honorably during the Pannonian revolt.
    See Velleius, *Compendium of Roman History*, CIX.

31 A good summary of this revolt can be found in Adrian Goldsworthy, *Pax Romana:
    War, Peace and Conquest in the Roman World* (New Haven, CT: Yale University Press,
    2016), pp. 208–9. See also Robert Samuel Rogers, "Notes on the Gallic Revolt,
    AD 21," *Classical Weekly*, 36, No. 7 (1942), pp. 75–6. On the potential for Sacrovir to
    have been a druid, see Jane Webster, "At the End of the World: Druidic and Other
    Revitalization Movements in Post-Conquest Gaul and Britain," *Britannia*, No. 30
    (1999), pp. 1–20.

32 Tacitus, *Annals*, III.44–7.

33 Ibid., II.52–4.

34 See Wouter Vanacker, "Adhuc Tacfarinas: Causes of the Tiberian War in North
    Africa (15–24 AD) and the Impact of the War on Roman Imperial Policy," *Historia:
    Zeitschrift für Alte Geschichte*, 64, No. 3 (2015), pp. 336–56. For a good overview of
    Rome's relations with client kings in Mauretania during this period, see Michele
    Coltelloni-Trannoy, "Rome et les rois amis et alliés du peuple roman, en Afrique
    (Ier siècle av. J.-C/Ier siècle ap. J.-C.)," *Pallas*, No. 68 (2005), pp. 117–44.

35 For a good contemporary and policy-relevant discussion of this insurgency, see
    Jakub Grygiel, "How to Fight an Elusive Enemy," *The American Interest*, May 11,
    2015, available at www.the-american-interest.com/2015/05/11/how-to-fight-an-elu-
    sive-enemy/, accessed 14 August 2023.

36 See Kimberly Kagan, "Redefining Roman Grand Strategy," *Journal of Military
    History*, 70, No. 2 (2006), pp. 333–62.

37 See Suetonius, "Tiberius Nero Caesar," *The Twelve Caesars*, XLI. On Tiberius' con-
    tinued close involvement in foreign policy from Capri, see Wolfgang Orth, *Die
    Provinzialpolitik des Tiberius* (Munich, Germany: Ludwig Maximilian University of
    Munich doctoral dissertation, 1970), and Levick, *Tiberius: The Politician*.

38 Tacitus, *Annals*, IV.13.

39 See Rebecca Edwards, *Divus Augustus Pater: Tiberius and the Charisma of Augustus*
    (Bloomington, IN: Indiana University doctoral dissertation, 2003), p. 216.

40 "To some governors who advised him to load the provinces with taxes, he
    answered, 'it is the part of a good shepherd to shear, not flay, his sheep.'" Suetonius,
    "Tiberius Nero Caesar," *The Twelve Caesars*, XXXII.

41 Some historians have suggested that Tiberius' harsher attitude toward provincial
    corruption may have exacerbated his unpopularity among Rome's ruling class. A
    Dutch historian writes, "He did concern himself greatly with the proper function-
    ing of the administration of the Empire, and with the uninterrupted supply of
    bread to the stomachs of Rome. That the manner in which he set about achieving
    those ends gave rise to incessant complaints about the princeps' arrogance—com-
    plaints issued from the mouths of those who profited most—reflected one undenia-
    ble fact: that the canny knack for public relations that had served Augustus so well

was completely lacking in his successor." Willemijn Van Dijk, *The Successor: Tiberius and the Triumph of the Roman Empire* (Waco, TX: Baylor University Press, 2017), Chapter 3.

42   Levick, *Tiberius: The Politician*, pp. 100–2.

43   Tacitus, *Annals*, I.81. Tiberius also abolished the *consilium principis*, a semiofficial advisory council or committee instituted by Augustus, and comprising leading senators (who served on a rotational basis) and imperial family members, preferring to draw on a select, handpicked group of advisors. As some classicists have noted, this may have been yet another attempt to draw a clearer separation between the Senate and the imperial executive, and to force senatorial consultations into a more open environment. Almost inevitably, however, it ended up reinforcing perceptions of growing regime opacity. See Wilkinson, *Republicanism During the Early Roman Empire*, Chapter 5. On the role of the consilium principis and advisors more broadly during the Principate, see the seminal work by Fergus Millar, *The Emperor in the Roman World* (London, UK: Bristol Classical Press, 1977).

44   Rebecca Edwards suggests that the fear over being prosecuted by delators or informers during the second half of Tiberius' reign may have paradoxically acted as a deterrent to provincial maladministration, every governor living in fear of being denounced on corruption charges by a rival. Edwards, *Divus Augustus Pater*, p. 222.

45   P.A. Brunt, "Charges of Provincial Maladministration under the Early Principate," *Historia: Zeitschrift für Alte Geschichte*, 10, No. 2 (1961), pp. 189–227.

46   Titus Flavius Josephus, *Antiquities of the Jews*, XVIII.2.5

47   Tacitus, *Annals*, II.2.

48   As Jacob Theodore Nabel notes, this was a recurring challenge, as Arsacids that had been raised in Rome often "deepened the very demarcation that their lives had done so much to efface. Political actors within Parthia and Rome turned the figure of the Arsacid hostage into a caricature of the empire on the opposite shore of the Euphrates. The Romans represented them as the barbarous inhabitants of an alter orbis, a different world; the Parthians repudiated their kingships, and perhaps even accused their former countrymen of acculturation to the mores of their Roman captors. Arsacid hostages were the negatives from which the imperial image of Parthia and Rome developed. They themselves connected, but the reaction against them divided." Jacob Theodore Nabel, *The Arsacids of Rome: Royal Hostages and Roman-Parthian Relations in the First Century ce* (Ithaca, NY: Cornell University doctoral dissertation, 2017), p. 3.

49   Germanicus was to die not long afterwards, in AD 19, following a mysterious illness. Many suspected that he had been poisoned by Piso, the governor of Syria, a former close associate of Tiberius and personal enemy of Germanicus. Piso was subsequently put on trial for treason and murder, and chose to commit suicide. The death of Germanicus, and Piso's suspected involvement, cast a great shadow over the remainder of Tiberius' reign, as many believed that the emperor, jealous of his stepson, had engineered an assassination. Most modern historians, however, find

this theory to be dubious at best, and believe that Germanicus most likely died of
an undetermined illness. On the historical debate over Piso's involvement, see
Cynthia Damon, "The Trial of Piso in Tacitus's *Annals* and the *Senatus Consultum de
CN. Pisone Patre*: New Light on Narrative Technique," *American Journal of Philology*,
120, No. 1 (1999), pp. 143–62, and Terence T. Rapke, "Tiberius, Piso, and
Germanicus," *Acta Classica*, 25 (1982), pp. 61–9.

50 Levick, *Tiberius: The Politician*, p. 146.

51 Tacitus, *Annals*, VI.32.

52 David Magie, *Roman Rule in Asia Minor to the End of the Third Century After Christ*
(Princeton, NJ: Princeton University Press, 1950), p. 495.

53 Suetonius, "Tiberius Nero Caesar," *The Twelve Caesars*, XXXVII.

54 Philo of Alexandria, *On the Embassy to Gaius*, XXL.

Great power retrenchment, military adaption, and the evolution of Rome's worldview

1   Strabo, *Geography*, I.17. Velleius also heavily stressed how terrain had played a
critical role in Rome's defeat, writing, "Hemmed in by forests and marshes and
ambushes, Rome's army was exterminated almost to a man by the very enemy
whom it had always slaughtered like cattle, whose life or death had depended solely
upon the wrath or the compassion of Romans." Velleius, *Compendium of Roman
History*, CXIX.

2   There is also a perfidious native, a "crafty and treacherous man," in Plutarch's
account of the Battle of Carrhae—an Arab chieftain named Ariamnes who deliber-
ately leads Crassus' army astray. See Plutarch, "Life of Crassus," *Parallel Lives*, 21.

3   Valerius Maximus, *Memorable Doings and Sayings*, VII.3–6.

4   Tacitus, *Annals*, III.21.

5   Plutarch, "Life of Crassus," *Parallel Lives*, 23.

6   Florus, *Epitome of Roman History*, II.XVIIII.

7   Gareth C. Sampson, *Rome and Parthia: Empires at War: Ventidius, Antony and the
Second Romano-Parthian War 40–20 BC* (Havertown, PA: Pen and Sword Books,
2020), p. 177.

8   For an excellent overview of Germanicus' campaigns, see Lindsay Powell,
Germanicus: The Magnificent Life and Mysterious Death of Rome's Most Popular General
(Barnsley, UK: Pen and Sword, 2012), Chapters 2–3.

9   Tacitus, *Annals*, III.74.

10 Ibid.

11 See Simon Elliott, *Romans at War: The Roman Military in the Republic and Empire*
(Oxford, UK: Casemate, 2020), p. 141, and J.C. Coulston, "Roman, Parthian, and
Sassanid Tactical Developments," in P. Freeman and D. Kennedy (eds), *The Defense
of the Roman and Byzantine East, Volume 1* (Oxford, UK: British Institute of
Archaeology, 1986), pp. 60–70.

12   See Karl Strobel, "Strategy and Army Structure Between Septimius Severus and Constantine the Great," in Paul Erdkamp (ed.), *A Companion to the Roman Army* (Oxford, UK: Wiley-Blackwell) pp. 267–86, and E. Gabba, "Sulle influenze reciproche degli ordinamenti militari dei Parti e dei Romani," in *Atti Del Convegno Sul Terma: La Persia e il mondo Greco-romano* (Rome, Italy: Accademia Nazionale dei Lincei, 1966), pp. 51–73.

13   See J.J. McLaughlin, *The Transformation of the Roman Auxiliary Soldier in Thought and Practice* (Ann Arbor, MI: University of Michigan doctoral dissertation, 2015).

14   For a seminal recent study, see Ian Haynes, *Blood of the Provinces: The Roman Auxilia and the Making of Roman Society from Augustus to the Severans* (Oxford, UK: Oxford University Press, 2013).

15   Nic Fields, *Roman Auxiliary Cavalryman: AD 14–193* (Oxford, UK: Osprey Publishing, 2006).

16   "He formed them so that the center was occupied by the auxiliary infantry, in number eight thousand, and three thousand horse were spread in the wings. The legions were stationed in the rear, before the entrenchments; a disposition which would render the victory signally glorious, if it were obtained without the expense of Roman blood." Tacitus, *The Life of Agricola*, 35. Recent scholarship has, however, begun to challenge some of the prevalent assumptions regarding the status and value of auxiliaries. As one classicist notes, "Auxiliary units have long been regarded as supplementary to the legions, the support that their name suggest. The noncitizen status of auxiliaries, at least in the early empire, estimates of their pay relative to that of legionaries, the attitude of the principal source for early imperial history, Tacitus, and the experiences and prejudices of modern imperialistic powers have led many historians to view auxiliaries as second-rate units of lesser value militarily than the legions. However, this is not necessarily the view now held, and auxiliary units would perhaps more accurately be considered as complementary to the legions: well-trained and reliable troops who could fight in the line of battle along with legionaries, as well as providing the diversity of forces vital to Rome's success, in the form of cavalry, camel riders, slingers, archers, and the skirmishing troops that had been lost to the legions with the manipular system." See Kate Gilliver, "The Augustan Reform and the Structure of the Imperial Army," in Erdkamp (ed.), *A Companion to the Roman Army*, p. 193.

17   Haynes, *Blood of the Provinces*, pp. 115–6.

18   Ibid., p. 193.

19   On the importance and tactical versatility of auxiliary light infantry in the early imperial era, see Adam O. Anders, *Roman Light Infantry and the Art of Combat: The Nature and Experience of Skirmishing and Non-Pitched Battle in Roman Warfare 264 BC–AD 235* (Cardiff, UK: Cardiff University doctoral dissertation, 2011), pp. 157–74.

20   See Catherine M. Gilliver, "Mons Graupius and the Role of Auxiliaries in Battle," *Greece and Rome*, 43, No. 1 (1996), pp. 54–67.

21   On the theory of "martial races" under the British Empire, see Gavin Rand,

"'Martial Races' and 'Imperial Subjects': Violence and Governance in Colonial India, 1857–1914," *European Review of History,* 13, No. 1 (2006), pp. 1–20. On Roman ethnic stereotypes, see Benjamin Isaac, *The Invention of Racism in Classical Antiquity* (Princeton, NJ: Princeton University Press, 2004).

22 See Emily Allen-Hornblower, "Beasts and Barbarians in Caesar's *Bellum Gallicum* 6.21–8," *Classical Quarterly,* 64, No. 2 (2014), pp. 682–93.

23 Tacitus, *Histories,* IV.10.

24 See McLaughlin, *The Transformation of the Roman Auxiliary Soldier,* p. 204.

25 For a seminal investigation of the status and role of Batavian auxiliaries, see Nico Roymans, *Ethnic Identity and Imperial Power: The Batavians in the Early Roman Empire* (Amsterdam, Netherlands: Amsterdam University Press, 2004).

26 Tacitus, *Histories,* IV.17.

27 See McLaughlin, *The Transformation of the Roman Auxiliary Soldier,* p. 405.

28 See *De Munitionibus Castrorum,* translation available online at http://www.intratext. com/X/LAT0347.htm

29 McLaughlin, *The Transformation of the Roman Auxiliary Soldier,* p. 321.

30 There is evidence of increased ethnic diversity among auxiliary regiments over the course of the second century AD, but this does not seem to be the result of a deliberate Roman policy to break up regimental ethnic fiefdoms.

31 It is worth noting, in passing, that the U.S. joint force faces similar recruitment difficulties in terms of meeting its end strength, with less than 30 percent of young American adults meeting enlistment eligibility criteria, and less than 10 percent expressing a potential desire to enlist. See Beth J. Asch, *Navigating Current and Emerging Army Recruitment Challenges: What Can Research Tell Us?* (Santa Monica, CA: RAND Corporation, 2019), and Amy Schafer, "Those Serving in the U.S. Military Don't Actually Represent the Country as a Whole," *Task and Purpose,* September 27, 2017, available at taskandpurpose.com/analysis/serving-us-military-dont-actually-represent-country-whole, accessed 14 August 2023.

32 Tacitus, *Annals,* IV.32.

33 There is a vast literature on the issues of credibility and reputational costs/gains in foreign policy. For a small sampling from the field of security studies, see Alex Weisiger and Keren Yarhi-Milo, "Revisiting Reputation: How Past Actions Matter in International Politics," *International Organization,* 69, No. 2 (2015), pp. 473–95, Daryl G. Press, *Calculating Credibility: How Leaders Assess Military Threats* (Ithaca, NY: Cornell University Press, 2007), and Robert Jervis, "Deterrence and Perception," *International Security,* 7, No. 3 (1982), pp. 3–30. On the importance of a country's "face" and "reputation for action," particularly in terms of managing and/or preserving foreign expectations, see Thomas C. Schelling, *Arms and Influence* (New Haven, CT: Yale University Press, 2008 edn), p. 124.

34 Tacitus, *Annals,* IV.24.

35 Pliny the Younger, *Panegyricus Traiani,* XVIII.

36 See Christopher J. Fettweis, "Restraining Rome: Lessons in Grand Strategy from Emperor Hadrian," *Survival,* 60, No. 4 (2018), pp. 123–50.

37   Cassius Dio, *Roman History*, LXIX.

38   Florus, "The Period of the Seven Kings, Beginning with Romulus," in *Epitome of Roman History*, 5.

39   For one such indictment, see Eutropius, *Abridgement of Roman History*, VIII.6. For Hadrian's foreign policy, see Anthony Birley, *Hadrian: The Restless Emperor* (New York, NY: Routledge, 2013 edn), Thorsten Opper, *Hadrian: Empire and Conflict* (Cambridge, MA: Harvard University Press, 2010), and Ronald Syme, "Hadrian and the Vassal Princes," *Athenaeum*, 59 (1981), pp. 273–83.

40   Frederick Jackson Turner, "The Significance of the Frontier in American History," in *The Annual Report of the American Historical Association* (Washington, DC: American Historical Association, 1893), pp. 199–227.

41   Tacitus, *Annals*, XII.12.

42   Seneca, *Selected Dialogues and Consolations*, IV.14.

43   Tacitus, *Germania*, II.

44   See Strabo, *Geography*, IV, and Philo of Alexandria, *On the Embassy to Gaius*, XXL.

45   In one revealing aside, Tacitus describes Parthia under the reign of Claudius as being an "allied power, which rivalled our [Rome's] power, but allowed our primacy out of respect." Tacitus, *Annals*, XII.10.

46   Velleius, *Compendium of Roman History*, II.CI.

47   Ibid.

48   Pompeius Trogus, *Justinus: Epitome of the Philippic History*, XLI.1, and Strabo, *Geography*, XI.9.

49   Livy, *History of Rome*, IX.18.

50   Lucan, *Pharsalia*, X.47.

51   See Randall J. Pogorzelski, "Orbis Romanus: Lucan and the Limits of the Roman World," *Transactions of the American Philological Association*, 141 (2011), pp. 143–70.

52   Susan Mattern-Parkes, "The Defeat of Crassus and the Just War," *Classical World*, 96, No. 4 (2003), pp. 387–96.

53   For another excellent treatment of the Roman mindset with regard to imperial hegemony and territorial control, see Claude Nicolet, *Space, Geography, and Politics in the Early Roman Empire* (Ann Arbor, MI: University of Michigan Press, 1991).

54   Guy de la Bédoyère, *Roman Britain: A New History* (London, UK: Thames & Hudson, 2013).

55   Cullen Murphy, *Are We Rome? The Fall of Empire and the Fate of America* (New York, NY: Houghton Mifflin, 2007), p. 63. On the archeological significance of the Vindolanda tablets, see Alan Bowman, *Life and Letters on the Vindolanda Frontier* (London, UK: British Museum, 1998).

56   Florus, "The German War," *Epitome of Roman History*, XXX.

57   Ibid, "The Sarmatian War," XXVIII.

58   See Zoe M. Tan, "Subversive Geography in Tacitus' Germania," *Journal of Roman Studies*, 104 (2014), pp. 184–214. For "shagged with forests or deformed by forests," see Tacitus, *Germania*, V.

59   Tacitus, *Germania*, I.1.

60 For discussions of Rome's evolving worldview, see Clifford Ando, *Imperial Ideology and Provincial Loyalty in the Roman Empire* (Berkeley, CA: University of California Press, 2000), pp. 277–355, and James J. Stewart, "The Geographical Definition of *Ultimus* from Julius Caesar to Domitian," *Acta Classica*, 43 (2000), pp. 129–37.

Conclusion

1 Montaigne, *Les Essais: Oeuvres Completes* (Paris, France: Gallimard, 2010 edn), p. 422.

2 "How wrong it is to cite the Romans at every turn [...] For any comparison to be valid it would be necessary to have a city with conditions like theirs, and then to govern it according to their example. In the case of a city with different qualities, the comparison is as much out of order as it would be to expect a donkey to race like a horse." Francesco Guicciardini, "Ricordi," in C. Grayson (ed.), *Francesco Guicciardini: Selected Writings* (Oxford, UK: Oxford University Press, 1965), p. 110.

3 John Lewis Gaddis, "Grammar, Logic, and Grand Strategy," in Hal Brands (ed.), *The New Makers of Modern Strategy: From the Ancient World to the Digital Age* (Princeton, NJ: Princeton University Press, 2023), p. 1120.

4 See Linda Dowling, "Roman Decadence and Victorian Historiography," *Victorian Studies*, No. 28 (1985), p. 595, and Sarah J. Butler, *Britain and Its Empire in the Shadow of Rome: The Reception of Rome in Socio-Political Debate from the 1850s to the 1920s* (London, UK: Bloomsbury, 2012).

5 Montagu Burrows, "Imperial Federation," *National Review*, 4 (1884–5), p. 369.

6 William Ewart Gladstone, "England's Mission," *Nineteenth Century*, 4 (1878), p. 584.

7 See Adam Kirsch, "The Empire Strikes Back," *New Yorker*, January 1, 2012, available at www.newyorker.com/magazine/2012/01/09/the-empire-strikes-back-adam-kirsch, accessed 14 August 2023.

8 "Everything which was in the past and is now, will be in the future, but the names change, and the outward appearance of things, so that anyone who lacks discernment does not recognize them and cannot draw conclusions or form an opinion for what he observes." Francesco Guicciardini, "Ricordi," p. 6.

9 On two-level games, i.e. the entanglements of domestic and international politics, see Robert D. Putnam, "Diplomacy and Domestic Politics: The Logic of Two-Level Games," *International Organization*, 42, No. 3 (1988), pp. 427–60.

10 See Nicholas Purcell, "The Non-Polis and the Game of Mirrors: Rome and Carthage in Ancient and Modern Comparison," *Classical Philology*, 112, No. 3 (2017), pp. 332–49.

11 Sallust, *The War with Catiline*, 10.

12 For a superlative examination of the deterioration of political vocabulary in times of political decay in the works of Sallust, Thucydides, and Tacitus, see Lydia Spielberg, "Language, *Stasis* and the Role of the Historian in Thucydides, Sallust and Tacitus," *American Journal of Philology*, 138, No. 2 (2017), pp. 331–73.

13 Florus, *Epitome of Roman History*, XLVII.6.

14   For a nuanced discussion of the evolution of America's post-Cold War grand strategy, see Hal Brands, "American Grand Strategy in the Post-Cold War Era," in Russell W. Glenn (ed.), *New Directions in Strategic Thinking 2.0* (Canberra: ANU Press, 2018), pp. 134–48. On the debates surrounding the 1992 DPG, see Eric S. Edelman, "The Strange Career of the 1992 Defense Planning Guidance," in Melvyn P. Leffler and Jeffrey W. Legro (eds), *In Uncertain Times: American Policy After the Berlin Wall and 9/11* (Ithaca, NY: Cornell University Press, 2011), pp. 63–78.

15   On how America's growing polarization risks hobbling its ability to devise and conduct an effective grand strategy, see Kenneth A. Schultz, "The Perils of Polarization for U.S. Foreign Policy," *Washington Quarterly*, 40, No. 4 (2017), pp. 7–28.

16   See, for instance, the *Texas National Security Review* roundtable debate on this very topic: Dr Iskander Rehman et al., "Policy Roundtable: Are the United States and China in a New Cold War?," *Texas National Security Review* (May 2018), retrievable at tnsr.org/roundtable/policy-roundtable-are-the-united-states-and-china-in-a-new-cold-war/tnsr_u-s-china-cold-war-roundtable/, accessed 15 August 2023.

17   Much of the following discussion is lifted from the author's previously published work on Sallust's relevance for contemporary policymakers. See Dr Iskander Rehman, "Metus Hostilis: Sallust, American Grand Strategy, and the Disciplining Effects of Peer Competition with China," *War on the Rocks,* May 3, 2021, available at warontherocks.com/2021/05/metus-hostilis-sallust-american-grand-strategy-and-the-disciplining-effects-of-peer-competition-with-china/, accessed 15 August 2023.

18   Daniel Kapust, *Republicanism, Rhetoric, and Roman Political Thought: Sallust, Livy, and Tacitus* (New York, NY: Cambridge University Press, 2011), p. 51.

19   See William J. Burns, "Polarized Politics has Infected American Diplomacy," *The Atlantic,* June 6, 2020, available at www.theatlantic.com/ideas/archive/2020/06/polarized-politics-has-infected-american-diplomacy/612778/, accessed 15 August 2023.

20   Jennifer Mitzen, "Ontological Security in World Politics: State Identity and the Security Dilemma," *European Journal of International Relations*, 12, No. 3 (2006), pp. 341–70, and Emily O. Goldman, *Power in Uncertain Times: Strategy in the Fog of Peace* (Stanford, CA: Stanford University Press, 2011).

21   For a good overview of different forms of defense planning frameworks, see Stephan Frühling, *Defense Planning and Uncertainty: Preparing for the Next Asia-Pacific War* (New York, NY: Routledge, 2014).

22   John Mueller, "Questing for Monsters to Destroy," in Leffler and Legro (eds), *In Uncertain Times*, p. 121.

23   Reinhold Niebuhr, *The Irony of American History* (Chicago, IL: University of Chicago Press, 2008 edn), p. 146.

24   See Steven Ward, "Because China Isn't 'Caucasian,' the US Is Planning for a 'Clash of Civilizations.' That Could be Dangerous," *Washington Post,* May 4, 2019, available at www.washingtonpost.com/politics/2019/05/04/because-china-isnt-caucasian-us-is-planning-clash-civilizations-that-could-be-dangerous/, accessed 15 August 2023.

25 See Nadege Rolland, *China's Vision for a New World Order* (Seattle, WA: National Bureau of Asian Research, 2020), and Julia Lovell, *Maoism: A Global History* (New York, NY: Knopf, 2019).

26 See John M. Friend and Bradley A. Thayer, *How China Sees the World: Han-Centrism and the Balance of Power in International Politics* (Lincoln, NK: Potomac Books, 2018), and Patrik Meyer, "Could Han Chauvinism Turn the 'Chinese Dream' into a 'Chinese Nightmare'?" *The Diplomat*, June 14, 2016, available at thediplomat.com/2016/06/could-han-chauvinism-turn-the-chinese-dream-into-a-chinese-nightmare/, accessed 15 August 2023.

27 Tsukasa Hadano, "China Purges School Libraries of 'Western Veneration,'" *Nikkei Asia*, April 18, 2021, available at https://asia.nikkei.com/Politics/China-purges-school-libraries-of-Western-veneration2.

28 Laura Silver, Kat Devlin, and Christine Huang, "Most Americans Support Tough Stance Toward China on Human Rights, Economic Issues," *Pew Research Center*, March 4, 2021, available at www.pewresearch.org/global/2021/03/04/most-americans-support-tough-stance-toward-china-on-human-rights-economic-issues/, accessed 15 August 2023.

29 See, for example, John Mueller, "The Impact of Ideas on Grand Strategy," in Richard Rosecrance and Arthur A. Stein (eds.), *The Domestic Bases of Grand Strategy* (Ithaca, NY: Cornell University Press, 1993), pp. 48–65, and Daphna Canetti et al., "What Does National Resilience Mean in a Democracy? Evidence from the United States and Israel," *Armed Forces and Society*, 40, No. 3 (2014), pp. 504–20.

30 See *2022 National Defense Strategy of the United States of America* (Washington, DC: U.S. Department of Defense, 2022), p.17. For more on this debate, see Jim Mitre, "A Eulogy for the Two-War Construct," *Washington Quarterly*, 41, No. 4, 2018, pp. 7–30, and Hal Brands and Evan Braden Montgomery, "One War is Not Enough: Strategy and Force Planning For Great-Power Competition," *Texas National Security Review*, 3, No. 2 (2020), available at tnsr.org/2020/03/one-war-is-not-enough-strategy-and-force-planning-for-great-power-competition/, accessed 15 August 2023.

31 Eric V. Larson, *Force Planning Scenarios, 1945–2016: Their Origins and Use in Defense Strategic Planning* (Santa Monica, CA: RAND Corporation, 2019), p. xiii.

32 On the challenges and risks associated with such force planning trade-offs, see *Providing for the Common Defense: The Assessment and Recommendations of the National Defense Strategy Commission*, November 2018, pp. 18–19, available at www.usip.org/publications/2018/11/providing-common-defense, accessed 15 August 2023.

33 On the potential for a recrudescence of proxy wars in an era of intensified great power competition, see Tyrone L. Groh, *Proxy War: The Least Bad Option* (Palo Alto, CA: Stanford University Press, 2019), Daniel Byman, "Why States Are Turning to Proxy War," *The National Interest*, August 26, 2018, available at nationalinterest.org/feature/why-states-are-turning-proxy-war-29677, and Zack Gold and William Rosenau, "The Future of Conflict is Proxy Warfare, Again," *Defense One*, July 25,

2019, available at www.defenseone.com/ideas/2019/07/future-conflict-proxy-warfare-again/158697/, accessed 15 August 2023.

34   Raphael S. Cohen, "Ukraine and the New Two War Construct," *War on the Rocks,* January 5, 2023, available at warontherocks.com/2023/01/ukraine-and-the-new-two-war-construct/, accessed 15 August 2023.

35   On the importance of the comparative advantage proffered by America's alliances, see Mira Rapp-Hooper, *Shields of the Republic: The Triumph and Peril of America's Alliances* (Cambridge, MA: Harvard University Press, 2020). See also Elbridge Colby and Jim Thomas, "Don't Scrap America's Alliances: Fix Them," *The National Interest,* June 29, 2016, available at nationalinterest.org/feature/dont-scrap-americas-alliances-fix-them-16788, accessed 15 August 2023.

36   Elbridge Colby and Wess Mitchell, "The Age of Great-Power Competition: How the Trump Administration Refashioned American Strategy," *Foreign Affairs*, 99, No. 1 (January/February 2020), pp. 118–31.

37   For an excellent recent example of a such an intellectual effort, see Ashley Townshend, Brendan Thomas-Noone, and Matilda Steward, *Averting Crisis: American Strategy, Military Spending and Collective Defense in the Indo-Pacific* (Sydney, Australia: United States Studies Center of the University of Sydney, 2019), available at www.ussc.edu.au/analysis/averting-crisis-american-strategy-military-spending-and-collective-defence-in-the-indo-pacific, accessed 15 August 2023.

38   See Philip H. Gordon and Amanda Sloat, "The Dangerous Unraveling of the U.S.-Turkish Alliance," *Foreign Affairs,* January 10, 2020, available at www.foreignaffairs.com/articles/turkey/2020-01-10/dangerous-unraveling-us-turkish-alliance, accessed 15 August 2023. Joseph Zeballos-Roig and Walt Hickey, "Barely 1 in 5 Americans View Saudi Arabia as a U.S. Ally—As Trump Weighs Military Action Against Iran Over Attacks on Saudi Oil Facilities," *Business Insider*, September 19, 2019, available at www.businessinsider.com/barely-one-in-five-americans-view-saudi-arabia-us-ally-2019-9, accessed 15 August 2023, and Jennifer Spindel, "The Case for Suspending American Arms Sales to Saudi Arabia," *War on the Rocks*, May 14, 2019, available at warontherocks.com/2019/05/the-case-for-suspending-american-arms-sales-to-saudi-arabia, accessed 15 August 2023.

39   Richard Nixon, "Asia After Vietnam," *Foreign Affairs*, 46, No. 1 (October 1967), pp. 114–15. On the so-called "Nixon Doctrine," see Robert S. Litwak, *Détente and the Nixon Doctrine: American Foreign Policy and the Pursuit of Stability, 1969–1976* (Cambridge, UK: Cambridge University Press, 1986).

40   See, for example, the role played by French troops accustomed to decades of desert warfare in stabilizing vast swathes of sub-Saharan Africa, or the growing presence of Nordic nation armed forces trained for operations in extreme cold in in the contested Arctic region. See Michael Shurkin, *France's War in Mali: Lessons for an Expeditionary Army* (Santa Monica, CA: RAND Corporation, 2014), Jackie Northam, "In a Remote Arctic Outpost, Norway Keeps Watch on Russia's Military Buildup," *NPR*, November 3, 2019, available at www.npr.org/2019/11/03/775155057/

in-a-remote-arctic-outpost-norway-keeps-watch-on-russias-military-buildup, accessed 15 August 2023, and Kevin McGwin, "In the Face of Uncertainty About Russia, A Nordic Gang of Four Emerges," *Arctic Today*, January 17, 2019, available at www.arctictoday.com/in-face-of-uncertainty-about-russia-a-nordic-gang-of-four-emerges/, accessed 15 August 2023.

41   In short, is the U.S. security establishment prepared to see their allies act with greater autonomy, including, in some cases, through structures or frameworks that may not systematically include the U.S.? See, for example, the sometimes heated debate over the issue of NATO and European strategic autonomy. For two opposing viewpoints, see Ronja Kempin and Barbara Kunz, "Washington Should Help Europe Achieve 'Strategic Autonomy': Not Fight It," *War on the Rocks*, April 12, 2018, available at https://warontherocks.com/2018/04/washington-should-help-europe-achieve-strategic-autonomy-not-fight-it/, accessed 15 August 2023, and Daniel Kochis, *Recent Strategic Autonomy Advances Threaten the Transatlantic Link* (Washington, DC: Heritage Foundation, 2020), available at www.heritage.org/europe/report/recent-eu-strategic-autonomy-advances-threaten-the-transatlantic-link, accessed 15 August 2023.

42   Henry A. Kissinger, *A World Restored: The Politics of Conservatism in a Revolutionary Era* (London, UK: Victor Gollancz, 1977), p. 213.

43   There is a vast literature on the importance of sustaining a strong elite consensus and of promoting a coherent, unifying narrative when charting a long-term strategy for geopolitical competition. See, for example, the academic analysis contained in the two following edited volumes: Rosecrance and Stein (eds), *The Domestic Bases of Grand Strategy*, and Peter Trubowitz, Emily Goldman, and Edward Rhodes, *The Politics of Strategic Adjustment: Ideas, Institutions, and Interests* (New York, NY: Columbia University Press, 1999).

44   For an excellent examination of how great powers have dealt with the simultaneity challenge over history, see Wess Mitchell, *Strategic Sequencing: How Great Powers Avoid Multi-Front War* (Washington, DC: The Marathon Initiative Working Paper, 2020), available at https://www.themarathoninitiative.org/wp-content/uploads/2022/02/ONA-Report_Mitchell_TMI_FINAL-220214.pdf, accessed 15 August 2023.

45   On this aspect of great power competition, see Aaron Friedberg, *The Authoritarian Challenge: China, Russia and the Threat to the Liberal International Order* (Tokyo, Japan: Sasakawa Peace Foundation, 2017), and Matthew Kroenig, *The Return of Great Power Rivalry: Democracy Versus Autocracy From the Ancient World to the U.S. and China* (New York, NY: Oxford University Press, 2020).

46   Alexandra Gajda, "Tacitus and Political Thought in Early Modern Europe, c.1530–c.1640," in A.J. Woodman (ed.), *The Cambridge Companion to Tacitus* (Cambridge, UK: Cambridge University Press, 2009), pp. 253–69, and J.H.M. Salmon, *Renaissance and Revolt: Essays in the Intellectual and Social History of Early Modern France* (Cambridge, UK: Cambridge University Press, 1987), pp. 27–54. On

the abiding insights Tacitus can provide for students of contemporary authoritarian systems, see Dr Iskander Rehman, "Thrones Wreathed in Shadow: Tacitus and the Psychology of Authoritarianism," *War on the Rocks,* July 1, 2020, available at warontherocks.com/2020/07/thrones-wreathed-in-shadow-tacitus-and-the-psychology-of-authoritarianism/, accessed 15 August 2023.

47   Justus Lipsius, dedication in *Ad Annales Cornelius Taciti Liber Commentarius* (Antwerp, Netherlands: 1581).

48   G.P. Baker, *Tiberius Caesar: Emperor of Rome* (London, UK: Cooper Square, 1929), pp. viii–ix.

49   Tacitus, *Annals,* IV.48.

BIBLIOGRAPHY

Classical sources

Appian, *Civil Wars*

Augustus, *Res Gestae Divi Augusti*

Cassius Dio, *Roman History*

De Munitionibus Castrorum

Eutropius, *Abridgement of Roman History*

Flavius Vegetius Renatus, *Of Military Matters*

Florus, *Epitome of Roman History*

Horace, *Odes*

Julius Caesar, *Gallic Wars*

Juvenal, *The Satires*

Livy, *History of Rome*

Lucan, *Pharsalia*

Ovid, *Tristia*

Philo of Alexandria, *On the Embassy to Gaius*

Pliny the Elder, *Natural History*

Pliny the Younger, *Panegyricus Traiani*

Plutarch, *Parallel Lives*

Polybius, *The Histories*

Pompeius Trogus, *Justinus: Epitome of the Philippic History*

Sallust, *The War with Catiline*

Seneca, *Essays*

Seneca, *Selected Dialogues and Consolations*

Sextus Propertius, *Elegies*

Strabo, *Geography*

Suetonius, *The Twelve Caesars*

Tacitus, *Annals*

Tacitus, *Germania*

Tacitus, *Histories*

Tacitus, *The Life of Agricola*

Titus Flavius Josephus, *Antiquities of the Jews*

Titus Flavius Josephus, *War of the Jews*

Valerius Maximus, *Memorable Doings and Sayings*

Velleius, *Compendium of Roman History*

Virgil, *Aeneid*

Virgil, *Georgics*

Modern sources

2022 National Defense Strategy of the United States of America, Washington, DC, U.S. Department of Defense, 2022

Aldhouse-Green, M., *Caesar's Druids: An Ancient Priesthood*, New Haven, CT, Yale University Press, 2010

Allen-Hornblower, E., "Beasts and Barbarians in Caesar's Bellum Gallicum 6.21–8," *Classical Quarterly*, 64, no. 2, 2014

Alston, R., *Rome's Revolution: Death of the Republic and Birth of the Empire*, Oxford, UK, Oxford University Press, 2015

Anders, A.O., *Roman Light Infantry and the Art of Combat: The Nature and Experience of Skirmishing and Non-Pitched Battle in Roman Warfare 264 BC–AD 235*, Cardiff, UK, Cardiff University doctoral dissertation, 2011

Ando, C., *Imperial Ideology and Provincial Loyalty in the Roman Empire*, Berkeley,

CA, University of California Press, 2000

The Annual Report of the American Historical Association, Washington, DC, American Historical Association, 1893

Asch, B.J., *Navigating Current and Emerging Army Recruitment Challenges: What Can Research Tell Us?*, Santa Monica, CA, RAND Corporation, 2019

Atkinson, J., "Ethnic Cleansing in Alexandria in 38," *Acta Classica*, 49, 2006

Atti Del Convegno Sul Terma: La Persia e il mondo Greco-romano, Rome, Italy, Accademia Nazionale dei Lincei, 1966

Baker, G.P., *Tiberius Caesar: Emperor of Rome*, London, UK, Cooper Square, 1929, and New York, NY, Cooper Square, 2001

Bakos, A.E., "Qui Nescit Dissimulare, Nescit Regnare: Louis XI and Raison D'Etat During the Reign of Louis XIII," *Journal of the History of Ideas*, 52, no. 3, 1991

Baldwin Bowsky, M.W., "Roman Arbitration in Central Crete: An Augustan Proconsul and a Neronian Procurator," *Classical Journal*, 82, no. 3, 1987

Balmaceda, C., "The Virtues of Tiberius in Velleius' *Histories*," *Historia: Zeitschrift für Alte Geschichte*, 63, no. 3, 2014

Balmaceda, C., *Virtus Romana: Politics and Morality in the Roman Historians*, Chapel Hill, NC, University of North Carolina Press, 2017

Bardon, H., *La Litterature latine inconnue, Tome II*, Paris, France, Klincksiek, 1952

Barnes, T.D., "The Victories of Augustus," *Journal of Roman Studies*, 64, 1974

Baronowski, D.W., "Roman Military Forces in 225 BC Polybius 2.23–24," *Historia: Zeitschrift für Alte Geschichte*, 42, no. 2, 1993

Baruah, P., "Military Developments in India 1750–1850," *Journal of Military History*, 58, no. 4, 1994

Beard, M., *SPQR: A History of Ancient Rome*, New York, NY, Liveright, 2015

Bird, H.W., "Laelius Sejanus and His Political Significance," *Latomus*, 28, no. 1, 1969

Birley, A., *Hadrian: The Restless Emperor*, 1997, New York, NY, Routledge, 2013 edn

Bishop, M.C. & Coulston, J.C.N. Coulston, *Roman Military Equipment from the Punic Wars to the Fall of Rome*, London, UK, Oxbow, 2006

Bishop, M.C., *Lorica Segmentata Volume I: A Handbook of Roman Articulated Plate Armour*, Oxford, UK, Armatura Press, 2003

Bowersock, G.W., "The Roman Emperor as Russian Tsar: Tacitus and Pushkin," *Proceedings of the American Philosophical Society*, 143, no. 1, 1999

Bowman, A.K., *Life and Letters on the Vindolanda Frontier*, London, UK, British Museum, 1998

Bowman, A.K., Champlin, E. & Lintott, A. (eds), *The Cambridge Ancient History, Volume X: The Augustan Empire 43 BC–AD 69*, Cambridge, UK, Cambridge University Press, 1996

Brands, H. (ed.), *The New Makers of Modern Strategy: From the Ancient World to the Digital Age*, Princeton, NJ, Princeton University Press, 2023

Brands, H. & Inboden, W., "Wisdom Without Tears: Statecraft and the Uses of History," *Journal of Strategic Studies*, 41, no. 7, 2018

Brands, H. & Montgomery, E.B., "One War is Not Enough: Strategy and Force Planning For Great-Power Competition," *Texas National Security Review*, 3, no. 2, 2020

Braund, D., *Rome and the Friendly King: The Character of Client Kingship*, New York, NY, St Martin's Press, 1984

Breeze, D.J., *The Frontiers of Imperial Rome*, Barnsley, UK, Pen and Sword, 2011

Brunt, P.A., "Charges of Provincial Maladministration under the Early Principate," *Historia: Zeitschrift für Alte Geschichte*, 10, no. 2, 1961

Brunt, P.A., *Italian Manpower 225 BC–AD 14*, Oxford, UK, Oxford University Press, 1971

Burgers, P., "The Role and Function of Senatorial Debate: The Case of the Reign of Tiberius AD 14–37," *Latomus*, 58, no. 3, 1999

Burrows, M., "Imperial Federation," *National Review*, 4, 1884–5

Busen, T. & Guner, A., "The Grotta di Matermania on Capri: Construction, Space and Atmosphere of an Imperial Pavilion," *Archäologischer Anzeiger*, 1, 2018

Butler, S.J., *Britain and Its Empire in the Shadow of Rome: The Reception of Rome in Socio-Political Debate from the 1850s to the 1920s*, London, UK, Bloomsbury, 2012

Campbell, B., *The Emperor and the Roman Army 31 BC–AD 235*, Oxford, UK, Oxford University Press 1984

Campbell, B. & Tritle, L.A. (eds), *The Oxford Handbook of Warfare in the Classical World*, New York, NY, Oxford University Press, 2013

Canetti, D., Waismel-Manor, I., Cohen, N. & Rapaport, C., "What Does National Resilience Mean in a Democracy? Evidence from the United States and Israel," *Armed Forces and Society*, 40, no. 3, 2014

Champion, C., "Empire by Invitation: Greek Political Strategies and Roman Imperial Interventions in the Second Century BCE," *Transactions of the American Philological Association*, 137, no. 2, 2007

Champlin, E., "Tiberius the Wise," *Historia: Zeitschrift für Alte Geschichte*, 57, no. 4, 2008

Champlin, E., "Sex on Capri," *Transactions of the American Philological Association*, 141, no. 2, 2011

Champlin, E., "Tiberius and the Heavenly Twins," *Journal of Roman Studies*, 101, 2011

Coats, R.M. & Pecquet, G.M., "The Calculus of Conquests: The Decline and Fall of the Returns to Roman Expansion," *Independent Review*, 17, no. 4, 2013

Colby, E. & Mitchell, W., "The Age of Great-Power Competition: How the Trump Administration Refashioned American Strategy," *Foreign Affairs*, 99, no. 1, 2020

Colledge, M.A.R., *The Parthians*, New York, NY, Praeger, 1967

Coltelloni-Trannoy, M., "Rome et les rois amis et alliés du peuple romain, en Afrique (Ier siècle av. J.-C./Ier siècle ap. J.-C.)," *Pallas*, no. 68, 2005

Connolly, J., *The State of Speech: Rhetoric and Political Thought in Ancient Rome*, Princeton, NJ, Princeton University Press, 2007

Cordovana, O.D., "Historical Ecosystems: Roman Frontier and Economic Hinterlands in North

Africa," *Historia: Zeitschrift für Alte Geschichte*, 61, no. 4, 2012

Cornwell, H., "The Construction of One's Enemies in Civil Wars (49–30 BCE)," *Hermathena*, no. 196/197, 2014

Cornwell, H., *Pax and the Politics of Peace: Republic to Principate*, New York, NY, Oxford University Press, 2017

Coulston, J.C.N., "How to Arm a Roman Soldier," *Bulletin of the Institute of Classical Studies*, 71, 1998

Cowan, E., "Tiberius and Augustus in Tiberian Sources," *Historia: Zeitschrift für Alte Geschichte*, 58, no. 4, 2009

Cowan, E. (ed.), *Velleius Paterculus: Making History*, Swansea, UK, Classical Press of Wales, 2011

Crowcroft, R. (ed.), *Applied History and Contemporary Policymaking: School of Statecraft*, New York, NY, Bloomsbury, 2022

Curchin, L.A., *The Romanization of Central Spain: Complexity, Diversity and Change in a Provincial Hinterland*, New York, NY, Routledge, 2004

D'Amato, R., *Imperial Naval Forces 31 BC–AD 500*, Oxford, UK, Osprey Publishing, 2009

D'Amato, R., *Roman Army Units in the Western Provinces*, Oxford, UK, Osprey Publishing, 2012

Damon, C., "The Trial of Piso in Tacitus's *Annals* and the *Senatus Consultum de CN. Pisone Patre*: New Light on Narrative Technique," *American Journal of Philology*, 120, no. 1, 1999

de Blois, L., "The Perception of Expansion in the Works of Sallust," *Latomus*, 47, no. 3, 1988

de Blois, L., Erdkamp, P., Hekster, O., De Kleijn, G. & Mols, S. (eds), *The Representation and Perception of Roman Imperial Power: Proceedings of the Third Workshop of the International Network, Impact of Empire: Roman Empire, 200 BC–476 AD (Rome, 20–23 March 2002)*, Leiden, Netherlands, Brill, 2003

de la Bédoyère, G., *Roman Britain: A History*, London, UK, Thames & Hudson, 2013

de Montesquieu, Baron G. (ed.), *Pensées et fragments inédits de Montesquieu*, Bordeaux, France: Imprimerie de G. Gounouilhou, 1899

Debevoise, N.C., *A Political History of Parthia*, Chicago, IL, University of Chicago Press, 1998

Dowling, L., "Roman Decadence and Victorian Historiography," *Victorian Studies*, no. 28, 1985

Drogula, F.K., *Commanders and Command in the Roman Republic and Early Empire*, Chapel Hill, NC, University of North Carolina Press, 2015

Dyson, S.L., *The Creation of the Roman Frontier*, Princeton, NJ, Princeton University Press, 1982

Earl, D., *The Moral and Political Tradition of Rome*, Ithaca, NY, Cornell University Press, 1984

Eckstein, A.M., *Moral Vision in the Histories of Polybius*, Berkeley, CA, University of California Press, 1995

Edmondson, J. (ed.), *Augustus*, Edinburgh, UK, Edinburgh University Press, 2014

Edwards, R., *Divus Augustus Pater: Tiberius and the Charisma of Augustus*, Bloomington, IN, Indiana University doctoral dissertation, 2003

Edwards, R., "Tacitus, Tiberius and Capri," *Latomus*, 70, no. 4, 2011

Edwell, P., *Between Rome and Persia: The Middle Euphrates, Mesopotamia and Palmyra Under Roman Control*, London, UK, Routledge, 2008

Elliott, S., *Roman Legionaries: Soldiers of Empire,* Oxford, UK, Casemate, 2018

Elliott, S., *Romans at War: The Roman Military in the Republic and Empire,* Oxford, UK, Casemate, 2020

Elman, C., *The Logic of Emulation: The Diffusion of Military Practices in the International System,* New York, NY, Columbia University doctoral dissertation, 1999

Erdkamp, P., "Polybius, Livy and the 'Fabian Strategy'," *Ancient Society,* 23, 1992

Erdkamp, P. (ed.), *A Companion to the Roman* Army, Oxford, UK, Blackwell, 2011

Erskine, A., *Roman Imperialism,* Edinburgh, UK, University of Edinburgh Press, 2010

Erskine, A. & Quinn, J.C. (eds), *Rome, Polybius and the East,* Oxford, UK, Oxford University Press, 2015

Everitt, A., *Augustus: The Life of Rome's First Emperor,* New York, NY, Random House, 2006

Farrell, T. & Terriff, T. (eds), *The Sources of Military Change: Culture, Politics and Technology,* Boulder, CO, Lynne Rienner, 2002

Ferguson, N. & Allison, G., *Applied History Manifesto,* Cambridge, MA, Harvard Belfer Center, 2016

Fettweis, C.J., "Restraining Rome: Lessons in Grand Strategy from Emperor Hadrian," *Survival,* 60, no. 4, 2018

Fields, N., *Roman Auxiliary Cavalryman AD 14–193,* Oxford, UK, Osprey Publishing, 2006

Fields, N., *The Roman Army: the Civil Wars, 88–31 BC,* Oxford, UK, Osprey Publishing, 2008.

Fields, N., *The Roman Army of the Principate: 27 BC–AD 117,* Oxford, UK, Osprey Publishing, 2009

Fishwick, D., *Cult, Ritual, Divinity and Belief in the Roman World,* New York, NY, Routledge, 2018

Fiske, G.C., "The Politics of the Patrician Claudii," *Harvard Studies in Classical Philology,* 13, 1902

Flint, W.W., "The Delatores in the Reign of Tiberius: As Described by Tacitus," *Classical Journal,* 8, no. 1, 1912

Flynn, G.Q., *Conscription and Democracy: The Draft in France, Great Britain and the United States,* Westport, CT, Greenport Press, 2002

Frank, R.I., "Augustus' Legislation on Marriage and Children," *California Studies in Classical Antiquity,* 8, 1975

Freeman, P. and Kennedy, D. (eds), *The Defense of the Roman and Byzantine East, Volume 1,* Oxford, UK, British Institute of Archaeology, 1986

Friedberg, A., *The Authoritarian Challenge: China, Russia and the Threat to the Liberal International Order,* Tokyo, Japan, Sasakawa Peace Foundation, 2017

Friend, J.M. & Thayer, B.A., *How China Sees the World: Han-Centrism and the Balance of Power in International Politics,* Lincoln, NE, Potomac Books, 2018

Frühling, S., *Defense Planning and Uncertainty: Preparing for the Next Asia-Pacific War,* New York, NY, Routledge, 2014

Fuhrmann, C.J., *Policing the Roman Empire: Soldiers, Administration and Public Order,* New York, NY, Oxford University Press, 2012

Galinsky, K., *Augustan Culture: An Interpretive Introduction,* Princeton,

NJ, Princeton University Press, 1996

Gambash, G., *Rome and Provincial Resistance*, New York, NY, Routledge, 2015

Garnsey, P.D.A. & Whittaker, C.R. (eds), *Imperialism in the Ancient World*, Cambridge, UK, Cambridge University Press, 1978

Garzetti, A., *From Tiberius to the Antonines: A History of the Roman Empire AD 14–192*, 1974, New York, NY, Routledge Revivals, 2014 edn

Gibbon, E., *The History of the Decline and Fall of the Roman Empire*, London, UK, Strahan & Cadell, 1776–89

Gilliver, C.M., "Mons Graupius and the Role of Auxiliaries in Battle," *Greece and Rome*, 43, no. 1, 1996

Gladstone, W.E., "England's Mission," *Nineteenth Century*, 4, 1878

Glenn, R.W. (ed.), *New Directions in Strategic Thinking 2.0*, Canberra: ANU Press, 2018

Goldman, E.O., *Power in Uncertain Times: Strategy in the Fog of Peace*, Stanford, CA, Stanford University Press, 2011

Goldman E. & Andres, R.B., "Systemic Effects of Military Innovation and Diffusion," *Security Studies*, 8, no. 4, 1999

Goldman, E. & Eliason, L. (eds), *The Diffusion of Military Technology and Ideas*, Stanford, CA, Stanford University Press, 2003

Goldsworthy, A., *Augustus: First Emperor of Rome*, New Haven, CT, Yale University Press, 2014

Goldsworthy, A., *Pax Romana: War, Peace and Conquest in the Roman World,* New Haven, CT, Yale University Press, 2016

Gowing, A.M., *Empire and Memory: The Representation of the Roman Republic in Imperial Culture*, Cambridge, UK, Cambridge University Press, 2005

Grayson, C. (ed.), *Francesco Giucciardini: Selected Writings*, Oxford, UK, Oxford University Press, 1965

Grise, Y., *Le suicide dans la Rome antique*, Paris, France, Les Belles Lettres, 1982

Groh, T.L., *Proxy War: The Least Bad Option*, Palo Alto, CA, Stanford University Press, 2019

Hammond, M., "The Sincerity of Augustus," *Harvard Studies in Classical Philology*, 69, 1965

Harris, W. (ed.), *The Imperialism of Mid-Republican Rome*, Ann Arbor, MI: University of Michigan Press, 1984

Hayes, W.M., "Tiberius and the Future," *Classical Journal*, 55, no. 1, 1959

Haynes, I., *Blood of the Provinces: The Roman Auxilia and the Making of Roman Society from Augustus to the Severans*, Oxford, UK, Oxford University Press, 2013

Heller, A., "Domination subie, Domination choisie: les cites d'Asie Mineure face au pouvoir romain, de la Republique à l'Empire," *Pallas*, 96, 2014

Holladay, A.J., "The Election of Magistrates in the Early Principate," *Latomus*, 37, no. 4, 1978

Holland, T., *Dynasty: The Rise and Fall of the House of Caesar,* New York, NY, Doubleday, 2015

Horowitz, M., *The Diffusion of Military Power: Causes and Consequences for International Politics*, Princeton, NJ, Princeton University Press, 2010

Houston, G.W., "Tiberius on Capri," *Greece and Rome*, 32, no. 2, 1985

Hyland, A., *Training the Roman Cavalry: From Arrian's Ars Tactica*, Stroud, UK, Sutton, 1993

Isaac, B., *The Invention of Racism in Classical Antiquity*, Princeton, NJ, Princeton University Press, 2004

Jameson, S., "Augustus and Agrippa Postumus," *Historia: Zeitschrift für Alte Geschichte*, 24, no. 2, 1975

Jervis, R., "Cooperation Under the Security Dilemma," *World Politics*, 30, no. 2, 1978

Jervis, R., "Deterrence and Perception," *International Security*, 7, no. 3, 1982

Kagan, K., "Redefining Roman Grand Strategy," *Journal of Military History*, 70, no. 2, 2006

Kamm, A., *Julius Caesar: A Life*, New York, Routledge, 2006.

Kapust, D.J., "On the Ancient Uses of Political Fear and its Modern Implications," *Journal of the History of Ideas*, 69, no. 3, 2008

Kapust, D.J., *Republicanism, Rhetoric, and Roman Political Thought: Sallust, Livy, and Tacitus*, New York, NY, Cambridge University Press, 2011

Karklins, R., *The System Made Me Do It: Corruption in Post-Communist Societies*, New York, NY, Routledge, 2005

Karwoski, M. & Ramsl, P.C. (eds), *Boii – Taurisci: Proceedings of the International Seminar, OberleisKlement, June 14th-15th, 2012*, Vienna, Austria, Austrian Academy of Sciences Press, 2016

Kelly, B., "Riot Control and Imperial Ideology in the Roman Empire," *Phoenix*, 61, no. ½, 2007

Kenty, J., "Messalla Corvinus: Augustan Orator, Ciceronian Statesman," *Rhetorica*, 35, no. 4, 2017

Keppie, L., *The Making of the Roman Empire: From Republic to Empire*, London, UK, Routledge, 1984

Kier, E., "Culture and Military Doctrine: France between the Wars," *International Security*, 19, no. 4, 1995

King, A., "On Combat Effectiveness in the Infantry Platoon: Beyond the Primary Group Thesis," *Security Studies*, 25, no. 4, 2016

Kissinger, H.A., *A World Restored: The Politics of Conservatism in a Revolutionary Era*, London, UK, Victor Gollancz, 1977

Krappe, A.H., "Tiberius and Thrasyllus," *American Journal of Philology*, 48, no. 4, 1927

Krepinevich, A.F. & Watts, B.D., *The Last Warrior: Andrew Marshall and the Shaping of Modern American Defense Strategy*, New York, NY, Basic Books, 2015

Kroenig, M., *The Return of Great Power Rivalry: Democracy Versus Autocracy From the Ancient World to the U.S. and China*, New York, NY, Oxford University Press, 2020

Lacey, J., *Rome: Strategy of Empire*, New York, NY, Oxford University Press, 2022

Lamp, K.S., *A City of Marble: The Rhetoric of Augustan Rome*, Columbia, SC: University of South Carolina Press, 2013

Larson, E.V., *Force Planning Scenarios, 1945–2016: Their Origins and Use in Defense Strategic Planning*, Santa Monica, CA, RAND Corporation, 2019

Last, H., "Rome and the Druids: A Note," *Journal of Roman Studies*, 39, no. 1, 1949

Lazenby, J., *The First Punic War*, New York, NY, Routledge, 2006

Le Bohec, Y., *The Imperial Roman Army*, 1994, London, UK, Routledge, 2001 edn

Le Teuff, B., "Les recensements augustéens, aux origines de l'Empire," *Pallas*, 96, 2014

Leffler, M.P. & Legro, J.W. (eds), *In Uncertain Times: American Policy After the Berlin Wall and 9/11*, Ithaca, NY, Cornell University Press, 2011

Lendon, J.E., *Empire of Honor: The Art of Government in the Roman World*, Oxford, UK, Oxford University Press, 2002

Levick, B., "The Beginning of Tiberius' Career," *Classical Quarterly*, 21, no. 2, 1971

Levick, B., "Tiberius' Retirement to Rhodes in 6 BC," *Latomus*, 31, no. 6, 1972

Levick, B., *Tiberius: The Politician*, London, UK, Thames & Hudson, 1976

Levick, B., *Augustus: Image and Substance*, London, UK, Routledge, 2010

Lintott, A., *The Romans in the Age of Augustus*, Oxford, UK, Wiley-Blackwell, 2010

Lipsius, J., *Ad Annales Cornelius Taciti Liber Commentarius*, Antwerp, Netherlands, Christopher Plantin, 1581

Litwak, R.S., *Détente and the Nixon Doctrine: American Foreign Policy and the Pursuit of Stability, 1969–1976*, Cambridge, UK, Cambridge University Press, 1986

Loewenstein, K., *The Governance of Rome*, The Hague, Netherlands, Martinus Nijhoff, 1973

Lovell, J., *Maoism: A Global History*, New York, NY, Knopf, 2019

Luce, T.J. & Woodman, A.J. (eds), *Tacitus and the Tacitean Tradition*, Princeton, NJ, Princeton University Press, 1993

Mackie, N.K., "Augustan Colonies in Mauretania," *Historia: Zeitschrift für Alte Geschichte*, 32, no. 3, 1983

MacMullen, R., "The Emperor's Largesses," *Latomus*, 21, no. 1, 1962

Magie, D., Jr., "The Mission of Agrippa to the Orient in 23 BC," *Classical Philology*, 3, no. 2, 1908

Magie, D., "Augustus' War in Spain 26–25 BC," *Classical Philology*, 15, no. 4, 1920

Magie, D., *Roman Rule in Asia Minor to the End of the Third Century After* Christ, Princeton, NJ, Princeton University Press, 1950

Mahnken, T. (ed.), *Net Assessment and Military Strategy: Retrospective and Prospective Essays,* Amherst, NY, Cambria Press, 2020

Maiuri, A., *Capri: Its History and Its Monuments,* Rome, Italy, Istituto Poligrafico e Zecca dello Stato, 1955

Marañón, G., *Tiberius: The Resentful Caesar,* New York, NY, Duell, Sloan and Pearce, 1956

Martin, J., "The Roman Empire: Domination and Integration," *Journal of Institutional and Theoretical Economics,* 151, no. 4, 1995

Mattern, S.P., *Rome and the Enemy: Imperial Strategy in the Principate,* Berkeley, CA: University of California Press, 1999

Mattern-Parkes, S.P., "The Defeat of Crassus and the Just War," *Classical World*, 96, no. 4, 2003

McLaughlin, J.J., *The Transformation of the Roman Auxiliary Soldier in Thought and Practice*, Ann Arbor, MI, University of Michigan doctoral dissertation, 2015

McNally, M., *Teutoburg Forest AD 9: The Destruction of Varus and his Legions*, Oxford, UK, Osprey Publishing, 2011

Metaxi-Mitrou, F., "Violence in the Contio during the Ciceronian Age," *L'Antiquite Classique*, 54, 1985

Miles, R., *Ancient Worlds: The Search for the Origins of Western Civilizations*, London, UK, Penguin, 2011

Millar, F., *The Emperor in the Roman World*, London, UK, Bristol Classical Press, 1977

Millar, F., "Government and Diplomacy in Imperial Rome During the First Three Centuries," *International History Review*, 10, no. 3, 1988

Millar, F., *Government, Society and Culture in the Roman Empire*, Chapel Hill, NC, University of North Carolina Press, 2004

Mitre, J., "A Eulogy for the Two-War Construct," *Washington Quarterly*, 41, no. 4, 2018

Mitzen, J., "Ontological Security in World Politics: State Identity and the Security Dilemma," *European Journal of International Relations*, 12, no. 3, 2006

Mommsen, T., *A History of Rome Under the Emperors*, New York, NY, Routledge, 1992

Mommsen, T., *A History of Rome Under the Emperors: Based on the Lecture Notes of Sebastian and Paul Hensen, 1882–86*, New York, NY, Routledge, 2005

Money, J., *Capri: Island of Pleasure,* New York, NY, Faber & Faber, 2011

Montaigne, *Les Essais: Oeuvres Completes*, Paris, France: Gallimard, 2010

Morley, N., *The Roman Empire: Roots of Imperialism,* London, UK, Pluto Press, 2010

Mountford, P., *Maecenas*, New York, NY, Routledge, 2019

Murphy, C., *Are We Rome? The Fall of Empire and the Fate of America*, New York, NY, Houghton Mifflin, 2007

Nabel, J.T., *The Arsacids of Rome: Royal Hostages and Roman-Parthian Relations in the First Century CE*, Ithaca, NY, Cornell University doctoral dissertation, 2017

Nicolet, C., *Space, Geography and Politics in the Early Roman Empire*, Ann Arbor, MI, University of Michigan Press, 1991

Niebuhr, R., *The Irony of American History*, 1952, Chicago, IL, University of Chicago Press, 2008 edn

Nixon, R., "Asia After Vietnam," *Foreign Affairs*, 46, no. 1, 1967

Norman, D., *Siren Land: A Celebration of Life in Southern Italy,* New York, NY, Bloomsbury, 2019) – first pub 1911

Ober, J., "Tiberius and the Political Testament of Augustus," *Historia: Zeitschrift für Alte Geschichte*, 31, no. 3, 1982

Opper, T., *Hadrian: Empire and Conflict*, Cambridge, MA, Harvard University Press, 2010

Orth, W., *Die Provinzialpolitik des Tiberius*, Munich, Germany, Ludwig Maximilian University of Munich doctoral dissertation, 1970

Osgood, J., *Caesar's Legacy: Civil War and the Emergence of the Roman Empire*, Cambridge, UK, Cambridge University Press, 2006

Osgood, J., *Rome and the Making of a World State 150 BCE–20 CE*, Cambridge, UK, Cambridge University Press, 2018

Parker, H.D., *The Roman Legions*, New York, NY, Oxford University Press, 1928

Phang, S.E., *Roman Military Service: Ideologies of Discipline in the Late Republic and Early Principate*, New York, NY, Cambridge University Press, 2008

Pitassi, M., *The Roman Navy: Ships, Men and Warfare 350 BC–AD 475*, Barnsley, UK, Seaforth, 2012

Pogorzelski, R.J., "Orbis Romanus: Lucan and the Limits of the Roman World," *Transactions of the American Philological Association*, 141, 2011

Poirot, J.J., *The Romano-Parthian Cold War: Julio-Claudian Foreign Policy in the 1st Century CE and Tacitus' Annals*, Baton Rouge, LO, Louisiana State University doctoral dissertation, 2014

Potter, D., "Empty Areas and Roman Frontier Policy," *American Journal of Philology*, 113, no. 2, 1992

Powell, L., *Eager for Glory: The Untold Story of Drusus the Elder: Conqueror of Germania*, Barnsley, UK, Pen and Sword, 2011

Powell, L., *Germanicus: The Magnificent Life and Mysterious Death of Rome's Most Popular General*, Barnsley, UK, Pen and Sword, 2012

Powell, L., *1st Century AD: Roman Soldier Versus Germanic Warrior*, Oxford, UK, Osprey Publishing, 2014

Press, D.G., *Calculating Credibility: How Leaders Assess Military Threats*, Ithaca, NY, Cornell University Press, 2007

Price, S., *Rituals and Power: The Roman Imperial Cult in Asia Minor*, 1984, Cambridge, UK, Cambridge University Press, 1985 edn

Purcell, N., "The Non-Polis and the Game of Mirrors: Rome and Carthage in Ancient and Modern Comparison," *Classical Philology*, 112, no. 3, 2017

Putnam, R.D., "Diplomacy and Domestic Politics: The Logic of Two-Level Games," *International Organization*, 42, no. 3, 1988

Raaflaub, K.A. & Toher, M. (eds), *Between Republic and Empire: Interpretations of Augustus and his Principate*, Berkeley, CA, University of California Press, 1990

Rand, G., "'Martial Races' and 'Imperial Subjects': Violence and Governance in Colonial India 1857–1914," *European Review of History*, 13, no. 1, 2006

Rapke, T.T., "Tiberius, Piso, and Germanicus," *Acta Classica*, 25, 1982

Rapp-Hooper, M., *Shields of the Republic: The Triumph and Peril of America's Alliances*, Cambridge, MA, Harvard University Press, 2020

Resende-Santos, J., "Anarchy and the Emulation of Military Systems: Military Organization and Technology in South America 1870–1990," *Security Studies*, 5, no. 3, 1996

Rich, J.W., "Drusus and the Spolia Opima," *Classical Quarterly*, 49, no. 2, 1999

Richardson, J.S., *Augustan Rome 44 BC to AD 14: The Restoration of the Republic and the Establishment of the Empire*, Edinburgh, UK, Edinburgh University Press, 2012

Ripat, P., "Expelling Misconceptions: Astrologers at Rome," *Classical Philology*, 106, no. 2, 2011

Rogers, R.S., "Notes on the Gallic Revolt, AD 21," *Classical Weekly*, 36, no. 7, 1942

Rogers, R.S., *Some Imperial Virtues of Tiberius and Drusus Julius Caesar,*

Baltimore, MD, Johns Hopkins
University Press, 1943

Rolland, N., *China's Vision for a New World Order*, Seattle, WA: National Bureau of Asian Research, 2020

Roller, D., *Empire of the Black Sea: The Rise and Fall of the Mithridatic World*, Oxford, UK, Oxford University Press, 2020

Rosecrance, R. & Stein, A. (eds), *The Domestic Bases of Grand Strategy*, Ithaca, NY, Cornell University Press, 1993

Roselaar, S.T. (ed.), *Processes of Cultural Change and Integration in the Roman World*, Leiden, Netherlands: Brill, 2016

Rosenstein, N.S., *Imperatores Victi: Military Defeat and Aristocratic Competition in the Middle and Late Republic*, Berkeley, CA: University of California Press, 1990

Roth, J., "The Size and Organization of the Imperial Legion," *Historia: Zeitschrift für Alte Geschichte*, 43, no. 3, 1994

Roth, J.P., *The Logistics of the Roman Army at War*, Leiden, Netherlands, Brill, 2012

Roymans, N., *Ethnic Identity and Imperial Power: The Batavians in the Early Roman Empire*, Amsterdam, Netherlands: Amsterdam University Press, 2004

Rutledge, S.H., *Imperial Inquisitions: Prosecutors and Informants from Tiberius to Domitian*, New York, NY, Routledge, 2002

Rutledge, S.H., "Tiberius' Philhellenism," *Classical World*, 101, no. 4, 2008

Sabin, P., "The Face of Roman Battle," *Journal of Roman Studies*, 90, 2000

Salisbury, N., "The Indians' Old World: Native Americans and the Coming of Europeans," *William and Mary Quarterly*, 53, no. 3, 1996

Saller, R.P., *Personal Patronage Under the Early Empire*, Cambridge, UK, Cambridge University Press, 1982

Salmon, E.T., *Roman Colonization Under the Republic*, Ithaca, NY, Cornell University Press, 1970

Salmon, J.H.M., *Renaissance and Revolt: Essays in the Intellectual and Social History of Early Modern France*, Cambridge, UK, Cambridge University Press, 1987

Salmon, J.H.M., "Stoicism and the Roman Example: Seneca and Tacitus in Jacobean England," *Journal of the History of Ideas*, 50, no. 2, 1989

Sampson, G.C., *Defeat of Rome in the East: Crassus, the Parthians, and the Disastrous Battle of Carrhae, 53 BC*, Barnsley, UK, Pen and Sword, 2008

Sampson, G.C., *Rome and Parthia: Empires at War: Ventidius, Antony and the Second Romano-Parthian War 40–20 BC*, Havertown, PA, Pen and Sword, 2020

Schelling, T.C., *Arms and Influence*, 1966, New Haven, CT, Yale University Press, 2008 edn

Schlude, J.M., *Rome, Parthia and the Politics of Peace: The Origins of War in the Ancient Middle East*, New York, NY, Routledge, 2020

Schultz, K.A., "The Perils of Polarization for U.S. Foreign Policy," *Washington Quarterly*, 40, no. 4, 2017

Seager, R., *Tiberius*, 2nd edn, Oxford, UK, Blackwell, 2005

Shannon, T.J., *Iroquois Diplomacy on the Early American Frontier*, New York, NY, Penguin Books, 1964

Shaw, B.D., "Bandits in the Roman Empire," *Past and Present*, 105, 1984

Shaw, M.C.G., *Drusus Caesar: The Son of Tiberius*, Vancouver, Canada, University of British Columbia doctoral dissertation, 1990

Sheldon, M.R., *Rome's Wars in Parthia: Blood in the Sand*, Portland, OR: Vallentine Mitchell, 2010

Shepphard, S., *Philippi 42 BC: The Death of the Roman Republic*, Oxford, UK, Osprey Publishing, 2008

Sherwin-White, A.N., "Violence in Roman Politics," *Journal of Roman Studies*, 46, 1956

Sherwin-White, A.N., "Rome the Aggressor?," *Journal of Roman Studies*, 70, 1980

Shotter, D., *Tiberius Caesar*, New York, NY, Routledge, 1992

Shotter, D.C.A., "Tacitus. Tiberius and Germanicus," *Historia: Zeitschrift für Alte Geschichte*, 17, no. 2, 1968

Shotter, D.C.A., "Tiberius and Asinius Gallus," *Historia: Zeitschrift für Alte Geschichte*, 20, no. 4, 1971

Shurkin, M., *France's War in Mali: Lessons for an Expeditionary Army*, Santa Monica, CA, RAND Corporation, 2014

Singh, A., *The First Anglo-Sikh War 1845–46*, Stroud, UK, Amberley, 2010

Singh, A., *The Second Anglo-Sikh War*, Stroud, UK, Amberley, 2016

Smith, D., T*he First Anglo-Sikh War 1845–46: The Betrayal of the Khalsa*, Oxford, UK, Osprey Publishing, 2019

Soll, J., "Amelot de la Houssaye and the Tacitean Tradition in France," *Translation and Literature*, 6, no. 2, 1997

Speidel, M., *Emperor Hadrian's Speeches to the African Army—A New Text*, Mainz, Germany, Römisch-Germanisches Zentralmuseum, 2007

Spielberg, L., "Language, Stasis and the Role of the Historian in Thucydides, Sallust and Tacitus," *American Journal of Philology*, 138, no. 2, 2017

Starr, C.G., "How Did Augustus Stop the Roman Revolution?", *Classical Journal*, 52, no. 3, 1956

Stewart, J.J., "The Geographical Definition of *Ultimus* from Julius Caesar to Domitian," *Acta Classica*, 43, 2000

Strachan, H., "Training, Morale and Modern War," *Journal of Contemporary History*, 4, no. 2, 2006

Sutherland, C.H.V., "Two Virtues of Tiberius: A Numismatic Contribution to the History of his Reign," *Journal of Roman Studies*, 28, no. 2, 1938

Syme, R., "Some Notes on the Legions Under Augustus," *Journal of Roman Studies*, 23, 1933

Syme, R., "The Spanish War of Augustus, 26–25 BC," *American Journal of Philology*, 55, no. 4, 1934

Syme, R., *The Roman Revolution*, New York, NY, Oxford University Press, 1939

Syme, R., "Hadrian and the Vassal Princes," *Athenaeum*, 59, 1981

Syme, R., "The Year 33 in Tacitus and Dio," *Athenaeum*, 61, 1983

Symonds, M., *Protecting the Roman Empire: Fortlets, Frontiers and the Quest for Post-Conquest Security*, Cambridge, UK, Cambridge University Press, 2018

Talmadge, C., *The Dictator's Army: Battlefield Effectiveness in Authoritarian Regimes*, Ithaca, NY, Cornell University Press, 2015

Tan, Z.M., "Subversive Geography in Tacitus' Germania," *Journal of Roman Studies*, 104, 2014

Tarver, J.C., *Tiberius the Tyrant*, Cambridge, MA, Harvard University Press, 1902

Taylor, M.J., "Visual Evidence for Roman Infantry Tactics," *Memoirs of the American Academy in Rome*, 59/60, 2015

Thiel, J.H., *A History of Roman Sea-Power Before the Second Punic War*, Amsterdam, Netherlands, North Holland, 1954

Thompson, E.A., "Early Germanic Warfare," *Past and Present*, 14, 1958

Townshend, A., Thomas-Noone, B. & Steward, M., *Averting Crisis: American Strategy, Military Spending and Collective Defense in the Indo-Pacific*, Sydney, Australia, United States Studies Center of the University of Sydney, 2019

Trubowitz, P., Goldman E. & Rhodes, E., *The Politics of Strategic Adjustment: Ideas, Institutions, and Interests*, New York, NY, Columbia University Press, 1999

Turcan, R., *Tibere*, Paris, France, Les Belles Lettres, 2017

Van Dijk, W., *The Successor: Tiberius and the Triumph of the Roman Empire*, Waco, TX, Baylor University Press, 2019

Vanacker, W., "Adhuc Tacfarinas: Causes of the Tiberian War in North Africa (15–24 AD) and the Impact of the War on Roman Imperial Policy," *Historia: Zeitschrift für Alte Geschichte*, 64, no. 3, 2015

Vasquez, J.P., III, "Shouldering the Soldiering: Democracy, Conscription and Military Casualties," *Journal of Conflict Resolution*, 49, no. 6, 2005

Wallace-Hadrill, A., "The Golden Age and Sin in Augustan Ideology," *Past and Present*, 95, 1982

Webster, J., "At the End of the World: Druidic and Other Revitalization Movements in Post-Conquest Gaul and Britain," *Britannia*, 30, 1999

Weisiger, A. & Yarhi-Milo, K., "Revisiting Reputation: How Past Actions Matter in International Politics," *International Organization*, 69, no. 2, 2015

Wells, P.S., *The Battle That Stopped Rome: Emperor Augustus, Arminius, and the Slaughter of the Legions in the Teutoburg Forest,* New York, NY, W.W. Norton and Company, 2015

White, R., *The Middle Ground: Indians, Empires and Republics in the Great Lakes Region, 1650–1815*, New York, NY, Cambridge University Press, 1991

Whittaker, C.R., *Frontiers of the Roman Empire: A Social and Economic Study*, Baltimore, MD, Johns Hopkins University Press, 1994

Whittaker, C.R., *Rome and Its Frontiers: The Dynamics of Empire*, New York, NY, Routledge, 2004

Wilcox, P., *Rome's Enemies: Parthians and Sassanid Persians*, Oxford, UK, Osprey Publishing, 1982

Wilkinson, S., *Republicanism During the Early Roman Empire*, London, UK, Continuum, 2012

Woodman, A.J., "Tacitus' Obituary of Tiberius," *Classical Quarterly*, 39, no. 1, 1989

Woodman, A.J., *Rhetoric in Classical Historiography: Four Studies*, 1988, New York, NY, Routledge, 2003 edn

Woodman, A.J., *Tacitus: The Annals: An Annotated Translation*, London, UK, Hackett, 2004

Woodman, A.J., *Velleius Paterculus: The Tiberian Narrative*, Cambridge, UK, Cambridge University Press, 2004

Woodman, A.J., "Mutiny and Madness: Tacitus Annals 1:16–1:49," *Arethusa*, 39, no. 2, 2006

Woodman, A.J., "Tiberius and the Taste of Power: The Year 33 in Tacitus," *Classical Quarterly*, 56, no. 1, 2006

Woodman, A.J. (ed.), *The Cambridge Companion to Tacitus*, Cambridge, UK, Cambridge University Press, 2009

Yihong, P., "Early Chinese Settlement Policies Towards the Nomads," *Asia Major*, 5, no. 2, 1992

Young, A.T., "From Caesar to Tacitus: Changes in Early Germanic Governance circa 50 BC–50 AD," *Public Choice*, 164, no. 3/4, 2015

Zisk, K.M., *Engaging the Enemy: Organization Theory and Soviet Military Innovation, 1955–1991*, Princeton, NJ, Princeton University Press, 1993

Image rights

Cover   DEA/V. Pirozzi/DeAgostini/Getty Images

14   Iskander Rehman
17   DEA/A. Dagli Orti/De Agostini/Getty Images
28   akg-images/TT
30–31   Mairie de Toulouse, Musée des Augustins
38–39   Andrea Jemolo/Electa/Mondadori Portfolio/Getty Images
42   The Metropolitan Museum of Art, New York/Bequest of Phyllis Massar, 2011
44–45   © Swanston Map Archive Limited
61   Alexandr Chernushkin/Shutterstock
69   © 2023 DeAgostini Picture Library/Scala, Florence
74–75   akg-images/TT
76:1   Eric Vandeville/akg-images/TT
76:2   E. Viadar/akg-images/TT
79   akg-images/TT
82–83   © Swanston Map Archive Limited
85   The Metropolitan Museum of Art, New York/The Elisha Whittelsey Collection,
          The Elisha Whittelsey Fund, 1949
100   Peace Palace Library/Wikimedia Commons
103   Daniel Martin, Photothèque du Musée Saint-Raymond, musée d'Archéologie de
          Toulouse/Wikimedia Commons
112   akg-images/TT
114–115   © Swanston Map Archive Limited
120–121   bpk | Bayerische Staatsgemäldesammlungen
124–125   akg-images/TT
130   Iskander Rehman
136   akg-images/TT
156   The Metropolitan Museum of Art, New York/ Gift of Mrs. Alfred J. Marrow, 1964
159   © 2023 Photo Smithsonian American Art Museum/Art Resource/Scala, Florence

ISKANDER REHMAN is an Ax:son Johnson Fellow at the Kissinger Center for Global Affairs and Senior Fellow for Strategic Studies at the American Foreign Policy Council. His work focuses on applied history, grand strategy, and US defense strategy in Asia. Over the course of his career, he has held fellowships at a number of different think tanks, such as the Brookings Institution, the Center for Strategic and Budgetary Assessments, the Carnegie Endowment for International Peace, and the German Marshall Fund of the United States. His first book, titled *Planning for Protraction: a Historically Informed Approach to Great Power War and Sino-US Competition*, was published in November 2023 as part of the International Institute for Strategic Studies, (IISS) Adelphi series. His current book project, *Phoenix Lords: Three Ministers, an Empire Shattered and a Kingdom Reforged* is a work of narrative nonfiction, and tells the story of more than a century of bitter Franco-Spanish rivalry through the lives of three legendary figures in the annals of French statecraft: Sully, Richelieu, and Mazarin. He lives in Washington DC, and holds a PhD, with distinction, from the Institute of Political Studies (Sciences Po), in Paris.

SIR PETER STOTHARD is the author of books on ancient and modern politics including *The Senecans, Four Men and Margaret Thatcher* (2016), *The Last Assassin, The Hunt for the Killers of Julius Caesar* (2020), *Palatine, An Alternative History of the Caesars* (2023), and *Thirty Days* (2004), a diary of his time with Tony Blair and George W. Bush during the Iraq War in 2003. He was editor of *The Times* (1992–2002) and of the *Times Literary Supplement* (2002–2016).

IRON IMPERATOR

Roman Grand Strategy under Tiberius

Published by Bokförlaget Stolpe, Stockholm, Sweden, 2024

Text: Iskander Rehman
Foreword author: Sir Peter Stothard
Text editor: Zoe Gullen
Picture editor: Susanna Mälarstedt
Design: Patric Leo
Layout: Pontus Dahlström
Cover image: *Saint Veronica Healing Tiberius with Her Veil*, painting by Lazzaro Baldi (1624–1703),
Galleri Spada, Rome. Photo: DEA/V. Pirozzi/DeAgostini/Getty Images
Prepress and print coordinator: Italgraf Media AB, Sweden
Print: Printon, Estonia, via Italgraf Media, 2024
First edition, first printing
ISBN: 978-91-89696-75-4

Bokförlaget Stolpe is a part of Axel and Margaret Ax:son Johnson Foundation for Public Benefit.

BOKFÖRLAGET STOLPE

AXEL AND MARGARET AX:SON JOHNSON

FOUNDATION FOR PUBLIC BENEFIT